05/07

UNIVERSITY OF
WOLVERHAMPTON

Also available from Continuum:

Understanding Christian–Muslim Relations: Past and Present

Fundamentalisms and the Media

Stewart M. Hoover and Nadia Kaneva

continuum

Continuum
Continuum International Publishing Group

The Tower Building   80 Maiden Lane
11 York Road   Suite 704
London SE1 7NX   New York NY 10038

www.continuumbooks.com

British Library Cataloguing-in-Publication Data
A catalogue record for this book is available from the British Library.

ISBN-10: HB: 1–8470–6133–8
        PB: 1–8470–6134–6

ISBN-13: HB: 978–1–8470–6133–1
        PB: 978–1–8470–6134–8

Library of Congress Cataloging-in-Publication Data
Fundamentalisms and the media.
p. cm.
  ISBN-13: 978–1–84706–133–1
  ISBN-10: 1–84706–133–8
  ISBN-13: 978–1–84706–134–8
  ISBN-10: 1–84706–134–6
  1. Religious fundamentalism.   2. Mass media—Religious aspects.
3. Fundamentalism.   4. Church and mass media.   I. Title.
BL238.F844 2009
201′.7—dc22

                            2008045475

Typeset by RefineCatch Limited, Bungay, Suffolk
Printed and bound in Great Britain by Cromwell Press Group, Trowbridge, Wiltshire

Contents

Contributors

R. Scott Appleby is the Director of the Joan B. Kroc Institute for International Peace Studies and Professor of History at the University of Notre Dame. He holds a Ph.D. from the University of Chicago. From 1988 to 1993 he co-directed the Fundamentalism Project, conducted under the auspices of the American Academy of Arts and Sciences, which resulted in the definitive five-volume work on fundamentalism, co-authored with Martin E. Marty.

Kwabena Asamoah-Gyadu is an Associate Professor and Dean at Trinity Theological Seminary in Legon, Ghana. He has been a Senior Research Fellow at the Center for World Religions at Harvard Divinity School, and Schiotz Visiting Professor of African Christianity at Luther Seminary in St. Paul, Minnesota, both in the USA. He was a member of the International Study Commission on Media, Religion and Culture, and is author of the book *African Charismatics* (2007) and numerous chapters and articles.

Dr. Claire Hoertz Badaracco is the author or editor of six books. Most recently, she edited *Quoting God: How Media Shape Ideas about Religion* (Baylor 2006), and wrote *Prescribing Faith: Medicine, Media and Religion in American Culture* (Baylor 2007). She teaches media and religion, media ethics and peace studies at Marquette University, where she is a Full Professor.

Leon Barkho is a lecturer at the Department of Languages and a doctoral student at the Media Management and Transformation Centre of Jönköping International Business School, Sweden. He taught English and translation at the University of Mosul until 1990. During the following decade he worked as a correspondent for Reuters and staff writer for the Associated Press.

David Haskell teaches journalism at Wilfrid Laurier University. His primary research interest is evangelical Christians and the Canadian news media. His work in this area has appeared in academic journals and in the popular press. Haskell has also enjoyed careers as a print features writer and as a TV news reporter.

Stewart M. Hoover is a Professor of Media Studies at the University of Colorado at Boulder, where he directs the Center for Media, Religion and Culture. His research centres on media and religion as they relate to meaning making and identities. He is author or co-author of five books and has co-edited several edited volumes. He has taught and lectured throughout the world on emerging issues in the study of religion and contemporary culture.

Robert Glenn Howard is an Associate Professor at the University of Wisconsin at Madison. He researches everyday expressive communication in network technologies. He has published on topics ranging from websites to the involvement of the printing press in the Protestant Reformation. Since 1994, his primary research interest has been an ethnographic study of the emergence of fundamentalist Christian communities online.

Kirsten Isgro (Ph.D., Communication and Women's Studies) is a contributing author in the anthology *Women and Children First* (SUNY Albany Press 2005). Her recent research examines an anti-feminist Christian organization as a way to study how religion intertwines with media and culture within the larger contexts of globalization and transnational politics.

Nadia Kaneva is an Assistant Professor in the Department of Mass Communications and Journalism Studies at the University of Denver. Her research draws on critical theories of culture and communication and explores the relationships between collective identities, power and ideology. She is currently working on a book that examines the phenomenon of nation branding in Eastern Europe and explores national and cultural identity struggles in this region after the collapse of the communist system.

Edward Michael Lenert is a graduate of the Department of Rhetoric, The University of California, Berkeley, *magna cum laude*. His Ph.D. (Radio Television Film) is from The University of Texas at Austin. He holds a law degree from Georgetown University Law Center, Washington, DC, and is a licensed attorney in California.

Susan Maurer holds a Bachelor's Degree in Music Performance and Theory (SUNY); Masters Degree in Theology and Religious Studies (St. John's University); Masters Degree in Modern World History (St. John's University), and is a candidate for Doctor of Arts in Modern World History (St. John's University) with specialization in History of Religion and particular interests in World Religions and Spirituality.

Jin Kyu Park has an M.A. in Journalism from the University of Texas and a Ph.D. in Communication from the University of Colorado. His research interests focus on: religion and audiences' cultural text reading; production and reception of religion/spirituality in Korean popular culture; globalization of religious symbolism in popular culture.

Pradip N. Thomas is an Associate Professor at the School of Journalism and Communication, University of Queensland, Brisbane, Australia. He has written widely on issues related to the political economy of communication. He is currently involved in a research project on Christian fundamentalism and the media in India.

Foreword

This book is intended to help open a new area of scholarly research and a new dialogue about emerging trends in media and religion. The perspective we offer here is innovative in a number of ways. First, we propose that the media play a central role in the constitution and evolution of religion and religious cultures. Second, we suggest that one of the most feared and controversial dimensions of religion – the movements that we call 'fundamentalisms' – is almost uniquely connected with the media and processes of mediation. Third, this is an inter-disciplinary perspective, holding that no single approach or discipline can fully address the complex issues involved. Fourth, it is an international perspective, convinced that the questions here are only fully addressed within a global context. Finally, we see the questions raised in this collection as being more than just 'academic'. These trends and issues are important well beyond scholarly discourse. They matter to local, regional, national and international civil society and politics.

This is clearly an ambitious agenda, and one that a volume such as this can only begin to address. As with many such efforts, this one began with a conference, the International Conference on Fundamentalism and the Media, which convened in Boulder, Colorado, in October 2006. That event brought together over 80 participants from throughout the world in a lively, substantive and creative dialogue. The range of perspectives, methods, learnings and approaches was truly impressive. The works in this volume represent the range and breadth of that meeting. Along with the conference, it is our hope that they have laid a foundation for further scholarly and intellectual work focused on these important questions and issues.

The conference would not have been possible without the interest and support of a number of organizations and individuals. Its genesis was in a global conversation on fundamentalism and the media undertaken by the World Association for Christian Communication (WACC), an international organization focused on communication, justice and cultural development. The Boulder meeting constituted the last in an international series of WACC consultations on the subject and benefited from the results of those prior events. WACC, and its North American Region, thus provided important financial and other support to the Boulder conference. We would like to recognize the efforts of

Randy Naylor, Philip Lee and María Teresa Aguirre from the WACC global staff and Adan Medrano and Paul Edison-Swift of the WACC North American Region.

This Boulder conference was the founding event of the Center for Media, Religion, and Culture (www.mediareligion.org), which operates within the School of Journalism and Mass Communication at the University of Colorado. We would like to recognize the financial and other support of the Center, the School and the University in these efforts. In particular, we note the roles of Dean Paul Voakes of the School of Journalism and Mass Communication and Mr. John Winsor, a key member of the Center's Advisory Board, in making this event, and thus this book, possible. We would also like to thank the University of Denver which provided important support during the preparation of this manuscript.

A number of other people were involved in detail work on the conference and on this book. These include Doña Olivier, the administrative coordinator of the Center; Pat Meyers and Catherine Larkins, the School's financial officers; the Center's Post-doctoral fellow Monica Emerich; and student workers Curtis Coats, Doug Crigler, and Annemarie Galeucia. For their work on this book, we'd like to thank Kimberly Eberhardt Casteline and Dawn Carmin.

This volume would not have been possible without the kind and patient support of our editors at Continuum Publishing, Rebecca Vaughan-Williams and her successor Kirsty Schaper, as well as Tom Crick.

Finally, we would like to thank the scholars and others who participated in the Fundamentalism and the Media Conference, and particularly those who appear in this volume. They have made an enduring contribution to scholarly and discursive progress on these important questions and issues. Whatever value there is in this work is the result of all of these efforts.

Stewart M. Hoover
Nadia Kaneva
July, 2008

Chapter 1

Fundamental Mediations: Religion, Meaning and Identity in Global Context

Stewart M. Hoover and Nadia Kaneva

One of the enduring conundrums of the contemporary era is the persistence of religion as a force in society, culture and politics. For most of the twentieth century, it was assumed that religions would decline in importance and influence. The secularization thesis, long held as canonical in the social sciences and humanities, assumed that the intellectual and moral fruits of modernity – education, economic liberalization, increasing human liberty and autonomy – would make religious faith less and less necessary. 'Religion' and 'modernity' were thought to be inversely related (Berger 1969). This idea is still tacitly accepted in much public discourse at the beginning of the twenty-first century.

There is also a received view of what we generalize as 'the media' in relation to religion in modernity. It is thought that media technologies are quintessentially 'modern'. In fact, the modern era in Western history is held to have resulted in part from the evolution of new media forms: the advent of printing and publishing. The political ideologies of modernity, especially Western European and specifically Anglo-American traditions of democratic practice, envision a central place for processes of mediation. These see media as an independent force, essential to the spread of knowledge, enlightenment and democratic values, and an important check on the institutional power of the state (and, by the way, religion).

The contemporary era thus presents us with a range of complexities and seeming contradictions. Not only has religion not faded away, it seems to be experiencing a resurgence along a variety of dimensions and in a variety of contexts. Furthermore, in many cases, this resurgence seems to involve the most emblematic instruments of 'the modern': the modern media of communication.

The events of 11 September 2001 are an obvious example of these trends. The attacks presented themselves as religiously-motivated, a particular expression of a particular religiously-based critique of modernity. Further, they posed a kind of existential challenge in that they seemed to be using the tools of modernity against modernity itself. Among the tools most effectively used were the media, which were integrated into the 9/11 saga in a variety of ways, not least as the context through which the horrors were experienced by global audiences (Hoover 2006).

For all of its singularity, however, 9/11 was evidence of what we have come to see as a broader, longer-term trend. For most of the last century, resistant religious movements that have come to be rather loosely grouped under the label 'fundamentalisms' have emerged onto the public stage. For those of us in the West, two particular examples have stood out. First, the prototype of 'fundamentalism' emerged in early twentieth century United States as a reaction against theological modernism in Protestantism. After a public repudiation in the 1920s, it seemingly went 'underground', re-emerging late in the century as one of the important political bases of a resurgent religious politics now known as 'neo-evangelicalism'.

The second major confrontation was a global, not a domestic one, signaled by the Islamic revolution in Iran of 1979.[1] The Iranian revolution was a major shock to the Western – and particularly the US – body politic. After a long period where it seemed obvious that religions no longer constituted a major force in national or global politics, political and media authorities were confronted by a situation that none of them had predicted: a political revolution motivated by religion. In diplomatic, security, intelligence and journalistic circles, the incident led to a widespread period of self-criticism and assessment (Rockefeller Foundation 1981). It may also have set the stage for a broader emergence of political Islam, though it can hardly be said that it was a sole cause, given the complexities involved. In addition to the rise of political Islam (sometimes referred to as 'Islamism') and the continuing evolutions in the Christian world, other 'fundamentalisms' have emerged, most notably in South Asia, where a resurgent Hindu nationalism has come to the fore in recent decades.

Fundamentalisms Considered

There is good reason to think of fundamentalisms in particular ways, three of which seem most prominent and relevant to our project here. First, fundamentalisms are *modern* movements. They emerged in modernity and most importantly as reactions to aspects of modernity. This is to say that, despite much of the incendiary political rhetoric today, fundamentalists are less interested in restoring the past than they are in shaping the present and future. This point is particularly strongly represented in the chapter by R. Scott Appleby in this volume as well as in much of his earlier work (e.g., Appleby 2002).

Second, fundamentalisms are *ideological* movements that seek to confront regnant secular and religious ideologies and are coming to exist on the same stage as (and to interact with) other, perhaps more familiar, ideologies such as communism, liberalism, capitalism and nationalism. This is not to say that their significance is primarily 'secular'. Each of them has important religious roots and a particularly religious agenda as well. But even this can be described as ideological in important ways, as fundamentalists have seen themselves as seeking to reform religious traditions that have lost their way (Marty and Appleby 1993).

Finally – and this is the unique argument proposed in this volume – fundamentalisms cannot be fully understood without reference to *the media*. They are all movements of what we might call 'the media age'. Both Christian Fundamentalism in the USA and the Islamic 'fundamentalism' behind the Iranian revolution used modern media of communication to great effect. In the US case, fundamentalists were best known through their media – pamphlets, books, tracts and most importantly radio – and the political evangelicalism that emerged later was encouraged by a powerful new media form: televangelism (Marsden 1982, Hadden and Shupe 1988). In the Iranian case, a variety of media technologies were brought to bear, but the innovative use of audio-cassettes and other 'small media', stood out (Sreberny-Mohammadi and Mohammadi 1994). But the role of media is not limited to the use of technologies by these groups. In each of these cases, and indeed in all cases we might call 'fundamentalisms', a broader process of mediation – or what some have begun to call 'mediatization' (cf: Hjarvard 2008, Schultz 2004) – has been significant.

Fundamentalisms and Media

In the first and most obvious instance, the media have been involved with fundamentalisms through their *coverage* of these movements. The ideological dimension of fundamentalisms is most important here, as journalism has seen them and covered them as political movements. What most of us know about them, about their truth claims, or about their presumed challenges to our own truth claims, we know through the media. There are implications of this that extend beyond the mere fact of how fundamentalisms are represented in the media and it is one of the goals of this volume to explore some of them. The most obvious is that in an era of media that are global and instantaneous at that, what once would have been local or national movements, now appear on a transnational stage. The fact of their coverage puts them into a broad context and connects them with other movements and trends thus, in a way, legitimizing their very existence. Increasingly, such movements are aware of this fact and act accordingly.

These movements interact with media technologies and the processes of mediation in a variety of ways, in a variety of contexts and through a variety of practices. There is a sense in which fundamentalisms and the media have co-evolved, and it is partly through the media that fundamentalisms have come to the fore in global political discourse. They are a twentieth century idea rooted in a specific context (the US prototype) that we can now see as a precursor to other movements in other contexts. And, there is evidence that the reflexivity of the media age – that is, the tendency for media discourses and media audiences to take on ideas such as 'fundamentalism' and treat them as generic categories – has led even movements that bear no relation to the Christian case to be relatively unproblematically labeled (and in some cases to label *themselves*) 'fundamentalisms'.

There has been a tendency to overlook or underplay the unique role of the media and mediation. Against this, we would argue that the significance of the media to these questions is based in certain characteristics of what we might call 'the media age'. By using this term, we do not intend to argue that the contemporary era is unique in the presence or importance of the institutions and processes of the media. Throughout Western history – in particular of the modern era – the media, from postal systems to printing to electric to electronic to digital communication, have played a vital (if often overlooked) role.

In using the term 'the media age', we intend to point to a set of conditions that have given modern media of communication a role in the constitution of contemporary politics, society and culture. This is a role that has evolved over time, but that increasingly deserves to be studied and understood on its own terms. It is of critical importance to recognize that technological, social, political and market conditions today constitute 'the media' as autonomous and authoritative forces that largely establish the conditions under which groups, movements and institutions function. The media today are a powerful 'third force' in relation to the state and to institutions such as religion. Their autonomy is rooted in, and is strengthened by, global market economics, which have favoured the emergence of transnational media institutions that are less and less subject to the regulation or control of state actors. This autonomy continues and extends their positioning in relation to religion, which in its institutional forms has suffered a decline in its authority and plausibility as the authority and plausibility of media sources have seemed to rise.

The Media and Religious Evolution

Seeing the media in these terms highlights some implications for religion and religious discourse. It has been widely noted that the media increasingly set the terms of political and social discourse (Gitlin 1980). Often the media are also the primary context within which public knowledge is produced and circulated. In other words, in many cases what we, as a global community, know we know through the media. Thus characteristics of media discourse, including its practices of framing and its genres of news and entertainment, establish the conditions for the construction of publicly-circulated 'truths'. What once were clearly-demarcated boundaries between journalism (to which we have traditionally attributed a level of facticity) and entertainment (which is increasingly looked to as a source of information) are today negotiated and nuanced.

The media also maintain – and at the same time blur – received distinctions such as that between 'private' and 'public'. Whereas fundamentalist movements might once have been limited to their local or national contexts, today they can also appear on a global stage and can have access to global audiences. As a result, no single or individual fundamentalism exists in isolation. And there are also putative pan-national fundamentalist movements, most obviously Islamism and Christian fundamentalism. Relations between these two, we should note, seem most portentous as they teeter towards a confrontation on their 'front line' – the 'Holy Land' of the Middle East – and prosecute their cases through the media.

Further, as discursive struggles over truth take place in the media context, they must take place using idioms and terms of reference established by that context. Transnational or global discourse is necessarily based on consensually-understood modes of representation and expression, modes that are determined and expressed by media discourse. In the case of fundamentalisms, for example, the widespread generic use of the term is itself a result of media practices of construction and representation.

The media are also implicated in establishing and maintaining important social and ideological conditions of late modernity. Anthony Giddens, for example, has suggested that late modern consciousness is characterized by a reflexive individualism that increasingly mistrusts authority and arrogates to itself the conditions of its own identity and selfhood (Giddens 1991). To Giddens and others, this sensibility is encouraged by the media which, through their scope and breadth of representation, convey a sense of instrumentality and autonomy over knowledge and the potential for action. Simply put, the media provide information in such a way that audiences become convinced that they understand the conditions of contemporary social and cultural life in a deeper way than publics might have in earlier times, and therefore feel empowered to articulate their interests in new and unprecedented ways.

Beyond Instrumentalism

Thus, the role of the media in fundamentalisms is more than just instrumental. The question moves beyond that of whether a given movement is effective in its use of media. Instead, we can see the media as integral to the evolution of religions in general and fundamentalisms in particular. Their use of media is an important issue, but there are also questions of the way media represent, define, construct and symbolize religions. It is thus not just how religion is mediated by the media, but how media practices of these various kinds contribute to the evolution or remaking of religion. Some observers have begun to use the term 'mediatization' to refer to this more complex, constitutive role for the media[2]:

As a concept mediatization denotes the processes through which core elements of a cultural or social activity (e.g., politics, religion, language) assume media form. As a consequence, the activity is to a greater or lesser degree performed through interaction with a medium, and the symbolic content and the structure of the social and cultural activities are influenced by media environments which they gradually become more dependent upon (Hjarvard 2007: 3).

It is beyond our scope here to assess the nature or extent of the mediatization of religion *per se*, but we might retain from arguments such as these that the relationship between religion and the media involves a complex interplay of practices and functions and, to an extent, religion today – along with many other institutions – is increasingly constituted by the media. In this regard, we might suggest that the interplay between fundamentalist movements and the media is a part of this process with reference to the larger religious traditions to which they relate.

Beyond these relations, there is an additional complexity in that the media seem to play a particular role in relation to fundamentalisms and their ideological projects *vis a vis* religious and secular authorities. Many fundamentalisms have at their base a vibrant critique of modern culture. As we have noted, and as some of the chapters in this volume document, they are typically movements against modernity, which see both the secular state and religious institutions as failing to adequately address trends which threaten fundamental beliefs and values. In many contexts, this involves as well a vibrant critique of the media as conveyors of beliefs and values. In the case of US fundamentalism and evangelicalism, this has been particularly obvious. Major conservative Christian institutions continue to identify 'the media' as a major opponent in the so-called 'culture wars' (Hunter 1992, Medved 1992).

This suggests yet another, less direct, context in which the media are active in relation to fundamentalist movements. As we have noted, the media are the central context of discourse today. As such, they are the place where social and cultural ideas are publicly represented. They are the global public sphere. To the extent that that sphere is a source of messages and symbols that do not respect religious traditions (which is often the case), the media themselves would be likely objects of fundamentalist scrutiny. There is ample evidence, for example, that the 9/11 hijackers were motivated in their critique of the amorality and immorality of Western culture by their exposure to things they saw in the media (Hoover 2006).

A Complex Picture

Thus, to raise the question of the media in relation to fundamentalisms is to open a complex and nuanced set of inquiries, as the contributions to this volume demonstrate. We can see three key valences of the relationship between fundamentalisms and the media. First, these movements are, at their base, mediated movements in that they aggressively and unproblematically use media to pursue their ends (Cf. Appleby, this volume). Second, there is a range of ways that these movements, and religion in general, are shaped by their interaction with media. Whether we call this 'mediatization' – where the media actually constitute these movements, the religions to which they relate, or the combination of these two – or merely an 'interaction' between fundamentalisms and the media, there is much evidence (much of it to be found in this volume) that we cannot understand these movements without understanding the media. Third, the media sphere's output almost necessarily constitutes a challenge to fundamentalisms rooted as it is in modernity and committed as it is to the expression of ideas and values that are typically not based in the doctrines of a specific faith. The media then challenge both traditional religious institutions and their structures of authority, and therefore the fundamentalisms that are directed at reform in those same institutions. These relations may well be even more complex and interrelated, as we will see presently.

Religious Change and Reform

As we further investigate the role that the media and mediation might play, we can suggest an additional implication for religions in relation to media and to fundamentalist movements. Fundamentalisms typically arise as reform movements within specific religions and religious contexts. The Christian Protestant prototype emerged to contest the drift of the US Protestant establishment towards modernism. The various forms of Islamism, from the founding of the Muslim Brotherhood onward, have arisen to contest secularizing or relativizing tendencies among various national Islams. The Khomeneist revolution in Iran had as its focus the recovery of a genuine Shiism over and against the accommodationism that had existed under the Shah. Fundamentalisms therefore see themselves as reform movements in relation to religion.

It seems that there is a tendency for all religions to undergo processes of reform. While we would not argue from the particular case of Christianity to the universal of all religions, the work of historians such as William McLoughlin is intriguing and perhaps indicative in this regard. McLoughlin (1978) has provided the most influential account of what are known as the 'Great Awakenings' of American Protestantism. He identified in this history a cyclic tendency for religions, over time, to become institutionalized, bureaucratic, and to lose their edge. Periodic reform movements then arise to call the faith back to its roots. Fundamentalisms can be seen to be such movements. We would argue that there is a complex interaction that implicates the media and processes of mediation in the evolution of religions, helping to create, in a sense, the conditions that bring about these reformist reactions.

Religions are not universal, immutable or fixed. They can be seen to evolve. Adam Smith noted in his account of urban religion in rapidly industrializing eighteenth century Britain that industrialization actually stimulated religion by creating conditions where atomized publics in the growing urban centres would be drawn to religion for stability and reassurance. From this, we might draw the conclusion that, rather than seeing modernity leading to a decline in religion, modernity might be said to co-evolve *with* religion. Rather than a pure process of 'secularization', industrialization in Britain (and the United States) also led to the rise of new forms of religion: specifically a revitalized urban form of evangelicalism. These evangelical movements of the nineteenth century are today established institutions, prone to calls for reform.

Today, it seems that a different set of pressures have come to bear on religions. Because they are social institutions, religions cannot be immune to the pressures of their social and cultural contexts. This is where the existence of the autonomous 'media sphere' comes into play in a more direct way. For a variety of reasons, contemporary media have become important sources of religious-symbolic 'supply'. Where religions might once have had a monopoly on religious or spiritual symbols and resources, the media today compete.

This situation is supported by three interacting trends. First, there has been a widely-observed decline in the authority and profile of religious institutions. Often confused with an overall process of 'secularization', religious authority has (along with other institutions) experienced a crisis of legitimacy (Roof 1999). Second, this trend has been accompanied by (and to an extent caused by) a change in the nature of religious belief and practice. Today there is a tendency towards 'autonomy' in religious practice. The turn towards social autonomy noted by Giddens above has a religious dimension to it, where the faithful are increasingly taking responsibility for their own religious and spiritual lives (Hammond 1992, Warner 1993, Hoover 2006). While this is a trend that is most observable in the West, there is evidence that it is a global trend, particularly among youth (Clark 2007). Third, the decline in religious authority and the rise of personal autonomy in matters of faith has been accompanied by trends in the media. The free media marketplace of symbolic 'supply' has been more than ready to accommodate itself to the developing demand for religiously-significant symbolic resources. The issue of commodification is also important here. While religions have been commodified to a greater or lesser extent for most of modern history, this process has come to play a more and more important role in defining the nature of religious symbols and resources since the mid-twentieth century (McDannell 1998). As a result of these trends, an ever-expanding inventory of religious and spiritual symbolic resources is now available, both locally and globally (Hoover 2006; Clark 2007; Sumiala-Seppänen, Lundby and Salokangas 2006).

The content of this religious 'supply' is necessarily less relevant to any particular faith than it is to faith and spirituality in general. As such, it constitutes yet another valence of the relativism that fundamentalists decry. The fact that the media sphere can be conceivable as a setting for the construction of religious and spiritual meaning is extended further by the emerging 'user-generated' content of the digital age. Today a dizzying array of voices are using media contexts such as YouTube as platforms for non-institutional, non-doctrinal religious products. The digital sphere has also encouraged the development of pan-national religious voices (self-conscious descendants of the American Televangelism of the 1970s) even in Islam (Wolfe 2008).

Competition from such sources, and the possibilities of presence on a global media stage constitutes an even more powerful source of social pressure for religions to 'adapt' and change, integrating themselves into their cultural contexts and (to fundamentalist eyes) watering down the purity of their truth claims. One of the sources of this pressure is political. In modernity, religions are pressured to accommodate to pluralism relativizing their messages in exchange for political ascendancy and power (Mead 2008). Religions and their contexts are intertwined, and often religions are seen to take on worldly commitments at the expense of 'the pure'. Again, the fundamentalist prototype, the twentieth-century American version, arose as a response to religious elites' seeming accommodation to modernism in science, education and social policy. Today, increasing personal autonomy in faith practice is an additional such pressure, encouraging religions to further relativize to compete in a secular-media-defined marketplace of ideas and discourses. The development of social networking media and Web 2.0 cannot help but further exacerbate this trend.

The result is yet another way in which the media sphere is interacting with fundamentalisms. The religious institutions which are in the first instance the targets of these movements are increasingly encouraged by the pressures of the media age in directions fundamentalists consider antithetical: towards pluralism, relativism and differentiation. Additionally, the overall trend towards 'personalized' religiosities and spiritualities are in themselves seen as threatening to tradition (and as advocates of tradition, fundamentalists are horrified by such trends). At the same time – as should be an obvious extension of our argument – fundamentalist movements are themselves examples of these pluralizing and relativizing trends and, as they become established as movements, might themselves become fractured and relativized by the same forces we see acting on formal religious institutions.

Media and Meaning-Making

These are largely structural and institutional questions surrounding fundamentalisms and the media, but there are also questions related to the actual practices of meaning construction in which these movements are engaged. Here, a set of issues rooted in ongoing theoretical debates in media scholarship provide some intriguing questions and potential insights. One way of looking at practices of mediation (and an obvious one at that) is in terms of the meaning of media texts themselves.

This is in a way related to the issues of instrumentalism and instrumental use of the media by these groups we discussed earlier. Media scholarship has tended to move beyond its earlier focus on instrumental 'effects' of media (and we have identified ourselves with this perspective), but there remain a set of questions and issues in relation to the cultural implications of media textual practice and the consumption of these texts. In the case of fundamentalisms, there is a direct relationship to long-standing concerns with questions of social *power* on the part of media studies and cultural studies scholars. This moves well beyond questions of particular and isolated 'effects' of media 'messages' to broader questions of the significance of media as systems of meaning and signification.

Theoretical work in these fields provides two distinct, yet related, ways of looking at questions of power in relation to fundamentalists' interactions with the media. Overall, the obvious concern is how, as competitive ideologies (as we have described them), these movements may find traction in global political and social discourse. This can be looked at along two rather broad dimensions. We can either focus on the meaning-constructive implications of the texts themselves, or we can look at how the textual and institutional practices of the media and mediation can serve as symbolic resources for the exercise of social power.

The poststructuralist philosopher and social critic Michel Foucault has been particularly influential in contemporary thought about the construction of symbolic meanings through discourses and texts. Foucault has argued that discourses do not exert direct control over specific truths and behaviours (an instrumentalist position) but exercise a domination over social ways of being and meaning-making that enforce certain modes of thinking and behaviour as the ones that become taken-for-granted (1972, 1977). In his own work, he demonstrated how important social categories such as mental illness and gender identity (1978) are socially-constructed and by extension involve the complicity of contexts of discourse such as the media in creating and maintaining such categories and definitions. This process is one that is constructive in a powerful and fundamental way. Discourses are, Foucault (1972: 49) argued, '. . . practices that systematically form the objects of which they speak . . . discourses are not about objects, they do not identify objects, they constitute them and in the practice of doing so conceal their own invention'. His theories envisioned a kind of elegant, multi-stage role of discourse in this regard. Not only do discourses shape the way we perceive the world and ourselves, they '. . . act more subtly by causing people to "police themselves"' (Mcnamara 2006: 9).

Religious discourse is clearly about meanings and about such fundamental questions as the meaning of life and the meaning of existential realities of various kinds (and, by extension, related subjectivities). It therefore is about the kinds of practices of subjectification that Foucault points to. Fundamentalist media discourses, as shown in a number of the contributions to this volume, aspire to precisely this same kind of function. Turning again to the American Protestant prototype, its various publications and productions intended to be definitive in this way (Hendershot 2004). The range of websites, television programmes, films and printed materials described by authors herein (and representing Christianity, Judaism, Islam and Hinduism) all share in common an aspiration to function as such determinative discourses. Many are a call to believers to return to the central tenets of the faith. Others seem to contemplate audiences beyond the already-convinced.

But there is a problem of scale when we apply poststructualist discourse theory (which contemplates meanings and subjectivities in whole cultures) to fundamentalisms (which are by their nature pragmatic and targeted at particular political agendas). While fundamentalisms might aspire to recover a role for ascendant religiously-based definitions of 'truth', their whole *raison d'etre* derives from their sense that their definitions are particular ones, not generally shared by their cultural or religious contexts. The motivation for their activism is to re-direct institutional and structural resources back to the 'fundamentals'.

Of course, it could be argued that the truth claims of Protestant Fundamentalists in the USA and Europe, Jewish Fundamentalists in Israel and Islamist groups in Turkey broadly coincide with meanings such as bourgeois sensibilities of personal morality. They thus contribute to the generalized sense of constructed truth of the kind to which Foucault might refer (1972). But their particular claims intend to be focused in more specific and pragmatic arenas.

Practices of Meaning

This pragmatism points to a second theoretical direction of concern to media scholars. On the one hand, represented by the work of Foucault, are all the questions surrounding the constitution of the texts of fundamentalist mediations and the way they, in turn, constitute audiences and ideologies or, more broadly, subjectivities. On the other hand, however, is the question of how mediations, symbols and texts are deployed by fundamentalist movements. To look in this direction, of course, denies the basic claim of determination implicit in Foucault's work, but there is ample evidence, including from the work detailed in this volume, that there is a great deal of social, cultural and political 'work' being done by adherents to these movements, using media materials and media practices. How might we account, theoretically, for these?

Here we might turn to the work of another French theorist, the sociologist and anthropologist Pierre Bourdieu. Bourdieu agreed with Foucault that language was at the centre of meaning, including social meanings. At the same time though, Bourdieu was more interested in the practical actions of individuals in relation to their contexts of life, and the ways in which they were active in deploying various symbols and meanings in the conduct of those lives.

He was also concerned primarily with questions of power, and of how such interactions and practices come to be locations where power is expressed. Believing that much such action involved symbols, he used the term 'symbolic violence' to describe how texts and symbols are deployed by some individuals and groups to exercise power over others.

In a conceptual turn that has been of particular interest to media scholars, Bourdieu used the metaphor of the market to describe the outlines of his theories of how individuals and groups engage in such practices and interactions. Rather than seeing media texts or other symbolic resources as realizing meanings in a process of consumption only, he saw such resources as being of primary significance when they are used and deployed by social actors in time and place. The market metaphor applies, for Bourdieu, in that not all resources are of equal value, and not all social actors are equally valued in their contexts of action. Rather, symbols become 'symbolic capital' that different classes of actors can use in the exercise of power. This is a complex process, which he theorized within the general framework of 'practice' (1998). Extending the market metaphor, Bourdieu held that there are certain logics that embed social actors in cultural and social exchange. His theoretical staging of the notion of 'practice' combines the notion of action in social space with the roles of individual and collective social actors whose practices of exchange become definitive of the meanings produced.

Bourdieu's (1984) reflections on the notion of 'taste' focused on the production of cultural and social value (and thus meanings) by such exchange. The exercise and judgement of taste, he argued, is not a trivial matter, but in fact acts to organize whole hierarchies of interpersonal and group relations with great effectiveness and efficiency. It is then '. . . a sort of social orientation, a "sense of one's place", guiding the occupants of a given . . . social space towards the social positions adjusted to their properties, and towards the practices or goods which befit the occupants of that position' (Bourdieu 1984: 466).

The way that individuals and groups deploy ideas, language, symbols and texts is thus in fact fundamental to the constitution of societies and cultures. Practices that can be said to be focused primarily on the conceptual level of language and symbols, then, are very important, and the kinds of struggles that are the focus of this volume – struggles over meanings, symbols and symbolic resources – are central questions of culture. And, many would argue, they are of critical political importance as they are involved in creating the contexts and languages through which actual struggles over power and authority are taking place today. We should note that Bourdieu himself identified the realm of religion as one location where these relations can be seen (cf: Swartz 1996). The important distinction we'd like to draw, though, is between a textual and determinative approach and Bourdieu's focus on practice. Power, he argued, is exercised by specific actors using symbolic resources in social space.

Fundamentalisms, Power and Ideology

The fundamentalist groups, movements and arguments we see here are about such struggles over ideas and power. And, while we think it is important to distance contemporary theoretical and empirical work in media and religion from naive assumptions about the instrumental power of specific and discontinuous media messages, we nonetheless want to acknowledge that media symbols do have determinative and definitive implications, if only in the aspirations of individuals and groups who wish to use them. But we think it is of further importance to see that the particularism of fundamentalist interests and movements wishes to address itself to historically located situations, actors and objects. How media resources come into play in this is the obvious essential question, and we would like to point to the ways in which media resources are produced, selected, made significant and used in practices of these movements and groups. This opens the door to a more complex and nuanced empirical approach to the mediation of these processes, something that is well demonstrated by the works included in this volume.

We are therefore suggesting that it is too simple to ask whether the question of fundamentalist media is about texts or, rather, about the use of cultural resources for purposes of social, cultural and political power. There is evidence of both taking place. Media are instruments of meaning construction and dissemination *and* they are contexts within which competing sets of symbols are proposed, promoted, circulated and consumed. They are a site of reflexive performance *and* spectatorship on a global stage. At the same time, fundamentalist media in this context are about particular arguments at particular historical moments and in particular places. The fact of global mediation substantially changes the stakes in these relations and their potential reach and significance, and it is our purpose here to try to lay out a scholarship that can address these issues in all their depth and complexity.

The Media as Practices

It is obvious that we and the contributors here wish to argue that media are integrated into these struggles over power, truth claims and the prospects of institutional authority within religions and beyond them. It is important, as we move to the specific scholarly contributions here, to look beyond the rather narrow and tacit way that the term 'the media' is often used (and we have admittedly used it here). The media are more than mere technologies or instruments. If we are to take seriously what we've said theoretically, we must recognize them as *practices*. They exist in specific times and spaces in history and function in specific ways. Their channels, genres, processes of production, political economy, practices of consumption and integration into social and cultural space and time are all significant.

This means that a range of issues – many of which are significant to the contributions here – need to be taken into consideration as we define 'media' in these regards and look for the implications of the media and of mediation here. We might call these conditions of the 'media age' relevant to the question of fundamentalisms and they should foreground our thinking about implications. Taking into account what we have said theoretically about media practice, at least the following issues seem to be of importance.

First, the issue of *reflexivity*. We mean this in the sense suggested by Giddens, Bourdieu and others that contemporary social actors are more self-conscious and autonomous in their modes of practice than may have been the case previously. Due in part to the ubiquity of modern media, people today feel a more keen sense of autonomy and knowledge over the constitution of society and culture and are consequently more active in what they see to be a project of crafting their own identity and self. Their relations to media are consequently altered over and against a received view of them as more or less subject to media messages and media manipulation. Today they are active, both in processes of production and in processes of consumption.

Second, struggles at the *private/public boundary*. As we noted, it is no longer possible to have a fully 'private' conversation. What once have been the internal discourses within specific movements or in bounded geographic locations are today accessible to global audiences. The capacity therefore exists for specific and particular interests to have access to a wider stage, and to articulate their truth claims and appeals for support well beyond their original boundaries.

Third, there are now a *myriad of producers*. The autonomous action we introduced above is not limited to audiences engaged in more or less passive consumption. Today, we all feel more empowered to create media and to have our voices heard on the media stage. There are both technological and socio-cultural reasons for this. There is a rising interest in and capacity for such autonomous action, of course. But at the same time, the new digital, social and Web 2.0 media are making it more and more standard practice all the time for individuals and groups to make, as well as consume, media. And perhaps most importantly, the new digital media have substantially lowered the barriers to access to the global media sphere.

Fourth, the media are largely *visual and symbolic*. Many observers of fundamentalisms have noted the more or less easy concordance between fundamentalist sensibilities and a media sphere that focuses more on hermetic and anachronistic symbols than it does on texts and doctrines. The natural inclination of the media sphere, it is argued, makes it a particularly salubrious environment for the articulation of specifically fundamentalist arguments. This may or may not be the case, and deserves careful empirical interpretation (some of which we see in these pages), but it remains a plausible and wide-spread perception of the particular capacities of fundamentalisms and the media to relate to one another.

Fifth, and perhaps most important for the prospects of religious authority, the media themselves constitute an *autonomous social and political sphere of authority*. We've already discussed the historical context for this reality, but want to emphasize it again here. Due to their political economy and market location, the media today are an inevitable actor on the social and political scene. Further, they are global and because of their market location they are increasingly beyond state control. Other spheres of (more traditional) institutional authority must necessarily accommodate themselves to the media more than *vice versa*. This means that the relations between these sectors in relation to fundamentalisms and the media is complexly multi-layered. Not only are media determinative in certain ways in terms of the conditions within which 'the church' and 'the state' must function, they are also more specifically and dynamically involved in interacting relations with specific political movements which seek to work out ideological struggles with these same institutions. It is not a simple matter, and we hope the contributions to this volume will make progress in describing and systematizing these complexities.

These Chapters

The project of bringing scholarly attention to fundamentalisms and the media deserves more attention than it has received heretofore. As an evolving field, the work that is emerging can seem eclectic. Strong, serious research and theory-building on some of the questions is well-advanced, while other areas still await attention. This volume is the first to focus in this area and a comprehensive view is still not possible. However, the works that follow cover a wide range of disciplines, locations, domains and approaches. There is thus a creative eclecticism to this collection that stems from the concrete reality of such a new field. We intend the structuring of what follows to help the reader enter into this scholarly discourse, not to impose a systematization where none is possible or even necessary at this point.

Much of what we have said would argue against an imposed structure. We have argued that the complexity of the field almost demands scholarly approaches that are rooted in the located practices of individuals, groups and movements. These practices emerge according to their own logics, not according to inductive theoretical categories. At the same time, there are received ways of looking at social science scholarship that can help us think about the scholarly and empirical domains within which these phenomena are encountered, and we have grouped these chapters within such very general categories.

The first three chapters appear in a section titled *Histories*. By this we mean to suggest that they describe material related to larger questions of the constitution of movements we might call 'fundamentalisms'. In the first of these, R. Scott Appleby, one of the singular international experts on fundamentalisms, brings a historical perspective to bear on a new set of questions necessitated by the highly politicized fundamentalisms that have emerged of the last

few decades. His particular concern is one that we should all share: what can
we learn from fundamentalist use of media that would help those who are
interested in reducing the trends towards conflict that are portents of many of
these movements? Appleby's account is both a serious and substantive review
of important trends in fundamentalist movements and a reflection that should
be of vital interest to those who wish to progress from this point to a situation
where global civil society is able to deal creatively and humanely with current
trends and pressures in the religious sphere.

Communication law scholar Edward Lenert follows with a review of one of
the most visible of recent controversies, the so-called 'Danish cartoons' episode
of 2006. This incident brought relations between Islam and the West into the
public eye in a new way. There had always been a sense that the issues were
large and significant. The publication of these images led to global responses
and reactions, and reinforced new stereotypes of the interests on both 'sides'.
Lenert lays out an argument for looking both beyond and between those
extremes. His expertise as a scholar of communication law and policy positions
him to be able to carefully re-think one of the 'absolutisms' in the debates over
the cartoons: the argument that Western press traditions should unequivocally
favour their unfettered publication, a position that he terms 'free expression fundamentalism'. It is clear that questions such as these will continue to figure
large in the mediation of religious politics for the foreseeable future, so a careful analysis such as Lenert's lays some important groundwork for the future.

The final chapter in the first section considers the prototype of American
Protestant Fundamentalism. As we have said, this movement is important to
our considerations here as it both represented the ways that conservative-
reformist impulses would come to interact with modernity over the succeeding
decades and became a kind of model for what has come after. Susan Maurer's
account of the history of this movement attempts a reconsideration that gives
special attention to processes and practices of mediation in that history.

The second section considers a range of *Mediations* of fundamentalisms
across a number of geographic, cultural and religious contexts. Journalist and
journalism educator Leon Barkho leads off with a study of the treatment of
fundamentalist ideas and movements by Arab and Muslim media. There has
been a good deal of concern expressed about the way that Islam in general, and
Islamist movements in particular, are covered by Western news media. Much of
the opinion has coincided with Edward Said's influential view of this coverage
as necessarily influenced by deterministic 'Western' framings. Barkho looks at
the ways that non-Western framings, and specifically those from the so-called
'Muslim world', also reveal systematic readings of the situation. His chapter
offers a rare look at fundamentalisms from 'the other side' of the symbolic line
that separates a 'Judeo-Christian' West from a 'Muslim' East.

Kirsten Isgro follows with a similar study focused on the Christian world and
the representation of Christian leaders in US news media. It has been widely
observed that there is a curious and confusing 'gap' between the preponderant

religiosity of politics and public culture in the United States and the relative inability of American journalism to deal with 'the religion story'. The central questions surround the specific and bounded ways that Christianity, as the dominant religious tradition in the USA, and its leaders are considered by journalism and the news media. Isgro's work suggests ways that journalistic treatment of conservative Christianity plays a role in the constitution and construction of its movements and leaders as politically significant.

Moving outside the US context, but remaining with the prototype Christian case, David Haskell presents a systematic study of the coverage of Fundamentalist Christianity in Canadian television news. Canada shares a great deal in common with the USA in cultural and religious terms, but is at the same time unique and distinct. Canadian media and media viewers are conditioned to think about news through the framing of the dominant culture to the South. This dualistic view of national and regional news is one factor unique to the Canadian case; the other is the nature of Canadian press traditions. Both of these are important factors in the way that topics like fundamentalisms are treated in Canadian news.

Robert Howard's chapter looks at the same religious tradition – Christian Fundamentalism – in a different medium: the digital realm. Howard conducts a detailed investigation of linked and related websites devoted to the specific Christian Fundamentalist theologies related to apocalyptic prophesies of the 'end times'. A significant feature of Howard's work is his account of the way that the production and consumption of these sites, which he labels 'vernacular Christian fundamentalism', contrast with those modes of practice in other media contexts, resulting in the constitution of new relations, networks and 'communities' online.

The final contribution to the *Mediations* section extends the notion of 'fundamentalism' to consideration of a traditionalist movement in a non-Protestant context. The Roman Catholic movement *Opus Dei* has received a good deal of attention – including prominent media attention – in recent years. Claire Badaracco is an accomplished observer of media in two professional contexts: journalism and public relations. Her expertise extends as well to contemporary Catholic cultural politics. Her chapter considers how the framing of this movement within Catholicism fits within received definitions conditioned by other contexts and movements. At the same time, Badaracco illustrates how *Opus Dei* has been an active agent in the shaping of the media discourse about the movement, exemplifying the argument we've made here about fundamentalists' pragmatic and strategic use of media.

The third section shifts perspective away from histories, institutions and traditions to the *Locations* where fundamentalisms can be said to interact with the media. This turn towards grounded contexts is both a theoretical and empirical contrast with the foregoing chapters. It also moves the discussion well beyond the prototypes of Christianity and American Protestantism to locations outside North America and the West more generally. The first of these chapters takes us to Africa, where Kwabena Asamoah-Gyadu describes the complex relations between traditional and more modern religions. Ghana, his study site, is one of the prime sites where the emerging global phenomenon of the Pentecostal 'megachurch' is finding its powerful African expression. Its development is layered on centuries of Christian and Muslim history in West Africa, each of which has encountered, and helped redefine, prior African trad- itional practices. Each of these layers persists in Ghanaian and West African contexts and is represented in various ways in symbol systems and mediations. What happens with these traditions may well be contingent on such medi- ations, and this chapter considers these processes in detail.

Next, Jin Kyu Park presents a study of the articulation of traditional religion and 'imported' religion through a specific genre – serial television drama – in contemporary South Korea. His study concerns a specific, wildly popular programme that brought into relief long-standing contrasts between the trad- itional Korean religious practice of shamanism and the more recently adopted, although presently holding a dominant socio-cultural status, Protestant Christianity. Since the beginning of Korean industrialization in the 1950s, Protestantism has grown in numbers and influence to the point that Korea is unique among East Asian nations for the proportion of Christians in its population. A widespread informal public discourse about this situation has continued for most of the last half-century, considering questions of the 'authenticity' of Christianity in Korean culture. The programme Park analyses, had the effect of bringing much of this discussion into the open and into public media. Through interviews with the programme's producers and writers, he is able to detail both competing ideas about the nature of religion and about the proper role of the media in interaction with 'traditional' and 'new' religions.

The final chapter of this section considers one of the locations where the term 'fundamentalism' has been frequently used to describe a non-Christian move- ment. Traditionalist Hindu groups have existed in India at least since the early twentieth century. They played an important role at the time of India's separ- ation from Britain and the process of partition in the 1940s. More recently, though, a resurgent Hindu nationalism has emerged (in part in response to global political and cultural pressures and stresses) and has taken on the guise of other 'fundamentalisms'. It has also done this in an era of intense growth in media in India, and has itself had important connections with the media and with processes of mediation (and 'mediatization'). In this chapter, Pradip Thomas investigates another 'fundamentalism' that has emerged in India in response to the larger movement. Christian groups which resemble 'funda- mentalisms' and which are also pursuing their interests through the media are becoming active. Thomas considers these trends and looks towards ways that the resulting tensions might be lessened, rather than intensified.

Taken together, the chapters in this volume are a beginning. They come as interest in, and scholarly consideration of, relations between 'religion' and 'the media' is rising on the public and research agendas. Historical circumstances have brought these questions to the fore and, as they have arisen, concerns about politics, ideology, conflict and violence have driven much of what has been known and said. At the centre of this, the problem of 'fundamentalisms' has been seen to be a major concern. It is our hope that this book can lay the groundwork for more extensive and comprehensive work both on fundamentalisms and on questions of religion and spirituality more generally. Much remains to be done, but the scholars here have already made great progress in thinking about not only the critical questions and issues, but also about the theoretical and methodological tools that are most appropriate to address them.

Notes

1   There has been a vibrant debate over the use of the term 'fundamentalism' to describe movements beyond the American Protestant twentieth-century case. As we will argue later, there are a number of reasons that we choose to conditionally apply the label. In general, we find ourselves agreeing with the argument of Appleby and his associates (Almond, Appleby and Sivan 2003) that the label has become generic, but that it is most appropriate to stipulate that when we use it we are intending to mean – paraphrasing here – 'movements that bear a family resemblance to fundamentalism'. The use of the term in the plural – 'fundamentalisms' – is also an attempt to signal a recognition that fundamentalism is not a unitary or ideal category, but rather a consensual one that has evolved from its passage through a number of local and global discursive contexts.

2   We acknowledge a developing scholarly debate about this term. Couldry's (2008) response has been especially relevant to our considerations here in that he raises important questions about the substantive view of the media implied by mediatization theory in the context of a media-scholarly discourse which has been increasingly skeptical of essentialized notions of the media. Our interest here is to raise the idea that the interaction between 'media' and 'religion' leads to a transformation of the latter, not to necessarily identify with the particular view taken by advocates for the notion of mediatization, a discussion that is beyond the scope of this essay.

References

Almond, G. A., Appleby, R. S. and Sivan, E. (2003), *Strong Religion: The Rise of Fundamentalisms Around the World*. Chicago: University of Chicago Press.

Appleby, R. S. (2002), 'History in the fundamentalist imagination', *The

Journal of American History, September, retrieved 26 June 2008 from
<http://www.historycooperative.org/cgi-bin/justtop.cgi?act=justtop&url=
http://www.historycooperative.org/journals/jah/89.2/appleby.html>.

Berger, P. (1969), *The Sacred Canopy: Elements of a Sociological Theory of Religion*. Garden City, NY: Doubleday.

Bourdieu, P. (1984), *Distinction: A Social Critique of the Judgment of Taste* (trans. Richard Nice). Cambridge: Harvard University Press.

Bourdieu, P. (1998), *Practical Reason: On the Theory of Action*. Palo Alto, CA: Stanford University Press.

Clark, L. S. (2007), 'Introduction: Identity, belonging, and religious lifestyle branding (fashion Bibles, Bhangra parties, and Muslim pop)', in L. S. Clark (ed.), *Religion, Media, and the Marketplace*. New Brunswick, NJ: Rutgers University Press, pp. 1–33.

Couldry, N. (2008), 'Mediatization or mediation? Alternative understandings of the emergent space of digital storytelling', *New Media and Society*, 10(3), 373–391.

Foucault, M. (1977), *Language, Counter-Memory, Practice*. New York: Cornell University Press.

Foucault, M. (1972), *The Archeology of Knowledge and the Discourse on Language*. New York: Harper and Row.

Giddens, A. (1991), *Modernity and Self-Identity: Self and Society in the Late-Modern Age*. Stanford, CA: Stanford University Press.

Gitlin, T. (1980), *The Whole World is Watching: The Mass Media in the Making and Unmaking of the American Left*. Berkeley, CA: University of California Press.

Hadden, J. and Shupe, A. (1988), *Televangelism: Power and Politics on God's Frontier*. New York: Henry Holt and Co.

Hammond, P. (1992), *Religion and Personal Autonomy: The Third Disestablishment in America*. Columbia, SC: University of South Carolina Press.

Hendershot, H. (2004), *Shaking the World for Jesus*. Chicago: University of Chicago Press.

Hjarvard, S. (2008), 'The mediatization of society', *Nordicom Review*, (29)2.

Hjarvard, S. (2007), 'Changing media, changing language. The mediatization of society and the spread of English and medialects', paper presented to the 57th ICA Conference, San Francisco, CA, 23–28 May.

Hoover, S. M. (1996), *Religion in the Media Age*. London: Routledge.

Hunter, J. D. (1992), *Culture Wars: The Struggle to Define America*. New York: Basic Books.

Marsden, G. (1983), 'Preachers of paradox: The religious New Right in historical perspective', in M. Douglas and S. M. Tipton (eds), *Religion and America: Spirituality in a Secular Age*. Boston: Beacon Press, pp. 150–168.

Marty, M. E. and Appleby, R. S. (1993), 'Introduction' in M. E. Marty and R. Scott Appleby (eds), *Fundamentalisms and the State: Remaking*

Polities, Economies, and Militance. Chicago: University of Chicago Press, pp. 1–9.

McDannell, C. (1998), *Material Christianity: Religion and Popular Culture in America*. New Haven, CT: Yale University Press.

McLoughlin, W. G. (1978), *Revivals, Awakenings and Reform*. Chicago: University of Chicago Press.

Mead, W. R. (2008), 'Born again: America's evangelicals are growing more moderate – and more powerful', *The Atlantic*, 301(2), 21–24.

Medved, M. (1992), *Hollywood vs. America: Popular Culture and the War on Traditional Values*. New York: Harper Collins.

Mcnamara, J. R. (2006), *Media and Male Identity: The Making and Remaking of Men*. New York: Palgrave Macmillan.

Rockefeller Foundation (1981), *The Religion Beat: The Reporting of Religion in the Media. A Rockefeller Conference Report*. New York: Rockefeller Foundation.

Roof, W. C. (1999), *Spiritual Marketplace: Baby Boomers and the Remaking of American Religion*. Princeton: Princeton University Press.

Schultz, W. (2004), 'Reconstructing mediatization as an analytical concept', *European Journal of Communication*, 19(1), 87–101.

Sreberny-Mohammadi, A. and Mohammadi, A. (1994), *Small Media, Big Revolution: Communication, Culture, and the Iranian Revolution*. Minneapolis: University of Minnesota Press.

Sumiala-Seppänen, J., Lundby, K. and Salokangas, R. (2006), *Implications of the Sacred in (Post) Modern Media*. Goteborg, Sweden: Nordicom.

Swartz, D. (1996), 'Bridging the study of culture and religion: Pierre Bourdieu's political economy of symbolic power', *Sociology of Religion*, 57(1), 71–85.

Warner, R. S. (1993), 'Work in progress toward a new paradigm for the socio-logical study of religion in the United States', *American Journal of Sociology*, 98(5), March, 1044–1093.

Wolfe, A. (2008), 'And the Winner is . . .', *The Atlantic*, 301(2), 56–63.

Part I

Histories

Chapter 2

*What Can Peacebuilders Learn
from Fundamentalists?*

R. Scott Appleby

Introduction

In the 1970s and 1980s the radical Jewish movement known as Gush Emunim ('Bloc of the Faithful') conducted a well-orchestrated public relations campaign in Israel to garner sympathy for the distinctive religious-political worldview underlying their controversial activities. Gush 'pioneers', as they liked to style themselves, had established the first wave of illegal settlements in the Palestinian territories occupied by Israel after the Six-Day War in June 1967. Composed of yeshiva students and Torah scholars from the Merkaz Harav school of thought, the original movement at its core was native born (70 per cent), Ashkenazic (82 per cent) and more religiously observant and better educated than the average Israeli Jew. A major goal of the public relations blitz, however, was to blur the boundaries between the 'fundamentalist' religious core of the movement and its expansionist allies, including other religious Jews (e.g., the Religious Zionists) and secular Israelis (e.g., the Land of Israel Movement), who were also dedicated to extending the boundaries of the State of Israel. In this way, Gush Emunim presented itself, inaccurately, as 'popular, heterogeneous and as embracing the majority of Zionists' (Aran 1991: 301).

By staging mass rallies and coordinating the illegal establishment of new settlement in the Territories with festive marches of Orthodox families across 'Judea' and 'Samaria', Gush Emunim encouraged sympathetic media coverage and exacerbated political rifts in the Knesset. The sociologist Gideon Aran, who was a participant-observer with the movement during its early years, comments on the extremists' 'media savvy':

Gush Emunim (GE) is aware of the value of public relations and excels in use of the mass media; the activists are not camera shy. The movement's campaigns receive extensive press coverage, and numerous forums are available for expression of its views. The Israeli public is extensively exposed to scenes of settlers ascending the hills of Judea and Samaria. Television viewers can recite GE slogans by heart and are almost intimately acquainted with the movement's spokesmen and activists, settlements, and institutions (Aran 1991: 311).

Indeed, the activism of the fundamentalists possesses an exhibitionist dimension. 'A less predictable phenomenon is the pretense and pomp that GE members often express in aspects of their religiosity otherwise free of radical significance', Aran writes. They 'enjoy parading not only their political initiatives but also their ritualistic lives, often in a demonstrative and essentially spiteful manner'. Habitual religious practices are performed by fundamentalists 'with a high level of awareness and some measure of presumptuousness'. Routine Orthodox rites may also be exploited 'as an expression of protest or provocation. For example, group members wear prayer shawls and long beards, identified traditionally with the ultra-Orthodox, as part of a distinctive ensemble combined with jeans or military fatigues' (Aran 1991: 312).

During the zenith of the secular Zionist ethos in the 1960s, Aran explains, Israeli nationals tended to conceal their religiosity, and the Orthodox sought integration into mainstream Israeli social, economic and political circles. They removed the traditional head covering altogether, replaced it with neutral headwear, or reduced the size of their skullcaps and moved them to the side where they could barely be seen. By contrast, 'the significant rise in self-esteem – or perhaps even vanity – among the Israeli Orthodox which accompanied the rise of GE may be measured according to the gradual increase in the skullcap's diameter and its assumption of increasingly blatant colours and forms' in the 1970s and 1980s (Aran 1991: 312).

To these fundamentalist Jews, 'Religion is politics and politics an expression of religiosity'. The activist surge, invested with motives 'that are not strictly religious but born of social and political frustration', Aran writes:

> exhibits such high levels of religious energy that existing religious structures cannot contain them, at which point they erupt and overflow, threatening civil order. Less acknowledged is the fact that the explosion carries seeds of subversion that threaten the existing religious order itself (Aran 1991: 313–314).

Indeed, the Gush Emunim worked diligently to downplay their marked departure from traditional orthodoxy. They used the media to make the radical appear normative. To the careful observer, however, the self-anointed true believers intentionally demonstrative and public performance of religion – enacted with what Aran calls 'a high level of awareness and some measure of presumptuousness' (1991: 312) – reflected a level of self-consciousness and calculation uncharacteristic of traditional religion. Rather fundamentalist activism is redolent of late modern propaganda, a style of activism thoroughly acculturated to a media-drenched culture of self-promotion and artifice.[1]

Fundamentalism's Media-Friendly Family Traits

The evolution of Jewish fundamentalism as embodied in Gush Emunim captures something of the genius of the militant anti-modernist movements that arose in the twentieth century within Judaism, Christianity and Islam. The comparative construct 'fundamentalism' encompasses the 'family resemblances' shared by these disparate movements, which have little in common beyond a striking and intriguing pattern of response to aspects of secular modernity they find threatening, indeed spiritually deadly. That pattern of response, in turn, is marked by five ideological traits which, taken together, constitute the logic of fundamentalist extremism: reactivity, selectivity, absolutism, dualism and millennialism (Almond et al. 2003).

The synergy generated by the interplay of *reactivity* and *selectivity* accounts for the fundamentalists' innate understanding of the persuasive power of mass media and their appropriation of its discursive patterns. Although they arise in radically different religious and political contexts, and do not share a world-view or specific doctrines, the religiously inspired activists who belong to what I am calling the family of fundamentalisms do share the conviction that organized religion and 'traditional' religious lifestyles, beliefs and practices have come under concerted assault in the modern era. An Iranian intellectual spoke for a generation of fundamentalists in Christianity and Judaism as well as Islam, when he characterized modern materialism, hedonism, secularism and feminism (with its attack on 'divinely ordained' patriarchy) as symptoms of 'Westoxication', a modern disease of the soul.

Such religious critics saw the hegemony of the secular nation-state, with its privatization of religion and differentiation of the religious from the political, as the inevitable and predictable culmination of a conspiracy of forces. For them, secular modernity is *not* a mere historical accident, but an intentional, coordinated, potentially lethal assault on theism, a juggernaut striving to loosen peoples' grip on tradition and faith.

In short, whatever presenting symptoms or consequences of aggressive secularization stir their initial response, those who are called, or who call themselves, 'true believers', 'ultra-orthodox', 'fundamentalists', etc., are reacting ultimately to *the marginalization of religion* (Almond et al. 2003: 93–94).

And yet the fundamentalists are themselves modern people, and they react by plumbing the repertoire of reactions available to moderns. The ranks of true believers include a significant proportion of engineers, computer software geeks, medical technicians and other practitioners of applied science. Not surprisingly, they tend to approach sacred scriptures and religious traditions in the manner of an engineer searching his tool-chest, selecting only the items that are useful for the constructive (or destructive) task at hand. Owing to their code of strict obedience to commandments and ethical injunctions enjoined by these sacred sources, however, fundamentalists are also *selective* in their intriguing adoption and adaptation of the most powerful products of techno-scientific modernity. The principle of selection is guided by a confidence that these products are largely instrumental, and can be turned from profane to sacred ends.

Thus the fundamentalists positioned themselves well ahead of the curve, throughout the twentieth century, when it came to appropriating media. Much earlier than their conservative, orthodox and liberal co-religionists, the modern anti-modernists within Christianity, Islam and Judaism identified 'the media' as the powerful ally of the encroaching secular nation-state and the most morally debilitating cultural weapon of the godless. They saw that radio, followed by television, cinema and, eventually, cyberspace, threatened to supplant the local church by making widely available alternative, de-sacralized spaces of popular communication and 'congregation'.

But the Bible-believing Christian televangelist, the fiery anti-Western Muslim cassette preacher and the media-genic Jewish settler propagandist also saw that the force of mass media could be turned, jujitsu-like, against the godless. Television and radio could be deployed to reinforce the very religious and communal identity under siege by Elvis, soap operas, *Dallas* and the like. Exploiting this insight led Biblical inerrantists to build an alternative media empire in the United States during the middle decades of the century (Carpenter 1997: 229–232). Islamic extremists discovered the propagandistic uses of the web early in its life, and used cyberspace as a virtual school of jihadist indoctrination (Hailman and Friedman 2003: 252–253). Gush Emunim mocked the staid print culture of their Haredi counterparts in the Jewish world, until even the passive messianists got their media act together and staged a tele-vised rally, featuring an address by Rabbi Eliezer Schach, in Israel's Yad Eliahu stadium (Schultze 2003). Even Hindu nationalists used the nationwide Indian television broadcast of the Ramayana – the epic of the Lord Ram, the sup-posed 'founder' of the Hindu nation – to raise cultural awareness of and support for their doctrine of *Hindutva* ('Hindu-ness') (van der Veer 1994: 172–178).

The origins of the fundamentalist courtship and appropriation of modern media coincided with the mass migration to cities, which transformed the lives of hundreds of millions of twentieth century pilgrims. Believers in Chicago, Cairo and Khartoum came to appreciate that modern media are ideal instru-ments for those who wish to reach the outsider, the marginalized. Through the media, the margin may become the centre, or one of many centres. North and South American Christian televangelism (and mass outdoor rallies by televangelists promoted on the airwaves) provide the obvious examples of the canny use of communications technology. Perhaps more striking to the American reader would be Donald Swearer's description of the skilful use of the media by Theravada Buddhists, on display in the lavish 'productions' at the Prathum Thani headquarters of the Wat Dhammakaya. Swearer notes that the broad-based popular support for the Dhammakaya movement:

> stems from an astute (media) packaging of a fundamentalistic form of Thai Buddhism that offers a way of embracing a secular modern life-style while retaining the communal identity once offered by traditional Buddhism – all the while maintaining that it is 'authentic' or 'true' Buddhism in contrast to its competitors (Swearer 1991: 666–667).

The believers who adopted the aggressive anti-modernism, reactive selectivity and dualist worldview intrinsic to fundamentalism were 'framers' of the highest order. They knew instinctively – one might say, psychologically and spiritually – how to identify, select, portray, project and enhance the drama inherent in their supernaturalist worldview. In this context the final three ideological traits or habits of mind, of 'fundamentalism' are relevant to our purposes here: absolutism, dualism and millennialism. Fundamentalists see themselves as righteous soldiers fighting a cosmic war, anointed agents of the divine plan. The vision is predicated on a *dualism* that views the world as separated into identifiable camps of sheep and goats, orthodox and infidels, elect and reprobate. Within such a cosmic worldview, the truths vouchsafed to the orthodox by God are not subject to revision or open to cultural or scientific criticism; their truth is inerrant, infallible, *absolute*. Added to this potent imaginary is the end-times or '*millennial*' scenario, a vision of final, apocalyptic vindication shared, *mutatis mutandis*, by Christianity, Judaism and Islam. The expectation of a special dispensation, a divinely ordained time of vindication for the righteous and punishment of their enemies, provides the charismatic leader with the necessary justification for a radical departure from ordinary ethical behaviours, including injunctions against murder or suicide.

What secular scenarios and self-images could possibly be more dramatic, more deeply driven by plot and suspense? Cherished by the producers of fundamentalist novels, comic books, movies and websites is the satisfying irony of it all: the technology of the infidels, which we created and they channelled to ill ends, is now turned against them! Their weapons of mass destruction are delivered unto their own heads! The Christian Messiah returns on clouds of glory, in the role of (incredibly violent) slayer of the anti-Christ and his minions. The Muslim Mahdi or Hidden Imam comes out of occultation to vanquish the Zionist interloper. The Jewish 'Land of Israel' is restored to its original biblical proportions by a miraculous process of the re-sanctification of the secular Zionists, who proceed to expel the Arab interloper. How Hollywood![2]

Creating the Imagined World by Projecting It

The fundamentalist approach to local, national and global media features a fascinating interplay between first order naiveté and second order naiveté. The first naiveté, which takes the media at functional face value, so to speak, as an uncomplicated instrument of education, formation and evangelism, is reflected in a rhetorical/discursive approach that is deceptively simple: saturate the air waves, the screen, the internet with the constituent elements of the religious imaginary. The strategy is to create, sustain and reinforce the total world of the religious imagination, using the same saturation mode employed by the madrasas, yeshivot and seminaries.

Accordingly, fundamentalists operating in this defensive mode strive to create and sustain a subculture that wraps the believer in a protective and nurturing cocoon of religious symbols, images, and discourse. In his book *God's Choice*, the educational anthropologist Alan Peshkin gives readers a glimpse into such an all-encompassing 'total world', that of the Christian evangelical and fundamentalist day schools and academies that blanketed sections of the country in the 1970s and 1980s. He quotes the pastor of a Christian academy:

> Without [such schools], we can't rightfully accent our biblical commitment ... The Christian schools, I think, are the only way we'll be able to have missionaries to send out to the world, provide preachers and train school-teachers for the Christian school movement (Peshkin 1986: 7).

Such institutions are 'total', in that they attempt to control the entire environment of the students, providing alternative media of instruction that will counteract the insidious influences of mainstream American culture. 'We can deal with the moral aspects of life ... and we can touch our students' total behaviour pattern', says the pastor. 'That's what makes us a twenty-four hour school. For us, this is a total life' (Peshkin 1986: 7).[3] The curriculum, Peshkin explains, is structured on the principle of the Christianization of knowledge. He quotes a teacher:

> Our classes here reflect the Word of God. We believe that history, for example, is *his* story, the unfolding of the word of Jesus Christ on the center stage of the world. A man trying to write a history textbook that presents Jesus Christ as just another historical figure has no concept of real truth. We don't teach that way in our history classes. Math is a study of orderliness. The Word of God says, 'Let everything be done decently and in order'. Try to keep a checkbook sometimes without using some order and organization. Science is an understanding of God's handiwork. Men deny the Word of God and try to make us believe that all that we see about us has come about just through a series of events. Sometimes, the general term of evolution is used to apply to all this, but the Word of God is different on that. It clearly

teaches that man was created from nothing: 'Out of nothing', God states. The evolution says that the dinosaur and man were epochs of time apart, but Dr. Henry Morris, a born-again man, a Christian man, has a picture in one of his books you won't find in the average, secular high school biology book. It shows in the same petrified streambed a footprint of a man and a footprint of a large dinosaur. So these creatures were on earth the same time as man. The evolutionists deny that, but here's a photograph that clearly shows the untruth of the evolutionary position. You'll get that kind of information in our schools; you'll see that kind of thing emphasized (Peshkin 1986: 50).

In her comparative sociological study of a Christian school sponsored by a working-class fundamentalist congregation, and the Christian academy sponsored by a middle-class independent fellowship, Susan Rose explains that such schools are responding to 'increased secularization in the public schools and larger society and greater privatization of religion' by enclosing them in 'constant and close-knit affiliations in a universe of shared symbols'. Censorship of materials from secular textbooks and the secular media is part of their strategy (Rose 1988: 192–193).

By the same token, 20 years later, the worldwide web is the fundamentalist's medium, for God is the author of the story and the creator of the technology. History remains His story. And yet, the fundamentalist, inevitably a political animal, also ventures beyond the 'sacred narrative' saturation mode of the first naiveté, to construct a second order discourse. This is, ultimately, a discourse of power, constructed via a self-aware, calculated manipulation of media and 'the media', which is acknowledged to be an indispensable means of claiming public space for one's political programme. In playing the game of politics and attempting to influence mainstream culture, the sacred myth and religious symbols may need to be masked, sublimated, de-contextualized or otherwise politicized in the interests of their own long-term survival.

Thus the devout may be led to cheer Iran's President as if he were a soccer star. What will Mahmoud Ahmadinejad do next, having brought Mike Wallace, *60 Minutes* and the trailing secular media to his doorstep to do his bidding, like an owner brings his dog to heel? Which will arrive first, the Hidden Imam or Iran's nuclear programme, both of which the Iranian president expects in the short term, and sees as accompanying pieces? What is the proper form of Shi'ite governance in the twenty-first century? How is the Islamic Republic of Iran positioning itself to support Shi'ite brethren in besieged Iraq? The answers to these and other questions of interest to the Islamic revolutionary can be found on Ahmadinejad's personal blog, which features, *inter alia*, reminiscences of his heroism as a critic of the Shah's government; anti-Zionist propaganda; a personal message to the American people, imploring them to deplore the Bush administration; and excerpts from the *Nahjul Balagha*, 'one of our most valuable religious texts [...] undoubtedly the greatest management charter of Islamic government' (Ahmadinejad 2007).

The urge to evangelize and proselytize, to create a dualistic world and situate one's disciples therein, is not confined to those who would forge a religious nationalist identity for believer-citizens. Today, transnational religious-political identities are the fashion, so vast and formative is the 'glo-local' media's reach. The capability meets the comprehensive mission aspirations of some Christians and some Muslims – and even some unconventional Jews, who hail from a religion not normally given over to converting outsiders (Ravitzky 1994: 310). Scholarly theses proliferate on the blossoming of Al Jazeera, for example, and its 'framing' of worldwide Islamic issues such as France's outlawing of the *hijab* for schoolgirls. Such sly representations constitute a strategy in creating a worldwide *umma* and, not least, a mass Muslim market (see Lynch 2005, Tatham 2006, Zayani 2005).

The strand of cynicism that is apparent in the crass manipulation of religious symbols and precepts does not mean, however, that the fundamentalist is a postmodernist. The fundamentalists have not abandoned the modernist's hope for Progress, Meaning and Order. Fundamentalists are, if not the world's last institution-builders, among the most vigorous ones still standing. Transforming the world through the media is the historical legacy of every fundamentalist, from the cassette-carrying Ayatollah Khomeini, to the klieg-light-loving denizens of Pat Robertson's *700 Club*. Among the radical messages of 9/11, the world's most notorious case of 'demonstration effect', was the Islamists' call to fellow Muslims to cooperate in the work of building militias, schools and new regimes in Pakistan, Afghanistan, Algeria, Saudi Arabia and elsewhere. Even a restored caliphate is now possible in the Islamist imagination, emboldened by the images of the rubble where once stood the World Trade Center (Lawrence 2005).

Indeed, many of the ideological and behavioural family resemblances shared by militant true believers from diverse backgrounds converge in fundamentalism's seemingly innate understanding and effortless manipulation of media of mass communication. The true believers' envy of the secular modernist and the desire to steal his thunder; the tactic of fostering a sense of crisis and urgency in order to force a decision upon the somnolent co-religionist or the potential recruit; the flair for the dramatic and symbolic act, which plays shrewdly to the popular appetite for sensational display – each of these tendencies can be traced, in part, to the fundamentalists' familiarity with the culture of techno-scientific modernity 'from the inside'.

A potentially debilitating irony plagues the fundamentalists' selective appropriation of secular modernity, however. In their utilitarian ransacking of both the storehouse of applied science *and the religious tradition itself*, the militant defenders of orthodoxy may be undermining the very practices and habits of mind essential to the tradition they seek to uphold. For the believer who genuinely reveres the religious tradition, will also inhabit it, accepting its demands without trying to rationalize or instrumentalize the internal contradictions, inconsistencies and ambiguities. The fundamentalist cannot be bothered with such complexity and internal pluralism; she is too much in a hurry, destroying or creating reality, to be absorbed by it. Yet in this irony lies a lesson for the peacebuilder, who might otherwise be instructed by the fundamentalists' approach to mass media.

Waging Peace Through the Media: The Work Ahead

Whereas fundamentalists excel in promoting their cause through the media and in mastering the latest techniques of propaganda, the advocates of nonviolent conflict transformation, including religiously inspired peacebuilders, find their efforts eclipsed by their more aggressive, agonistic, headline-stealing counterparts. Rather than heighten a global sense of dread, as the fundamentalists attempt, faith-based peacebuilders seek to heighten a global sense of hope. How might they do so?

It is possible, of course, that this is the wrong question. Why should peacebuilders seek publicity or wish to disseminate their message broadly? Holiness is hidden, while scandal and sin, violence and vengeance play to mass audiences, in the public spotlight. And even if peacebuilders sought greater coverage and outreach, their message may be considered far less 'newsworthy' or popularly appealing than wars and rumours of war. Imminent Armageddon is interesting, while 'building peace' is often painstaking, incremental, long-term and sometimes tedious work.

In the parlance of professional peacebuilders, 'peace' is understood as the set of conditions that enable people to manage or resolve conflicts nonviolently or with a minimum of violence. Positively, peace is understood as a set of conditions in which authentic human flourishing is possible; such conditions are variously defined to include access to clean drinking water, health care and education, basic human security and protection of human rights, transparent and accountable governance, sustainable economic development, the right of political self-determination and the like. 'Building' indicates that peace is an ongoing process, engaging a range of actors at every level of society and across disciplines and cultural, religious and class borders (Lederach 1997).

In order to sustain the conditions that make for peace, the professional knows, the community must never stop building. What is being built, ultimately, is a network of sustainable human relationships – partnerships and friendships sufficiently robust to survive, and to help the community survive, the attempt by extremists to exploit differences of race, religion, ethnicity and privilege that divide communities and exacerbates conflict that turns deadly when resources are strained and tribal mentality prevails. In an influential study of communal conflict in India, the political scientist Ashutosh Varshney found that, in communities that were not torn by communal violence, the establishment of personal relationships across boundaries was the most effective antidote to politically or racially motivated exploitation of differences. In particular,

Hindus and Muslims overcame media stereotypes and were able to resist pressures to compete violently for resources, when they had participated together in the institutions and programmes fostered by civil society – the associational forms of civic life – such as business partnerships, parent–teacher associations, professional guilds and the like (Varshney 2002).

This example raises an important question, however, precisely in its seeming lesson that *unmediated*, person-to-person relationships strengthen the conditions for peace – or, at least, the conditions for resistance to political manipulation rooted in extremist 'othering' – while 'media' comes between people, (mis)representing them to one another from a distorting distance.

Yet the peacebuilder who thinks and acts **strategically** ranges across distances, across levels of society, seeing the field in both its horizontal/local and vertical/global dimensions. Horizontally, she endeavours to comprehend the dynamics that shape the proximate conflict setting, be it a village, town, city, nation or region. In this mode she is trained to diagnose the facts in the field, to comprehend the interrelated parts of the organic whole, which is a discrete community, however broken or dysfunctional. Arms trade, forms of local governance, water rights, strength of media, ethnic and religious profile, educational system, international politics and the like: all factors that shape a society are the strategic peacebuilder's area of expertise. The peacebuilder is always looking for allies in the community, partners in establishing and sustaining cross-ethnic, cross-religious relationships. While building person-to-person, face-to-face relationships and alliances are the goal of this mapping exercise, in all but the smallest communities it cannot be conducted successfully merely through personal lobbying. Effective communication and persuasion across time and space is essential to the task.

Moreover, the strategic peacebuilder seeks such partnerships not only 'horizontally', in the conflict setting itself, but 'vertically' as well, at the regional, national and global levels. In this context the appropriate partners are transnational NGOs, intergovernmental and governmental agencies, humanitarian organizations, the World Bank, US-AID, the Aga Khan Foundation, the United Nations, the Vatican, the Organization of Islamic Conference – whoever and whatever might serve as a source of resources, from funding to food to expertise, in the effort to tilt the balance of power towards the reduction or ending of violence, the creation of economic and political opportunity, the sowing of hope. In this effort communication media is clearly essential (Lederach and Appleby 2009).

The strategic peacebuilder, to be effective, must think of the field as a battlefield of sorts; by disposition, some peace people reject this metaphor. But it is the reality we face. Concede this perception to the fundamentalist: we *are* in a cosmic battle, a struggle for hearts and minds and, yes, for souls – certainly, a contest to shape what peacebuilding theorist and practitioner John Paul Lederach calls 'the moral imagination' (Lederach 2005). The strategic peacebuilder needs recruits for her nonviolent, constructive, inclusive, bridge-building approach to the root causes of conflict, including structural violence and systemic injustice, just as surely as does the fundamentalist.

The peacebuilder must think and act strategically in the political sense as well: how do I frame *our* story, *our* vision, *our* worldview, *our* sense of the tradition and the scriptures? In response to the 'holiness is hidden' argument, one might invoke no less righteous a 'propagandist' than Jesus: 'Hide not your light beneath a bushel-basket' (Matthew 5: 14); 'be as shrewd as serpents and as innocent as doves' (Matthew 10: 16). Strategic peacebuilders sometimes have their ears closed to such counsel, owing to a misguided sense of humility. Closely related is the faith-based peacebuilder's respect for human dignity and particularly the ineffable core of human agency: like Muslim philosophers who forbade icons and other representations of the divine, lest God be reduced to a flawed and incomplete and ultimately distorting human image or sign, some Christian, Muslim and Jewish peacebuilders wince at the prospect of 'framing' a complex human story, thereby reducing it to images, sound bites and modes of discourse that fail to capture, ambiguity, irony, uncertainty and other dimensions of human beings caught in conflict and war. A final inhibition strategic peacebuilders bring to the question of utilizing media is the fear that relationship building is not well served by publicity; it is a far more subtle and delicate vocation, best pursued in personal and face-to-face encounters.

Yet each of these objections fails to address the underlying challenge facing peacebuilders: without effective communications and media relations, they are under-equipped to achieve the task at hand. Reconciliation is a weak child who needs to be nurtured, not only in person but also in public, because, as the fundamentalists understand: *fides ex auditu*: faith comes from hearing – and seeing. We are mimetic people; we watch and imitate those we wish to emulate.

In addition, effective use of the media is central to any sound strategy in waging a war of ideas about how best to manage conflict over resources, the direction of social change, political philosophies and public priorities. The peacebuilder who thinks and acts strategically must blend activism and relationship building, in part because unjust laws and structures can often impede relationship building across classes, races and religions. The activist, in turn, must become practiced at employing media, for public advocacy for social, legal and political change is both the result and the ultimate goal of constructive relationship-building across divides.

Not least, peacebuilding falls squarely within the arena of the imagination. In order to build a better, more humane, just and peaceful society, one must envision it. The media, precisely as a showcase and framer of images, emotions and sensibilities, is a potential ally to peacebuilders whose first and foremost task is to inspire hope by constructing a common narrative that makes sense of peoples' striving and suffering for justice. In his treatise on 'the art and soul of building peace', *The Moral Imagination*, John Paul Lederach writes compellingly of the need to 'create spaces, construct platforms and build webs of relationships'; less developed in the literature of peace studies are recommendations for the effective use of media in creating and reinforcing an underlying vision and narrative that would inform these tasks (Lederach 2005).

In framing our discussion in this way, it is my hope that scholars and practitioners of modern communications will redouble their efforts to enhance the use of media in two ways. First, communicators are called to craft sophisticated, nuanced examinations of the complex social and political problems facing conflicted and war-torn societies. Second, and even more challenging, peacebuilders are called to employ media effectively to 'frame the myth' – that is, to convey, via symbol-laden narratives that evoke the depth dimensions of human experience, the nature of human suffering and the riveting tale of the ongoing striving for justice in settings of obvious oppression and deprivation. If the human story of the struggle for justice and peace is conveyed via media that capture even a substantial portion of the story's inherent moral power, such 'propaganda' will serve the essential peacebuilder's goals of legitimating constructive social and political reform, mobilizing people to work for the desired transformations, and providing 'demonstration effect' of the benevolent consequences that follow upon relationship-building in the service of nonviolent social change.

The world does not present itself to us as a coherent plot or self-evident Truth. It demands to be interpreted. It could well be a tale told by an idiot, signifying nothing – but this possibility is rejected by both religious militants for peace and fundamentalists who endorse righteous violence. Both camps assume, seek, construct meaning and live according to the myths they create. Both are idealists, believing that their constructed meaning is true for all humankind. What is the meaning of 9/11? Of the Bosnian war of 1992–1995 and its outcomes? Does the Oslo Process constitute a precedent for a real Road Map to peace in the Middle East, or was it a detour? Were the Argentinian mothers of the Disappeared who made Cinco de Mayo a feast of remembrance and ritual for justice poignant embodiments of the dispossessed and abandoned, or heralds of global people power?

In peacebuilding, no less than in the cosmic war waged by the fundamentalists, hermeneutics is all. And for better or worse, in the twenty-first century, the mass media, especially the electronic media, is *a*, perhaps *the*, paramount interpreter, framer, creator of meaning and mobilizer. Strategic peacebuilders would do well to understand and accept this somewhat inconvenient fact. The fundamentalists did so a century ago.

Notes

1   For analyses of fundamentalists' media activism, see Rebecca Moore (2005), Heather Hendershot (2004) especially pp. 1–14, and Linda Kintz and Julia Lesage (1998).

2   See the bestselling novels, several of which have been made into movies,

in the 'Left Behind' series, which popularizes the fundamentalist Christian apocalypticism known as premillennial dispensationalism. The first of sixteen novels in the series by Tim LaHaye and Jerry B. Jenkins is *Left Behind: A Novel of the Earth's Last Days* (1995). On the Mahdi and graphic novels regarding the Dajal or anti-Christ figure in Sunni Islam, I am indebted to a lecture by Barbara Stowasser, delivered at Georgetown University in August 2002; on Jewish sanctification of the secular Zionists, see Aran (1991: 290–295).

3   The pastor's school is part of America's fundamentalist Christian school movement, Peshkin explains. 'More particularly, it belongs to the nation-wide American Association of Christian Schools, (AACS) and to its state branch, the Illinois Association of Christian Schools (IACS). The AACS began with approximately 125 member schools and 25,000 students in 1972 and grew to more than 1,000 schools and 150,000 students by 1982. It became a full-service organization for its affiliated schools who must 'subscribe without reservation' to the AACS Statement of faith. This statement holds to the Bible's inerrancy, and emphasizes, among other doctrine, Christ's Virgin Birth and Second Coming, salvation only 'by grace through faith', and the necessity of the 'New Birth' (Peshkin 1986: 35).

References

Ahmadinejad, M. (2007), 'A guideline for Islamic governance', *Mahmoud Ahmadinejad's Personal Memos* [online], 1 December 2007, retrieved 22 June 2008 from <http://www.ahmadinejad.ir/en>.

Almond, G. A., Appleby, R. S. and Sivan, E. (2003), *Strong Religion: The Rise of Fundamentalisms in the Modern World*. Chicago: University of Chicago Press.

Aran, G. (1991), 'Jewish Zionist Fundamentalism: The bloc of the faithful in Israel (Gush Emunim)', in M. E. Marty and R. S. Appleby (eds), *Fundamentalisms Observed*. Chicago: University of Chicago Press, pp. 265–344.

Carpenter, J. A. (1997), *Revive Us Again: The Reawakening of American Fundamentalism*. New York: Oxford University Press, pp. 229–232.

Heilman, S. C. and Friedman, M. (1991), 'Religious Fundamentalism and Religious Jews: The Case of the Haredim', in M. E. Marty and R. S. Appleby (eds), *Fundamentalisms Observed*. Chicago: University of Chicago Press, pp. 252–253.

Hendershot, H. (2004), *Shaking the World for Jesus: Media and Conservative Evangelical Culture*. Chicago: University of Chicago Press.

Kintz, L. and Lesage, J. (eds) (1998), *Media, Culture, and the Religious Right*. Minneapolis: University of Minnesota Press.

LaHaye, T. and Jenkins, J. B. (1995), *Left Behind: A Novel of the Earth's Last Days*. Carol Stream, IL: Tyndale House Publishers.

Lawrence, B. (ed.) (2005), *Messages to the World: The Statements of Osama Bin Laden*. London: Verso.

Lederach, J. P. (1997), *Building Peace: Sustainable Reconciliation in Divided Societies*. Washington, DC: US Institute of Peace Press.

Lederach, J. P. (2005), *The Moral Imagination: The Art and Soul of Building Peace*. New York: Oxford University Press.

Lederach, J. P. and Appleby, R. S., 'Strategic Peacebuilding: An Overview', in D. Philpott (ed.), *Strategic Peacebuilding*. New York: Oxford University Press. Forthcoming 2009.

Lynch, M. (2005), *Voices of the New Arab Public: Iraq, al-Jazeera, and Middle East Politics Today*. New York: Columbia University Press.

Moore, R. (2005), 'A Framework for Understanding Fundamentalism', in C. H. Badaracco (ed.), *Quoting God: How Media Shape Ideas About Religion and Culture*. Waco, TX: Baylor University Press, pp. 87–99.

Peshkin, A. (1986), *God's Choice: The Total World of a Fundamentalist Christian School*. Chicago: University of Chicago Press.

Ravitzky, A. (1994), 'The Contemporary Lubavitch Movement: Between Conservatism and Messianism', in M. E. Marty and R. S. Appleby (eds), *Accounting for Fundamentalisms*. Chicago: University of Chicago Press, p. 310.

Rose, S. D. (1988), *Keeping Them Out of the Hands of Satan: Evangelical Schooling in America*. New York: Routledge, pp. 192–193.

Schultze, Q. (2003), *Televangelism and American Culture: The Business of Popular Religion*. Eugene, OR: Wipf and Stock Publishers.

Swearer, D. (1991), 'Fundamentalistic Movements in Theravada Buddhism', in M. E. Marty and R. S. Appleby (eds), *Fundamentalisms Observed*. Chicago: University of Chicago Press, pp. 666–667.

Tatham, S. (2006), *Losing Arab Hearts & Minds: The Coalition, Al-Jazeera & Muslim Public Opinion*. London: Hurst & Co.

Van der Veer, P. (1994), *Religious Nationalism: Hindus and Muslims in India*. Berkeley: University of California Press, pp. 172–178.

Varshney, A. (2002), *Ethnic Conflict and Civic Life: Hindus and Muslims in India*. New Haven, CT: Yale University Press.

Zayani, M. (2005), *The Al Jazeera Phenomenon: Critical Perspectives On New Arab Media*. Boulder, CO: Paradigm Publishers.

Chapter 3

Are Free Expression and Fundamentalism Two Colliding Principles?

Edward Michael Lenert

Introduction

The Danish cartoons controversy began 30 September 2005, when the *Jyllands-Posten*, Denmark's highest-circulation newspaper, published 12 editorial cartoons depicting the Islamic Prophet Muhammad. One of the cartoons featured a drawing of Muhammad with a bomb in his turban, fuse lit and the Islamic creed written on the bomb. Almost immediately a serious situation developed. Islam forbids depictions of Muhammad and critics of the cartoons described them as hateful and blasphemous to people of the Muslim faith. When challenged, the newspaper refused to retract the cartoons or apologize, citing its right of free expression. In the course of various related confrontations, at least 139 people were killed and, almost three years later, the Danish cartoons controversy continues. In 2008, Danish police arrested three persons on charges of plotting to kill Kurt Westergaard, one of the 12 cartoonists whose pictures of Muhammad were published in the *Jyllands-Posten* (Kimmelman 2008).

The longevity of the Danish cartoons controversy suggests a need to examine further the fundamental principles held by the two sides in the conflict. This is precisely the goal of this chapter which will look at this heated dispute in the context of two potentially colliding principles: a religious (Islamic) fundamentalist insistence on observing certain standards of right and wrong, and an equally strong secularist (and Western) insistence on upholding unlimited freedom of expression in the media of mass communication.

The Danish cartoon controversy immediately presents two questions: First, do followers of any religion have the right to threaten or kill others based on their beliefs? Second, are their actions justified if they are responding to direct challenges to those beliefs? I cannot find any justification for the destructive and deadly behaviours of Islamic fundamentalists, and my answer to both of these questions is 'no'. However, equally importantly, the cartoon controversy raises a third and more complex question, namely: Is the Western liberal conception of free expression so absolute that it supports insults to religious fundamentalists? In others words, even in the context of a Western tradition of free expression, was the *Jyllands-Posten*'s publication of the 12 cartoons an impermissible and direct provocation?

Answering this last question is a complicated matter because in the West there is a long history of imagining and arguing that unfettered mass media are central to the survival of democracy and should therefore be protected by law. This is more than a legal doctrine but also a very powerful cultural myth that excites passions among many but particularly among media professionals. As I would argue in this essay, however, a strict adherence to an absolute freedom of the press is far from what most Western legal texts propose. Therefore, the debate about the significance of what the *Jyllands-Posten* editors did is more nuanced than may appear at first sight and has to do with the way we interpret the legal doctrine of freedom of expression.

To explore this problematic, this essay examines current trends in Western legal regulation and in social responses to hateful expression by drawing examples from particular texts of legal rules against hateful speech in various Western European countries and the United States. In the course of the analysis, the case of the Danish cartoons and the public discourse around it are used to illuminate these trends more clearly. Ultimately, the goal of this chapter is to illustrate that there may be alarming similarities between a fundamentalist way of interpreting religious beliefs and an absolutist (or 'fundamentalist') way of interpreting the legal doctrine of freedom of expression. However, the essay also hopes to demonstrate that such interpretations are not the ones intended by most legal codes in contemporary Europe and the USA and are certainly not the only possible ones.

What is Fundamentalism?

Let me now return to the analysis. Before we can answer the question of whether the Danish cartoons were an impermissible provocation, we must address an important clarifying question, namely: What is *fundamentalism*? Fundamentalism is a contested term that means different things to different people and the meaning is often controlled by the context. For the purposes of this chapter, however, I would propose that it would be illuminating to focus on the way so called fundamentalists interpret the surrounding reality. Hence, this chapter's working definition of fundamentalism holds that: *fundamentalism is a rigid style of interpretation, reliant on authoritative texts, to discover rights and duties.* Importantly, this essential trait of fundamentalism-as-interpretation is shared by both Christian and Muslim societies. For those in the West, fundamentalism most often refers to Protestantism that depends on a strict and literal interpretation of the Bible, including its narratives, doctrines, prophecies and moral laws. For Muslims, fundamentalism means that Islamic law is central to state and society, advocating strict adherence to the Koran at all costs and in all spheres of life.

Within a strict interpretation of Islam, visual depictions of the Prophet Muhammad constitute blasphemy and are forbidden, subject to the most severe penalties. To give just one recent example, a British primary school teacher in Sudan, Gillian Gibbons, allowed her pupils to name a teddy bear after the Prophet Muhammad as part of a class assignment. When officials discovered this transgression, Gibbons was arrested and imprisoned under strict blasphemy laws for showing 'contempt and disrespect against the believers'. Had the British government and others not intervened, she could have faced penalties of up to 40 lashes and a year in jail (Judd 2007).

As extreme as this may seem, it is important to realize that the West has not been exempted from the influence of fundamentalism either. In fact, Western traditions have long regarded blasphemy as an offence against the community. When religious faith is at the heart of a society, it is common for the law against blasphemy to protect the fabric of the society, and its faithful, from a perceived challenge or threat (Columbia Encyclopedia 2007). While no European nation today enforces its laws against blasphemy, these laws are indisputably part of Western legal tradition. For example, the British law of blasphemy, based on decisions made by nineteenth-century courts, is restricted to protecting the 'tenets and beliefs of the Church of England' (BBC News 2004). Presently this law is not enforced, and the BBC reports that the last British man to be sent to prison for blasphemy was in 1922 for comparing Jesus with a circus clown (BBC News 2004).

Free Expression Fundamentalism

Using the working definition of fundamentalism proposed above, one could conceive of the strict interpretation of the legal principle of free expression in Western law as a form of 'free expression fundamentalism'. In a similar vein, Richard Webster, author of *A Brief History of Blasphemy* (1990), we can observe that the battle over the Danish cartoons can be characterized as two kinds of rigidity, two forms of fundamentalism (Webster 2002). He asserts that the more closely we examine liberal rhetoric, the more it seems that we are indeed dealing not with a battle between religion and secular liberalism but with a clash between two forms of essentially religious ideology. According to Webster, an analysis of rhetoric such as in the Danish cartoon controversy shows that advocates for the freedom of expression often depict the events as part of a battle to be fought out in terms of 'implacable antitheses' – a war between 'humanity and the forces of inhumanity' and between 'the forces of light and the forces of dark' (Webster 2002).

A fundamentalist style of interpreting texts takes the announced principles as being without limitation or compromise against potentially competing values. In a fundamentalist interpretation, the freedom of expression is an absolute, a principle that must be adhered to. Failure to abide by its clear mandates endangers an entire civilization. Whether Western or Islamic, a fundamentalist style of interpretation is based on bedrock principles. Language is seen as a concrete and unchanging vessel of meaning and does not permit ambiguity, paradox, contradiction or irony.

Free expression fundamentalism is not an advocacy of freedom within the law; rather, it is the law of absolute individual freedom, a moral law that takes precedence over competing considerations. Consider how this way of interpreting free expression factors into the debate over the appropriateness of the publication of the Danish cartoons. It is a form of strict free expression fundamentalism which allowed the editors of various European newspapers, many of which reprinted the offensive Danish cartoons, to conceive of culturally insensitive expressions of opinion as an expression of the ultimate right of every free citizen, rather than as an evil to be avoided whenever possible. For example, Niklas Ekdal of the *Dagens Nyheter*, the largest-circulation Swedish morning newspaper, expresses a fundamentalist interpretation of the right of freedom of expression in the following passage:

> Here it only concerns the defense of an open society against those who want to use violence to send us back to the Middle Ages. There are both similarities and differences with the Rushdie case, 20 years ago. Now just as then, the defense of freedom of speech must be absolute, and now just as then, it is a national issue to protect those who are affected (World Association of Newspapers 2008).

In this passage, Mr. Ekdal seems to be imagining a system that places inerrant faith in the unalloyed benefits of complete freedom of expression. It is strict, unqualified and true; as he puts it 'the defense of freedom of expression must be absolute'.

Another recent example demonstrating some of the qualities of a fundamentalist interpretation of freedom of expression is the position taken by European Commission President José Manuel Barroso. In a February 2006 debate over the Danish cartoons in the Strasbourg Plenary Session, Mr. Barroso stated that, 'Freedom of speech is part of Europe's values and traditions. Let me be clear. Freedom of speech is not negotiable' (European Parliament 2006).

Similarly, Iranian-born professor Afshin Ellian of Leiden University in the Netherlands, has argued that all of Europe should show solidarity with the principles of freedom of expression, regardless of the degree of insult or offense contained in the expression. In an opinion piece in *The Wall Street Journal*, professor Ellian discusses how in March 2008 hardliner Geert Wilders, a Dutch politician who has publicly stated that the Koran is a 'fascist book', made a film with the message that the Koran motivates murderous jihadists. The film includes one of the most famous of the Danish cartoons which depicts Muhammad wearing a bomb-filled turban. Defending this display, Ellian argues that 'any weakness in the resolve' to defend the freedom of expression that permits the publication of the film would be 'betrayal and cowardice' (Ellian 2008).

Speaking on another occasion, and not at all in reference to the Danish cartoons, author Salman Rushdie offered his own unconditional and dogmatic defence of freedom of expression to rebut his Islamic critics: 'free speech is a non-starter says one of my Islamic extremist opponents. No, sir, it is not. Free speech is the whole thing, the whole ball game. Free speech is life itself' (Rushdie 1991). No doubt, Rushdie has unique credentials to argue that 'free speech is life itself'. Following the publication of Rushdie's novel *The Satanic Verses*, Iran's Ayatollah Khomeini called for everyone involved in the book's publication to be punished. The result: Rushdie's Japanese translator was murdered, his Italian translator stabbed, and his Norwegian publisher shot. However, his statement, although made significantly before the time of the Danish cartoons controversy, illustrates the unequivocal nature of what I have termed in this chapter 'free expression fundamentalism'.

A Non-Fundamentalist Style of Interpretation

As the argument so far suggests, libertarian and religious fundamentalisms share a style of interpretation that does not tolerate ambiguity or nuance in the application of rules. By contrast, some texts, by the very way that they are written, require a non-fundamentalist style of interpretation. Consider, for example, the International Covenant on Civil and Political Rights whose Article 18(3) declares that:

Freedom to manifest one's religion or beliefs may be subject only to such limitations as are prescribed by law and are necessary to protect public safety, order, health, or morals or the fundamental rights and freedoms of others (International Covenant on Civil and Political Rights 1966).

In other words, this freedom is not an absolute right, and is subject to balancing against other social interests. Moreover, Article 19 also recognizes that the right of freedom of expression 'carries with it special duties and responsibilities. It may therefore be subject to certain restrictions, but these shall only be such as are provided by law and are necessary . . .' (International Covenant on Civil and Political Rights 1966), including respect for the rights and reputations of others and protection of public order and morals. This text resists a fundamentalist style of interpretation because it uses wording that requires thoughtful consideration and a balance of competing individual and social interests.

In a similar way, in the course of history the practice of American courts has been to move away from a fundamentalist style of interpretation of the constitutional principle of freedom of expression. An exception to this trend can be seen in the opinion of Supreme Court Justice Hugo Black who once dogmatically said that:

> The phrase 'Congress shall make no law' is composed of plain words, easily understood. It is my belief that there are 'absolutes' in our Bill of Rights, and that they were put there on purpose by men who knew what words meant, and meant their prohibitions to be 'absolutes'. In other words, 'If the text of the Constitution prohibited government from taking some action, then that was it' (Black 1960).

However, Justice Black's absolutist (or 'fundamentalist') views do not represent current American interpretation. Indeed, the American legal tradition is complicated in this case; once you start to apply the easy answers of dogma to real life, you can get really stuck in the details. In practice, the law of free expression almost always involves balancing rights.

For example, in *Beauharnais v. Illinois* (1952), the US Supreme Court upheld a state group libel law that made it unlawful to defame a race or class of people. The court rejected the protection of free speech in a case concerning white supremacists. Indeed, the Justices seemed to contextualize their decision within the history of racial strife in Illinois; the legislature reasonably feared substantial evils would come from unrestrained racial utterances.

Contemporary American law no longer recognizes *Beauharnais* as a binding precedent, trumped by the rulings in *R.A.V. v. City of St. Paul* (1992) and *Virginia v. Black* (2003). In *R.A.V. v. City of St. Paul* a majority of the Court struck down a law that prohibited the display of a symbol which one knows or has reason to know 'arouses anger, alarm or resentment in others on the basis of race, colour, creed, religion or gender' (*R.A.V. v. City of St. Paul* 1992). The Court reasoned that since the statute isolated certain words based on their content or viewpoint it therefore violated the First Amendment. Later, in the *Virginia v. Black* case, a majority of the US Supreme Court held that, under certain circumstances, a state could outlaw the display of symbols that intentionally intimidate any person or group of persons. Once again, the majority found that the specific law in question was invalid, but said that in general principle the First Amendment permits government to outlaw particularly virulent forms of symbolic intimidation – such as cross burning – when the intention is intimidation. However, the Supreme Court insisted on a distinction between illegal 'threats of intimidation' and cases like the Ku Klux Klan's constitutionally protected display of symbols and messages of shared ideology, even if hateful in the view of others (*Virginia v. Black* 2003). And so the rule in the USA has arisen that the principle of free expression protects someone who displays controversial symbols as long as the element of intimidation is absent.

These rules, taken together, illustrate the dictum of Justice Holmes that essentially 'the life of the law is experience' and that legal results cannot be reached by the mere rigorous application of logic (Holmes 1880). By admitting a reasoned exception to a general principle, the Supreme Court adopted a non-fundamentalist approach. In other words, the Court went beyond the First Amendment's literal meaning to find the deeper human truths that underlie its general principle.

Limitations in the West: Human Rights vs. Freedom of Expression Rights

In present-day Britain, for example, it is illegal to use the right of free expression to foment racial hatred, and propagation of such attitudes is subject to prosecution and suppression. Recently, Parliament extended the reach of this limitation on free expression to include religious beliefs. The bill approved in 2006 makes it a criminal offence to use threatening words or behaviour with the intention of stirring up hatred against any group of people because of religion or atheism (Home Office 2008).

Throughout Europe there is continuing disagreement whether religious beliefs or faith should be protected. For example, Norwegian law forbids threats and insults to persons on the basis of their skin colour, nationality, outlook on life or sexual preference but excludes religious beliefs (*Aftenposten* 2006). Without attempting to be comprehensive, a quick review shows that many Western nations have laws in place that could be used to limit the socially adverse consequences of freedom of expression directed at religious faith. Nations such as Germany, Ireland, Canada and Sweden all have laws within their freedom of speech traditions that prohibit inciting hate and ridicule towards certain groups or minorities. In Germany, *Volksverhetzung* (the incitement of hatred against a minority under certain conditions) is a punishable offence under Section 130 of the *Strafgesetzbuch* (Germany's criminal code) and can lead to up to five years of imprisonment (Federal Ministry of Justice 2008). In Ireland, the Prohibition of Incitement to Hatred Act proscribes words or behaviours which are 'threatening, abusive or insulting and are intended or, having regard to all the circumstances, are likely to stir up hatred' against 'a group of persons in the State or elsewhere on account of their race, colour, nationality, religion, ethnic or national origins, membership of the traveling community or sexual orientation' (Office of the Attorney General 1989). In Canada, advocating genocide or inciting hatred against any 'identifiable group' is an offence under the Criminal Code of Canada. An 'identifiable group' is defined as 'any section of the public distinguished by colour, race, religion, ethnic origin or sexual orientation' (Department of Justice 2008). The Code makes exceptions for cases of statements of truth and subjects of public debate and religious doctrine (Department of Justice 2008). Sweden prohibits hate speech defined as publicly making statements that threaten or express disrespect for an ethnic group or similar group regarding their race, skin colour, national or ethnic origin, faith or sexual orientation (Legislation online.org n.d.).

So, across the European continent, there is a split of opinion on whether religion should be legally protected. However, there is a reason to believe that the trend is shifting in favour of more rather than less protection for religion and faith. An example of this can be seen in a measure adopted recently by The Council of Europe which could criminalize 'any written material, any image or any other representation of ideas or theories, which advocates, promotes or incites hatred, discrimination or violence, against any individual or group of individuals, based on race, colour, descent or national or ethnic origin, as well as religion if used as pretext for any of these factors' (Scheeres 2002). While the Council of Europe is not a legislative body, its opinions carry some per-suasive force. According to its mission statement, the 47 member countries seek to develop throughout Europe common and democratic principles based on the European Convention on Human Rights and other reference texts on the protection of individuals (Council of Europe 2008).

In the particular case of the republishing of the Danish cartoons by various newspapers, it is instructive to observe that official US voices did not side with the right of freedom of expression. For example, State Department spokesman Kurtis Cooper said, 'These cartoons are indeed offensive to the belief of Muslims' and added that, 'we all fully recognize and respect freedom of the press and expression but it must be coupled with press responsibility. Inciting religious or ethnic hatreds in this manner is not acceptable' (Hudson 2006). Mr. Cooper's comments compare favourably with other comments made by US officials, where politicians often take a hard-line against Muslims. Indeed, there is often a pronounced and regrettable fundamentalist tendency present in aspects of US discourse about Islam and Muslims. To give just one example, Richard T. Cooper, writing in *The Los Angeles Times*, has observed that at the highest levels, there is a pronounced tendency in US political discourse to frame the Middle East conflict in terms of good and evil. For example, he observes that immediately after the 11 September 2001 attacks against the US, President Bush said he wanted to lead a 'crusade' against terrorism (Cooper 2003). When more culturally sensitive critics called attention to the negative public relations consequences of the President's characterization of US intentions, this statement was later retracted.

Others in positions of power in the USA have gone further towards a dogmatic stance, positing the values of Christianity against those of Islam. For example, when discussing the battle against a Muslim warlord in Somalia, Lt. Gen. William G. Boykin, as Deputy Undersecretary of Defence for Intelligence, told a public audience, 'I knew my God was bigger than his. I knew that my God was a real God and his was an idol' (BBC News 2003). He has also said of President Bush, 'He's in the White House because God put him there' (BBC News 2003). Boykin's characterization of the situation is unfortunate because one of the most significant dangers of a fundamentalist point of view is that it permits one socially intolerant group to demonize another. Demonizing an individual, group or culture generally involves a suspension of the normal considerations of humane behaviour and respect. Given that the subjects of demonization are portrayed as evil and/or subhuman beyond any dispute, then any means of self-defence is considered legitimate, in proportion to the threat represented (Nasheed 2007). Recent evidence suggests that many Americans believe that American Muslims constitute a threat to the United States. According to a 2006 poll, 39 per cent of respondents believe that American Muslims aren't loyal to the United States and nearly a third believe that American Muslims are sympathetic to al-Qaida (Haynes 2006). As First Amendment scholar Charles C. Haynes has observed,

> More Americans than I imagined, it appears, are so frustrated, fearful and angry about the terrorist threat that they're no longer willing to sort out what is and isn't authentic Islam. For growing numbers of people in this country, the 'war on terrorism' is now seen as a 'war on Islam'. This characterization of the war is exactly what al-Qaida has worked for years to achieve in its battle for the hearts and minds of Muslims worldwide (Haynes 2006).

From a very practical point of view, public statements that demonize other nations and religions are clearly against American interests. As Yoji Cole has pointed out, these conditions, along with official statements that the United States 'is at war with Islamic fascists', may result in effectively bringing together groups that would otherwise be opposed to partnering, such as Hamas and Hezbollah, with al-Qaeda (Cole 2006).

Fundamentalist Interpretations of Rights and Duties

We now return to the question, 'Does the liberal conception of the absolute right to freedom of expression include the right to offend deeply held religious beliefs?' In the case of the Danish cartoons, some have answered this question affirmatively. For example, when asked to reflect on the costs and benefits of the incident in early 2006, Joern Mikkelsen, political editor at the *Jyllands-Posten*, said, 'Yes, it was worth it' (Tynes 2007). In a similar way, Flemming Rose, *Jyllands-Posten*'s culture editor who commissioned the 12 cartoons, has stated:

> [Some Muslims] demand a special position, insisting on special consideration of their own religious feelings. It is incompatible with contemporary democracy and freedom of speech, where you must be ready to put up with insults, mockery and ridicule (Tynes 2007).

In essence, the editors of the newspaper take the position that its publication of the cartoons was not intended as an offense but should instead be seen as a contribution to debate regarding criticism of Islam and self-censorship.

As to this point, Professor Jorgen S. Neilsen has indicated that there is a substantial irony here: modern European nation-states were often constructed through centuries of conflict in which 'religious differences and oppression were explosive' (Nielesen 2008). This works against the argument that the West needs to teach others the value of free expression. He further explains that contemporary European culture and discourse has become secularized, and as a result, the West is less aware of peoples who hold religion central to their lives and identities.

For advocates of free expression in a multicultural world, it seems unwise to advance the doctrine that the principles of freedom of expression require acceptance of expression of hatred and bigotry. A better course for the West is to retain its regard for freedom of expression by building a foundation of education and mutual understanding that would make the insult or abuse of another person's core beliefs unacceptable public behaviour. Indeed, it is interesting to note that while the Danish Director of Public Prosecutions' Decision on Possible Criminal Proceedings in the case of *Jyllands-Posten's* article 'The Face of Muhammad' upheld the finding of no liability, he concluded his decision with the words, 'to the extent publicly made expressions fall within the scope of these rules [of Danish law] there is, therefore, no free and unrestricted right to express opinions about religious subjects' (Fode 2006).

Limiting Freedom of Expression: Social Sanction

In 2006, Joseph Ratzinger, after ascending to the papacy as Benedict XVI, quoted a source in a speech that called Muhammad 'evil'. Following his public statement, enraged rioters burned churches and killed a nun in Somalia. In response, rather than insisting on freedom of speech in the service of theological inquiry, the Pope retracted his statement and entered into a dialogue with Islamic clerics. As *Time Magazine* reported, 'none of the parties are departing from their theology, but out of frankness, a tenuous bridge seems to have been built' (Van Biema 2008). In this case, the strategic choice of the Pope is a useful example and calls to mind the possibility of social, as opposed to legal, sanction of intolerant and transgressive remarks.

An interesting example of a penalty imposed from outside of a legal system is a recent incident concerning comments made by James Watson, the 1962

Nobel Prize winner. In a 2007 interview with the *London Times*, Watson was quoted as saying that there was no reason to believe different races separated by geography should have evolved identically, and that while he hoped everyone was equal, 'people who have to deal with black employees find this is not true' (CNN 2007). In response, London's Science Museum cancelled Watson's talk there, saying that his words had 'gone beyond the point of acceptable debate' (CNN 2007). In full agreement, the board of trustees at New York's Cold Spring Harbor Laboratory, which Watson has led for nearly four decades, suspended his administrative responsibilities pending a review of his comments (CNN 2007). In this case concerning race rather than religion, Watson crossed the boundaries of acceptable debate and there were immediate and powerful consequences. This clearly signalled social sanction against unacceptable speech. The Watson incident helps us realize that even in a society that places a high value on free expression, the concept of democracy is not synonymous with absolute individual liberty; indeed, often the will of the majority is at odds with the needs and rights of specific individuals.

Similarly, in reference to the Danish cartoons, former Danish Prime Minister Poul Nyrup Rasmussen has discussed this point and it is constructive to cite him at length. He began his remarks by saying that he had been shocked to see people attacked, flags burned, embassies trashed and innocent people losing their jobs. He further said:

> This is sad because our history is based on tolerance, solidarity and development. We have fought for justice, and for peaceful co-existence in Palestine. Violence must stop. I want to thank President Barroso for his signal of solidarity to my country. Any attack on one Member State is an attack on the whole EU. [But the] EU should not be deemed to be [a] Union of intolerance. Through our long and bloody history, we have learned values of peaceful co-existence the hard way (Rasmussen 2006).

The cartoon episode, Rasmussen said, cannot be used to create new myths about each other or to stimulate xenophobic and populist movements in Europe or in the Islamic world.

> It is not a matter of them and us. For too long extremists have played the tune, it is time for moderate and responsible voices to set an agenda for another way and not to add fuel to fire. We should unite all forces for a new dialogue with the Islamic world, for mutual respect beyond all borders to all religions. It is not them against us, we are one (Rasmussen 2006).

In sum, Rassmussen said that this event should be the last act of provocation and that instead there should be a permanent, political, open and constructive dialogue (Rasmussen 2006).

Indeed, when speaking in Qatar, former US president Bill Clinton strongly criticized the publication of the Danish cartoons, comparing historical anti-Semitism in Europe with anti-Islamic feeling today. He asked, 'So now what are we going to do? [. . .] Replace the anti-Semitic prejudice with anti-Islamic prejudice?' (AFP 2005).

Conclusion

The case of the Danish cartoons thus calls into focus a clash of two competing principles: the right of freedom of expression and the right of a society to impose restrictions on expression in order to create a foundation for tolerance and mutual accommodation. In its most extreme instances, the example of the Danish cartoons incident shows a fundamentalist turn in the West concerning interpretation of rights and duties. In this context, many have advocated a doctrine of freedom of expression that privileges a rigid adherence to the doctrine of abstract individual freedom. Rather than asking which interpretation of an absolute right prevails over the other, perhaps the best way forward is to attempt to reach an accommodation between the competing principles of fundamentalism and free expression.

In this essay I have tried to document a fundamentalist turn in interpreting the principle of freedom of expression, as evidenced by statements like those of the *Jyllands-Posten*'s editors Mikkelsen and Rose. Such statements have been called into question by many participants in the debate over the Danish cartoons who have insisted that freedom of expression is not an absolute within any culture, and it is a problematic absolute in any multicultural environment.

Tolerance is a prerequisite for the free flow of information, and no rational society would choose a rule of law that leads to sectarian strife or civil war. So starting with the assumption that globalization – coexistence – calls for a climate of mutual respect to favour peace among people and nations, I have suggested that free expression and religious fundamentalism collide most irreconcilably when the followers of each doctrine use the same inflexible principles of fundamentalism in rigidly interpreting rights and responsibilities. It is the fundamentalist quality of the debate that makes the words used so harsh and the destructive responses so intense.

However, coming from a Western tradition, we also need to be aware of our own tendency towards a fundamentalist interpretation of the right of free expression. History shows that the actual limits on free expression are democratic decisions, guided as much by historical context as by logic and reason. What's more, the best view seems to deny that free expression is a universal principle unchecked by society. While in the USA the First Amendment protects even vicious and cruel parodies of public figures – *Hustler Magazine* once published a parody of the Reverend Jerry Falwell getting drunk before preaching and then having sex with his mother in an outhouse (*Hustler Magazine v.*

Fallwell 1988) – it would be intolerant to force this broad interpretation of the right of free expression upon other communities and nations. Indeed, there is a critical difference between asking another society to accept one set of principles and values and demanding so.

While the recent trend in the USA has been towards a legal regime that protects hateful speech, there is ample evidence of a sharp decrease in its social acceptance. In other words, one does not need the participation of the legal system to create effective social limitations on free expression. In the West, legal restrictions of freedom of expression are unlikely to be workable solutions especially when grounded upon content-based distinctions. So, ultimately, the tension between faith and reason must be counterbalanced by dialogue and respect – and we must call upon the 'better angels of our nature' to guide us in this dialogue (Lincoln 1861). A healthy relationship between rights and responsibilities in the context of freedom of expression will not come from a legal regime alone, with its unyielding interpretations of rights and duties. What we need is a deeper understanding of the characteristics of fundamentalism and the range of appropriate responses, especially in the realm of international communications.

There is no society that guarantees absolute freedom of expression. What actually exists in all cases is the freedom of expression within the law, which varies from nation to nation. So while no society should unilaterally compromise its most valued freedoms, it ultimately makes little sense to fight Islamic intolerance with secular Western intolerance.

References

AFP (2005), 'Clinton warns of rising anti-Islamic feeling', retrieved 7 June 2008 from <http://www.breitbart.com/article.php?id=060130151546. v8vrasnt&show_article=1>.

Aftenposten [Norway] (2006), 'Norwegian Muslims want blasphemy law', 1 February, retrieved 21 March 2008 from <http://www.aftenposten.no/english/local/article1211932.ece>.

BBC News (2003), 'US is "battling Satan" says general', 17 October, retrieved 1 June 2008 from <http://news.bbc.co.uk/2/hi/americas/3199212.stm>.

BBC News (2004), 'Q & A: Blasphemy law', 18 October, retrieved 2 March 2008 from <http://news.bbc.co.uk/2/hi/uk_news/3753408.stm>.

Beauharnais v. Illinois (1952), 343 U.S. 250.

Black, H. (1960), 'The Bill of Rights', Lecture at the New York University School of Law, 17 February, retrieved 2 March 2008 from <http://www.saf.org/LawReviews/Black.html>.

CNN (2007), '"Race row" Nobel winner suspended', 18 October, retrieved 18 May 2008 from <http://edition.cnn.com/2007/TECH/science/10/19/uk.race>.

Cole, Y. (2006), 'Islamic fascism: Fact or fiction?', retrieved 3 June 2008 from <http://multicultural.syr.edu/home.php?inc=news&mode=details&id=40>.

Columbia Encyclopedia (2007), 'Blasphemy', retrieved 15 March 2008 from <http://www.bartleby.com/65/bl/blasphemy.html>.

Cooper, R. (2003), 'General casts war in religious terms', *Los Angeles Times*, 16 October, retrieved 14 March 2008 from <http://www.commondreams.org/headlines03/1016-01.htm>.

Council of Europe (2008), 'About the Council of Europe', retrieved 1 June 2008 from <http://www.coe.int/T/e/Com/about_coe>.

Department of Justice [Canada] (2008), *Criminal Code (R.S., 1985, c. C-46)*, retrieved 23 June 2008 from <http://laws.justice.gc.ca/en/C-46>.

Ellian, A. (2008), 'Criticism and Islam', *Wall Street Journal*, 31 March, p. A18.

European Parliament (2006), 'MEP's debate freedom of expression and respect for religious belief', retrieved 18 June 2008 from <http://www.europarl.europa.eu/sides/getDoc.do?language=EN&type=IM-PRESS&reference=20060214IPR05265>.

Federal Ministry of Justice [Germany] (1998), 'Strafgesetzbuch, StGB', retrieved 1 June 2008 from <http://www.iuscomp.org/gla/statutes/StGB.htm>.

Fode, H. (2006), 'Decision on possible criminal proceedings in the case of *Jyllands-Posten*'s article "The Face of Muhammad"', Director of Public Prosecutions [Demark], retrieved 21 June 2008 from <http://www.dendanskeforening.dk/side327.html>.

Haynes, C. (2006), 'Islam is not the enemy', The First Amendment Center, retrieved 1 June 2008 from <http://www.firstamendmentcenter.org/commentary.aspx?id=17289>.

Holmes, O. W. (1880), *The Common Law*. Available online at <http://www.law.harvard.edu/library/collections/special/online-collections/common_law/Contents.php>.

Home Office [United Kingdom] (2008), 'Hate crime', retrieved 25 June 2008 from <http://www.homeoffice.gov.uk/crime-victims/reducing-crime/hate-crime/>.

Hudson, S. (2006), 'US backs Muslims in cartoon dispute', *Boston Globe*, 3 February, retrieved 28 June 2008 from <http://www.boston.com/news/nation/washington/articles/2006/02/03/us_sides_with_muslims_in_cartoon_dispute>.

Hustler Magazine v. Falwell (1988), 485 U.S. 46.

International Covenant on Civil and Political Rights (1966), 'General Assembly resolution 2200A (XXI) of 16 December 1966', retrieved 16 January 2008 from <http://www.unhchr.ch/html/menu3/b/a_ccpr.htm>.

Judd, T. (2007), 'Teacher held for teddy bear blasphemy', retrieved 5 March 2008 from <http://www.independent.co.uk/news/world/africa/teacher-held-for-teddy-bear-blasphemy-760590.html>.

Kimmelman, M. (2008), 'Outrage at cartoons still tests the Danes', *The New*

York Times, 20 March, retrieved 15 June 2008 from <http://www.nytimes.com/2008/03/20/books/20cartoon.html>.

Legislationonline.org [Sweden] (n.d.), 'Incitement to hatred/Dissemination of racist ideas', retrieved 22 March 2008 from <http://www.legislationline.org/?jid=48&less=false&tid=218>.

Lincoln, A. (1861), 'First inaugural address', 4 March 1861, retrieved 6 June 2008 from <http://www.bartleby.com/124/pres31.html>.

Nasheed, M. (2007), 'Like the Jews were called vermin', 22 May, retrieved 30 January 2008 from <http://www.mnasheed.com/2007/05/like_the_jews_were_called_verm.php>.

Nielsen, J. (2008), 'Dialogue of the deaf: Europe's Muslim "problem"', *Newsweek.Washington Post.com*, 28 March, retrieved June 14 2008 from <http://newsweek.washingtonpost.com/postglobal/needtoknow/2008/03/europes_muslim_problem.html>.

Office of the Attorney General [Ireland] (1989), *Prohibition of Incitement to Hatred Act*, retrieved 1 June 2008 from <http://www.irishstatutebook.ie/1989/en/act/pub/0019/index.html>.

R.A.V. v. City of St. Paul (1992), 505 U.S. 377.

Rasmussen, P. (2006), 'Fundamental rights', 15 February, retrieved 3 June 2008 from <http://www.abhaber.com/haber.php?id=10107>.

Rushdie, S. (1991), 'Excerpts from Rushdie's Address: 1,000 Days "Trapped Inside a Metaphor"', *The New York Times*, 12 December, retrieved 2 February 2008 from <http://www.nytimes.com/books/99/04/18/specials/rushdie-address.html?_r=2&oref=slogin&oref=slogin>.

Scheeres, J. (2002), 'Europeans outlaw net hate speech', *Wired*, 11 September 2002, retrieved 8 June 2008 from <http://www.wired.com/news/business/0,1367,56294,00.html>.

Tynes, N. (2007), 'Chairman of Danish daily stands by decision to publish prophet cartoons, criticizes U.S. Media', International Center for Journalists Website, 16 April 2007, retrieved 2 June 2008 from <http://ijnet.org/Director.aspx?P=Article&ID=306188&LID=>.

Van Biema, J. (2008), 'The American Pope', *Time Magazine*, April 14, p. 50.

Virginia v. Black et al. (2003), 538 U.S. 343.

Webster, R. (1990), *A Brief History of Blasphemy*. Oxford, UK: The Orwell Press.

Webster, R. (2002), 'Liberalism's holy war', retrieved 15 March 2008 from <http://www.richardwebster.net/liberalismsholywar.html>.

World Association of Newspapers (2008), 'WAN critical of death threats related to Mohammad cartoon', retrieved 7 March 2008 from <http://www.wansweden2008.com/articles.php?id=341>.

Chapter 4

A Historical Overview of American Christian Fundamentalism in the Twentieth Century

Susan A. Maurer

This essay surveys the origins, the birth and the history of American Christian Fundamentalism during the twentieth century. It includes a historical background of religious ideas in the United States that contributed to the formation of twentieth-century Fundamentalism; and it analyses the changes in religious attitudes that occurred as a reaction against modernity, particularly during the decade prior to the outbreak of World War I, and which resulted in the formation of the broad movement that came to be known as 'Christian Fundamentalism'. The special relationship of the media to the dissemination of the Christian message is also considered, as well as the contributions of some of the major figures in the creation and dissemination of fundamentalist ideas. The essay concludes with an analysis of the historical impact of these ideas, and the media's role in their dissemination, on twentieth-century American society.

Media and American Fundamentalism

Evangelical cultural identity has been shaped in great measure by the use of media by Christians who are eager to disseminate the message, or messages, of their religious faith, their political agendas, and their critiques of what is perceived to be American secular society. As early as the 1880s, Christian preacher Dwight L. Moody took the innovative step of purchasing newspaper space in order to advertise his revival meetings. The Moody Bible Institute's radio station, WMBI, is among the oldest currently broadcasting radio stations in the United States (Hendershot 2004: 147). Indeed, the success in Britain of Moody's 'Great Revival' of 1873 represents the beginning of a communications revolution in modern religion (Monteiro 2006).

In addition to radio and television programmes, the ever-increasing availability of Christian music and books, such as LaHaye's *Left Behind* series, in large American chain stores illustrate the power of Christian media to influence American culture. Heather Hendershot, in *Shaking the World for Jesus* (2004), demonstrates how American culture is influenced simply by the predominance of Christian materials on the store shelves. She points out that as 'family-friendly' stores like Sam's Club and Wal-Mart continue to thrive, 'more and more retail shelf space is being filled by Christian media, leaving less room for other kinds of media' (Hendershot 2004: 211).

Even Hollywood, which has long been the object of criticism by Christians who see it as a centre of immorality and secular values, has been appropriated by Christian evangelists as a means of reaching the American public. Dr. Charles Fuller's *Old Fashioned Revival Hour*, a nationwide radio programme originally broadcast from Hollywood, aired for over 30 years on over 650 stations.

During the 1920s, Aimee Semple McPherson's 5,300-seat capacity Angelus Temple was filled seven days a week by audiences that included many from the entertainment business who looked forward to McPherson's dramatic sermons. And in the early twenty-first century, Christian evangelical personalities like Joyce Meyer, who has written over 70 books on Christianity, and whose radio programmes are broadcast in over 20 languages in 200 countries, command the attention of a large segment of the modern population.

Christian evangelists like Moody, McPherson and Meyer – not to mention the likes of Billy Sunday and Billy Graham, who has been the advisor to several US presidents, and whose radio and television broadcasts have reached millions of people over a span of more than 50 years – have certainly been instrumental in creating a religious communications revolution, spreading the evangelical, and indeed, the fundamentalist message through the open channels of radio, television and print media.

While the use of the term 'fundamentalist' can sometimes be problematic, in a Pew Research Center survey conducted 17–21 March 2005, 40 per cent of American Christians and 34 per cent of the general public do classify themselves as 'born-again'; and according to the 2004 National Election Pool exit poll, President George W. Bush received 78 per cent of the vote among white evangelicals ('Religion and the Presidential Vote' 2004). Clearly, religion and lifestyle are intimately connected, and socio-political policies are necessarily determined by the same religious ideals that inform the worldview of a society.

Without a doubt, religious beliefs have always played an important role in American society and politics; and the growing number of evangelical mega-churches attests to the increasing popularity of evangelical values and community in the United States (Mahler 2005). *The New York Times* reports that in 1970, there were only 10 non-Catholic mega-churches in the United States. By 2005, the number had reached 282 and continues to rise at a rapid rate (Mahler 2005). This dramatic increase in attendance at evangelical churches, in contrast to the decline in attendance at mainstream Protestant churches, is indicative of the ever-growing popularity of evangelical and fundamentalist ideas among Americans. The huge success of novels like *The*

Late Great Planet Earth and the *Left Behind* series, and television programmes like NBC's 2005 *Revelations* attests to the popularity of Christian fundamentalist ideas in contemporary pop culture. (Even though the premiere received bad critical reviews, the Nielsen ratings showed that *Revelations*, which concerns two characters, described by the network as 'one who worships God and one who worships Science', won the night among households, averaging a 9.6 rating as contrasted with 9.5 for Fox's top-rated *American Idol*, shown in the same time slot on the same evening.)

Early American Christian Influences and Millennial Thinking

Christopher Columbus has been described as one who saw himself as 'a man of providential destiny'. Dr. Christopher Kauffman (1992) explains that, influenced by the *Book of Revelation* and the vision of a 'liberated Jerusalem' ruled for a thousand years by the returned Christ: 'It was he [Columbus] who introduced the millennial motif into the character of America history'. (*Millennialism* refers to the religious belief in the immanent return of Christ to Earth, where he will rule in peace and harmony for a thousand years.) Catherine Keller (1994), in her translation of Columbus' *Professies*, notes that Columbus expected the world to end in the year 1650; he therefore took his mission as 'Christ-carrier' (as he began to sign his letters after 1498) very seriously, working to bring Christianity to as many of the 'unsaved' pagans of the new world as he could before the end of the world and the return of Christ.

During the mid-sixteenth century, the Puritans, who zealously believed in the authority of scripture, became disappointed and angry with what they believed to be Queen Elizabeth I's compromising of English religion for political purposes. Persecuted by the Anglican Church and led by John Winthrop, they sailed for the New World, which they hailed as the perfect place for a new beginning; a special place provided to them for their sacred work of preparing the world for the coming of the Kingdom of God. For the Puritans, there was no separation of religious and civic life; all of life was to be lived in accordance with Christian principles and beliefs. They spoke of this sacred duty in biblical terms, describing what they saw as their holy obligation to be a 'light to the world' and a 'city upon a hill', which would stand as an example upon which the eyes of the entire world would be directed and would thus see the works of God made manifest on Earth (Albanese 1996[1992]: 435). Ironically, the Puritans, who fled England to escape the religiously repressive policies of Elizabethan England, created, in their new home, a society regulated by their own religious beliefs; and they instituted repressive policies against non-Puritans in the New World, even to the point of executing those who refused to conform with Puritan beliefs and customs, as was the case in 1669 with Mary Dyer, a supporter of theological dissenter Anne Hutchinson. The Massachusetts Bay Colony in particular flourished as a Puritan theocracy, even though other colonies like Rhode Island permitted religious freedom.

This millennial vision of a world where evil has been defeated and righteousness prevails motivated the creation of a society based on the belief that the days of the Earth were numbered and that there was no time to be lost in the work of preparing the world for the return of Christ. Thus, early American Christians aimed to create a Christian society where they could be free to reject worldly ideas of a secular, unreligious society, and to prepare for the end times which they believed to be imminent.

In addition to persecution by the Church of England, the Puritans felt threatened by an even greater and infinitely more sinister enemy: modernity. Enlightenment thought and the advances of science had brought about a new, empirical approach to the study and evaluation of human experience. Religion, including scripture, was to be subject to the same empirical scrutiny as was the physical world. For many, such attitudes seemed to be a denial of faith in God, and therefore unacceptable to any person who desired to live a truly Christian life. In response, reform movements were undertaken in order to enable people to return, and to hold on to, the traditional religious values that were perceived to be in danger of being lost.

In the United States, some Christian sects did adopt the individualistic thinking of the European Reform movements. George Fox, who founded the Society of Friends (Quakers), believed that personal experience, and not institutionalized teachings, should be the basis for Christian life; and he exhorted his followers to 'make use of their own understanding, without direction from another' (Lovejoy 1985). John Wesley, who declared that religion was 'not a doctrine in the head but a light in the heart', also believed in the value of personal experience over doctrine, and his Methodists also followed the practice of reading their own Bibles and relying on their own understanding of scripture (Armstrong 2000: 77). The humanistic influences of Enlightenment Europe had helped to bring about a desire to return to the original texts and message of scripture; and the influence of Martin Luther especially had raised the importance of scripture over tradition. Thus, the individual's reading of, and relationship with, scripture became a key issue among Christians.

Karen Armstrong has described a very interesting and ironic aspect of the new emphasis on scripture. The religious reformers were concerned about the perceived dangerous and faith-denying advances of modern thought and values, and their resistance included a return to the 'original' message of scripture. However, Armstrong writes:

[T]he reformers claimed to be returning, conservative-wise, to the primary source, the Bible, but they were reading Scripture in a modern way. The reformed Christian was to stand alone before God, relying simply on his

Bible, but this would not have been possible before the invention of printing had made it feasible for all Christians to have a Bible of their own and before the developing literacy of the period enabled them to read (2000: 66).

So, it was only through the modern invention of the printing press that the newly literate faithful were able to approach scripture without the mediation of a church cleric. Ironically, the emerging sense of individuality, which came about as a result of Enlightenment and Renaissance thought, was key to the desire of the anti-modern Christian to be able to 'stand alone before God, relying simply on his Bible', as Armstrong (2000: 66) points out. Christian ambivalence towards modernity was therefore evident from the beginning of the reform efforts of the Enlightenment period, and it has continued to the present, in which evangelical Christians have made effective use of modern technology and media to disseminate the Christian message even as they continue to view their secularizing influence with suspicion (Hendershot 2004: 4).

By the beginning of the eighteenth century, religion in the United States continued to increase in popularity, and the 1730s saw the eruption of the First Great Awakening, sparked by the emotional and charismatic sermons of preachers like Jonathan Edwards (1703–1758) and George Whitefield (1714–1770). Whitefield, who was born in Gloucester, England, conducted a preaching tour in the United States in 1739 that was so well received that the churches could not hold the numbers of people who came to hear him. As a result, he was forced to move his gatherings to outdoor sites, where he often drew audiences that were so large that they exceeded the populations of the towns in which he preached (Stout 1993).

Both Whitefield and Jonathan Edwards believed that the revival of religious fervour in the United States was evidence of God's work in the world and that in this way Christians would be able to help bring about the establishment of God's Kingdom on Earth (Armstrong 2000: 79).

The appeal to human emotional response has been an enduring feature of Christian evangelical preaching even until the present, with both positive and negative results. While deep religious feelings have often found expression in social programmes designed to improve human life, human emotions have also sometimes been manipulated, and in some cases co-opted, by racist or nationalist groups, such that they have erupted into violence and destruction, as in the cases of the Ku Klux Klan, Jim Jones, Christian Identity, Ruby Ridge and Heaven's Gate, to name just a few. Mark Twain attacked religious emotionalism in many of his works, notably in *Captain Stormfield's Visit to Heaven* (1909), which was written as an indignant reaction to a series of novels by Elizabeth Ward that glorified the Christian vision of heaven.

Eighteenth-century Americans spent many hours in the company of their religious congregations. Churches were the places where people would go, not only for worship, but also for social interaction. For many, the weekly worship service was also the social event of the week. According to one author, the average colonial churchgoer 'would have listened to some 7,000 sermons in his or her lifetime, totaling nearly 10,000 hours of concentrated listening' (Stout 1993). During the 1770s, some members of the Protestant clergy, over 600 of whom had by then been educated at the seminaries of Harvard and Yale, began to preach about the 'idolatry' of British rule and the obligation of American Christians to resist it. This was based on the idea that British rule violated the concept of *sola scriptura* ('scripture alone') as reflecting God's will for humanity. Soon, the conflict between the American colonies and Great Britain began to be seen among many churchgoing Christians as a cosmic struggle between good and evil; and with the exception of the Quakers and the Mennonites, who believed that Christians should never take up arms (and who, in turn, were persecuted for not supporting the war effort), a number of religious groups began to perceive resistance to British rule as a religiously validated cause.

Some preachers, such as Samuel Sherwood, went so far as to draw connections between Britain and the figure of the anti-Christ from the *Book of Revelation*. In a sermon entitled, *The Church's Flight into the Wilderness*, Sherwood presented American Christians as the 'church in the wilderness' whose responsibility it was to fight and defeat the anti-Christ in the form of Britain, who, he said, 'appears to have many of the features and much of the temper and character of the image of the beast' (Stout 1993). Thus, the expectation naturally followed among those Christians who accepted Sherwood's ideas that defeat of the enemy would hasten the arrival of Christ's millennial reign.

Many American Christians saw the Revolutionary War as evidence of the coming millennial Kingdom, when Christ would return and peace would prevail. However, as the war dragged on into the 1780s, people began to lose confidence in the Kingdom to come, and millennial enthusiasm waned as the end of the century approached.

As independence from Britain became a reality, Americans began to turn their faces westward to the expanding American frontier. The Louisiana Purchase of 1803 had doubled the area of the young United States, and the spirit of individualism had taken firm hold.

Concerned that religion might be lost on the frontier, preachers began to move west along with the pioneers. In 1800, preacher James McGready (1758–1817) held the first frontier 'camp meeting' at Gasper River, Kentucky. By 1801, the popularity of this new kind of religious gathering was such that they would draw as many as 20,000 people, as did the Cane Ridge revival of 1801.

Camp meetings, or 'revivals', were often highly emotional events lasting several days, where attendees would pitch tents and set up camp for several days on the outskirts of frontier towns. After listening to preachers (sometimes from several different denominations) speak during the day, people would, during the evenings, come forward to publicly acknowledge their sins and repent, frequently displaying extreme physical reactions to their conversion experiences.

The camp meetings were part of a greater wave of religious revival that occurred during the early nineteenth century. The Second Great Awakening of 1800–1830 saw large numbers of itinerant preachers from several new religious sects swarm across the newly acquired western frontier. The Methodists, followers of John Wesley, who figured prominently in the First Great Awakening, the Quakers and the Baptists were just a few of the denominations that played a major role in the revivalist preaching of the Second Great Awakening, which extended across the entire country and included converts from almost every social group, rich, poor, immigrants and native-born Americans.

The Church of Latter Day Saints (Mormons), founded by Joseph Smith of Vermont (1805–1844), was one new religious movement to be born as a result of nineteenth-century revivalism. Smith was convinced that the end of the world was near, as evidenced by what he saw as a decline in religion and culture, and that the return of Christ in glory was at hand. After Smith was killed in 1844, his disciple Brigham Young led the Mormons westward to what is now Utah, with the intention of establishing a millennial society apart from the rest of the United States (Bulman 1999: 99–102).

As people moved westward into new territory, the American population grew from about 4 million in 1780 to 10 million in 1820, and to 31 million in 1860, about an eightfold increase. However, the growth of Christian religious congregations far exceeded the increase in population. From 2,500 congregations in 1780, the number increased to 11,000 in 1820, and by 1860, the number of Christian congregations in the United States had reached a staggering 52,000 – an almost 21-fold increase (Armstrong 2000: 93).

American religion, from its beginnings until the years of the Civil War, had been based mainly on the belief that the new world was a place provided by God for the creation of a new, Christian society, to be ruled by Christ in peace and harmony; and that Christians would help to create the social circumstances that would bring about that society. The Civil War, however, was to have an impact that would bring about a pivotal change in the hopes and attitudes of American Christians.

Many nineteenth-century American Christians became involved in activities that intended to bring about societal conditions necessary for the inauguration of the hoped-for-divine Kingdom; and these included a variety of social reform efforts, including, for example, the abolitionist movement.

Another concern of mounting importance was the issue of slavery, which increasingly divided Protestant churches, both in, as well as between, the North and the South. Advocates in both camps used biblical ideas and language to support their positions, and ideas concerning the meaning and the parameters of life in a Christian society caused believers to become ever more polarized. Harriet Beecher Stowe, daughter of the President of Lane Theological

Seminary, wrote *Uncle Tom's Cabin*, an argument against slavery that is based on a radical Christian vision she shared with many others, particularly in the Northeast. By the time the war itself finally broke out in 1863, both sides were convinced that they were fighting in a holy cause, and that their victory would mean divine approbation and favour in the coming Kingdom. In the North, this is evidenced by the immense popularity of the apocalyptic Civil War song, *Mine Eyes Have Seen the Glory*, also known as the *Battle Hymn of the Republic*.

As the war continued unmitigated and increasingly destructive, however, ideas about the coming millennial Kingdom began to take on a different and darker aspect. The immense loss of life and property and the utter destruction of families and communities perpetrated during the war began to be perceived by some as evidence of the apocalyptic 'end times' described in the *Book of Revelation*. President Lincoln himself regularly used apocalyptic and millennial imagery, describing the war as a 'fiery trial' through which the nation must pass (Bulman 1999: 102). His Gettysburg Address used the religious imagery of 'consecration' and referred to the sacredness of the sacrifices made by 'this nation under God'; and his Second Inaugural Address also invoked the idea of divine judgement in retribution for the sins of the nation.

When the war finally ended, hopes were high that the period immediately following would auger in the much-awaited era of peace and prosperity that wartime millennial thought had promised. Novels with religious themes, such as Charles Sheldon's *In His Steps* (1897), Margaret Deland's *John Ward, Preacher* (1888), Lew Wallace's *Ben Hur* (1880) and Edward P. Roe's *Barriers Burned Away* (1873), became best sellers during the post-war years among readers harboring millennial expectations.

However, Lincoln's assassination in 1865 was the first in a series of disappointments that would bring about a radical shift in American religious expectations. (Among other results, the 'martyrdom' of Lincoln helped to bring about the birth of 'American civic religion', a secularized version of millennialism that increasingly justified the political agenda of the United States in religious and/or biblical terms. The idea of 'Manifest Destiny', for example, presented the American expansionist policy as having divine origins and approbation.) The miseries of the newly freed slaves, who relocated in large numbers from the South to the North, the continued movement westward and the increase in the numbers of cities, the second phase of American industrialization, and the ever-increasing numbers of immigrants all combined to impose considerable stress on American society (Bulman 1999: 103). As in previous times of uncertainty, many people turned to the Bible and to biblical prophecy in order to find meaning in the apparent post-war chaos.

The horrors and utter destruction carried out during the Civil War and the deep disappointment experienced after its conclusion left an indelible impression in the evangelical consciousness; in light of this, events foretold in the *Book of Revelation* began to take on a new importance. American post-Civil-War society was searching for some meaning in its suffering and misery; and meaning was found in the biblical interpretations of John Nelson Darby (1800–1882), an English preacher whose ideas gained great popularity and spread from Europe to the United States.

Darby, ordained to the priesthood of the Church of Ireland in 1826, was convinced that the church had succumbed to the liberalizing, faith-denying ideas of the Enlightenment and that as a result, Christianity had declined, along with the rest of the modern world, into a desperate state where the secularizing trends of modernity had resulted in the marginalization of religion and had resulted in a world where the salvation of modern Christians was seriously threatened.

Darby presented several theological ideas that he considered to be non-negotiable for believing Christians in the face of liberal modernism. Among these was the idea of the dispensations. Darby and his later interpreters found biblical clues that divided human history into seven distinct eras, or dispensations, which would end in the thousand-year period of peace described in Revelation 20: 1–7. Darby's innovative ideas represent the introduction of *premillenial dispensationalism* into American Christian thinking.

The concept of the dispensations was widely disseminated and became very popular among Christians who were feeling increasingly threatened by the idea of the primacy of human reason over the inerrancy of scripture and traditional Christian belief, and who considered the ideas of modernity to be a threat to the validity of faith and the authority of religion.

This fear was not limited to Protestants. In 1907, Pope Pius X issued the encyclical *Pascendi dominici gregis*, in which he condemned the ideas of modernism as a collection of heresies. The conservative pontiff rejected any attempts to reconcile traditional Catholicism with the modern world; and in particular, he rejected the ideas of historical criticism as applied to scripture and the elevation of human reason over the supernatural. In addition, Charles Darwin's theory of evolution appeared to many to deny the truth of the biblical creation stories. Darwin's ideas would themselves bring about a legal confrontation in the 1920s that would have a lasting impact on American society. As will be discussed, as these events occurred, and Darby's beliefs became more popular and more widely disseminated, so did public rejection of modern, secular views.

In a public statement intended to reject unequivocally the ideas of modernity, which were perceived as a diabolical threat to Christian culture and society, a series of pamphlets was published during the first and second decades of the twentieth century by Lyman and Milton Stewart in cooperation with the Rev. A. C. Dixon of the Moody Church in Chicago. These pamphlets, entitled *The Fundamentals*, were intended to challenge and to defeat the heresies of modernism and secularization and to work towards the re-establishment of the true, traditional faith among Christians in the United States. The pamphlets, three million of which were distributed free of charge to Christian churches and leaders, consisted of articles written by a number of authors expounding the five fundamental beliefs, derived from Darby's thought, that must be accepted in order to be a 'true' Christian. The five main fundamentals, as described in the pamphlets, were: 1) The virgin birth of Christ; 2) The substitutionary atonement of Christ for the sins of humanity; 3) The reality of the Resurrection; 4) The reality of miracles and of the Second Coming of Christ and 5) The literal inerrancy of the Bible (Torrey and Dixon 2003[1917]). Each of the five fundamental beliefs represented an article of faith that stood in opposition to scientific probity, and therefore demonstrated a rejection of modern thought and secular principles. Christians who adopted the principles outlined in these pamphlets became known as 'fundamentalists'.

While, as previously discussed, Christian millennial beliefs had always been present in American society and had undeniably influenced the development of social and political policies, the teachings of Charles Darby and the resulting emergence of American Fundamentalism marked the appearance of a new, darker, and much more pessimistic view of the Christian relationship with the world. Whereas the previous Evangelical mindset was one that charged Christians with responsibility concerning the improvement of social conditions, the dispensationalist views of emerging fundamentalism denied the value of any attempts to save the world from its predestined decline into disaster and ruin.

This dark outlook would have ominous repercussions in the period immediately preceding World War I; where Germany, the home of higher criticism, was already perceived by many American Christians as the birthplace of satanic ideas that rejected true religion and espoused secularity. Also, World War I saw an outbreak of American patriotism that, later in the century, would ironically be shared by fundamentalists, a group whose premillennialist ideas held that no earthly government had authority over Christians, who were, first and foremost, citizens of the divine Kingdom of Christ (Marsden 1980: 141). George Marsden explains that this paradoxical turn of events took place as:

> [. . .] German *Kultur*, where the doctrine of evolution had bred the twin evils of modernism and militarism, showed the inevitable result of such doctrines . . . evolution and modernism were tied together and seen as a cultural as well as a specifically religious threat. Out of these concerns, to which anti-communism was soon added, fundamentalist super-patriotism began to grow.

As anti-war premillennialism came under sharp attack during the war years as unpatriotic, post-war fundamentalists were forced to rethink their position. Therefore, during and after World War I, American Fundamentalism, originally a religiously inspired phenomenon focused ostensibly on doctrinal purity, would take a much stronger social and political turn that was characterized by the battle to save American civilization from modernism and secularity. One result of this change in attitude on the part of American fundamentalists was the eventual co-opting, during the second half of the twentieth century, of the idea of patriotism as reflective of Christian ideals.

In the years immediately following World War I, this commitment to protect American Christian society from secular thought became especially focused on the dangers presented by Darwin's evolutionism. Fundamentalism's first major public cultural battle was the Scopes 'Monkey' Trial of 1925. Charles Darwin's publications concerning evolution had evoked deep anxiety among Christians who felt that to accept the idea of evolution was to invalidate the truth of the Bible, which was read and understood as the literal word of God as well as a literal history of the universe and humanity. Christians in the South mobilized in large numbers to protest the teaching of evolution in public schools, which represented to them an insult and a danger to Christian culture. By 1923, several Southern states had passed laws restricting the teaching of evolution, and the law that was passed in Tennessee in 1925 forbade it absolutely. John Scopes, a biology teacher in the Tennessee public school system, defied the law and was brought to trial in July of 1925. He was defended by lawyers Clarence Darrow and Dudley Field Malone. In spite of arguments and cross-examinations that proved embarrassing to William Jennings Bryan, the prosecuting attorney, and which made fundamentalists out to be ignorant, backward laughingstocks, Scopes was convicted of violating the Tennessee statute and was fined $100. (The verdict was reversed on a technicality in 1927, but the anti-evolution law stayed on the books in Tennessee until 1967.)

The Scopes trial, one of the first major media events of the twentieth century, epitomized the opposing values of liberals, who represented modernity and secular culture, and fundamentalists, who supported a culture dominated by religious ideas and values. Although fundamentalism scored a legal victory in the Scopes trial, public opinion tended strongly to support the modern, secular ideas represented by Scopes and Darrow. An editorial referring to the Scopes trial in Dayton, Tennessee, and published during the summer of 1925 in *The Nation*, described what it saw as the real point of contention:

At bottom, the issue is whether the separation of church and state shall be maintained. To be sure, there is no mention of this at Dayton. The fundamentalists are not saying, even among themselves, 'There should be a Protestant state church in America'. No such monstrous ambitions are consciously entertained by fundamentalists, but the significance of fundamentalism lies not in what it is consciously but in what it is unconsciously. Unconsciously it puts the church above the state (cited in *Christian History* 1997: 19).

The trial was broadcast on live radio and covered by hundreds of news-papers. Consciously or not, American Christian Fundamentalism had engaged in its first committed large-scale act of attempting to bring American civic life into congruence with its interpretation of scripture, and radio and print media played a central role in bringing the Christian message to the American public.

Media and the Resurgence of American Fundamentalism

In the years following World War I, American Fundamentalism seemed to weaken considerably in intensity. Burned by the backlash of public opinion, which, after the Scopes trial, tended to perceive fundamentalists as somewhat naïve and misinformed, many Christians quietly withdrew from the public struggle against modernity. They did not, however, relinquish their commitment to fundamentalist thinking and ideals, and efforts to spread anti-modern ideas continued to flourish, especially in the South.

In their attempts to continue the dissemination of anti-modern and anti-secular fundamentalist ideas, Christians were not reluctant to employ modern secular technology to perpetuate the Christian message. In spite of the Bible's view of Satan as the 'prince of the power of the air' (Hendershot 2004: 5), fundamentalists were among the first preachers to make use of radio as a tool to reach large numbers of Christian listeners. Pentacostalist Aimee Semple McPherson appropriated the Hollywood movie culture and familiar Hollywood symbols as useful tools in spreading the message.

World War II and the years following presented new opportunities and challenges to American Fundamentalism. For the first time, the United States awarded Conscientious Objector status to those who objected to military service based on religious principles. This enabled anti-military Christians to serve in work camps or as medical providers or chaplains rather than as soldiers. The Evangelical Youth for Christ organization ministered to soldiers and to displaced young women. Among those who ministered to the soldiers was the young Billy Graham.

The Cold War and the presence of nuclear weapons also helped to bring about a strengthening of Fundamentalist, and especially millennial dispensationalist, ideas. Communism, perceived as secular and anti-religious, became the enemy against which all Christians must struggle in order to preserve Christian culture. In *The Irony of American History* (1985), Reinhold Niebuhr presented Communism and the Soviet Union as absolutely evil and demonically motivated. According to Martin Marty, Niebuhr wrote that religious faith was the only means through which repentance could be experienced for 'the false meaning which the pride of nations and cultures introduces into the pattern' of history (Marty 1996: 124).

The opposition to the threat of Communism produced a number of anti-communist groups and organizations, among them the Christian Anti-Communism Crusade, founded in 1955, the Christian Crusade, founded by the Rev. Billy

James Hargis, and the American Council of Christian Churches, founded in 1941 by the Rev. Carl McIntire. Although most of these groups were created by Evangelicals, another influential group, the Cardinal Mindszenty Foundation (CMF), founded in 1958, comprised mostly Catholics (Berlet and Lyons 2000: 201). The John Birch Society, also founded in 1958, advanced an agenda of anti-Communist, American Christian nationalism.

In addition to anti-Communist organizations, the post-World War II era saw the production of 30 films by Christian filmmaker Irwin S. Moon and produced by the Moody Bible Institute. These 'scientific' and 'non-sectarian' films, shown in secular venues such as public schools and air force training camps, nevertheless put forth a strong salvation message contained in the vehicle of 'scientific exposition' which included mention of a 'Creator' (though there was no specific mention of Jesus). Although these films were not shown in commercial movie theater venues, they were seen by millions in elementary schools, foreign missions, world's fairs and churches, and were required viewing for air force recruits as part of President Truman's Character Guidance Program (Hendershot 2004: 145–147).

The Fundamentalist Political Agenda of the Latter Twentieth Century

Partly because of the apparent weakening of Christian Fundamentalism after the Scopes trial of 1925, scholars expected that the trend of secularization that had become apparent in Western Europe would also take root in the United States and that this would result in the eventual demise of religion in the United States. But this was not to be the case. Indeed, religion, and especially Evangelical Christianity, has continued to flourish despite the expectations of secularization theorists (Finke 1992).

By the 1970's, Evangelical Christians (who, although they still believe in the priority of the Bible, had for the most part rejected the term 'fundamentalist' as pejorative) had identified *secular humanism* as a major threat to American morality. Evangelical Christians tended to see secular humanism as an atheistic, 'parody' type of religion that intended to eliminate Christianity from American public life. As believers in evolution, secular humanists denied the validity of scripture, according to Evangelicals, and thus stood in opposition to Christianity and its moral principles. Evangelicals believed that secular humanism pervaded all aspects of American life, and that it was especially insidious and prevalent in the political environment. The legalization of abortion, the removal of prayer from the public schools and the feminist movement were seen as secular humanist advances that eroded Christian morality in the United States.[1] The increasingly pluralistic nature of American society with its increased tolerance of non-Christian religions also seemed to Evangelical Christians to threaten the American Christian lifestyle.

In 1979, an organization called the Moral Majority was formed by Jerry Falwell, a fundamentalist Baptist preacher from Lynchburg, Virginia. Falwell had enjoyed considerable success through the *Old Time Gospel Hour*, a television and radio show that featured his preaching. The Moral Majority was dedicated to 'reestablishing traditional religious values in the national consciousness through support of conservative political candidates' ('Jerry Falwell' n.d.). The key issues addressed by the Moral Majority were school prayer, abortion, homosexuality, the integrity of the family and feminism. It allied itself with the Republican Party as the party of conservative values, and it contributed to the successful election campaign of Ronald Reagan in 1980. Conservative Republican strategist Paul Weyrich claimed that the Moral Majority registered over nine million new voters during the Presidential campaign of 1980. During that campaign, the Moral Majority successfully supported Republican Ronald Reagan against the Democratic President Jimmy Carter, a self-professed born-again Southern Baptist. This support of Reagan, an actor and a divorced man whose current wife was known to dabble in astrology, underscores the level of distrust and antipathy the Moral Majority harboured towards the Democratic Party, which it considered to be the party of demonic liberalism and secular humanism, in spite of the fact that the bearer of the Democratic Party's banner at the time was a born-again Southern Baptist.

The Moral Majority was, however, disappointed with the Reagan administration's failure to reverse abortion laws and to reinstate school prayer. Nevertheless, in spite of a number of sex and money scandals during the late 1980s that contributed to the eventual dissolution of the organization at that time, the new Christian Right continued to support its chosen candidates; among them Christian televangelist Pat Robertson.

The latter years of the twentieth century also saw the creation of other groups espousing the principles of the Moral Majority, which rose from the ashes of scandal to develop into the movement now known as the Christian Right. Among these groups are the Christian Coalition, Phyllis Schlafly's Eagle Forum, Beverly LaHaye's Concerned Women for America, Tim LaHaye's American Coalition for Traditional Values, the Conservative Caucus, Summit Ministries and the previously mentioned Christian Anti-Communism Crusade and John Birch Society (Berlet and Lyons 2000: 209). All these groups have as their purpose the protection of American Christian society from the ravages of secular and liberal thought and activities, and all are part of the Christian Right as defined by Clyde Wilcox: 'The Christian Right is a social movement that attempts to mobilize evangelical Protestants and other orthodox Christians into conservative political action' (2000: 5).

Wilcox continues to explain that, while many Christian Right leaders prefer the term 'Religious Right', the movement 'remains concentrated primarily among white evangelical Christians' (Wilcox 2000: 5). Nevertheless, it appears that the primary agenda of the Christian Right remains that of, consciously or unconsciously, putting religious principles into prominence where political action is concerned. In its manual, the Christian Coalition, for example, describes it purposes as follows: 1) To train Christians for effective political action; 2) To inform Christians of timely issues and legislation; 3) To speak out in the public arena and the media and 4) To protest anti-Christian bigotry ('Christian Coalition Leadership Manuel' n.d.).

Clearly, the Christian Coalition, along with the other groups previously mentioned, is concerned with promoting a Christian political agenda. However, the special concern of these groups with what may be called Christian 'moral' issues, abortion, homosexuality and the family (read: women's rights), demonstrate most clearly the religious reaction to what it considers to be anti-religious (i.e., secular) ideas. The power that such groups have to mobilize and to motivate voters is considerable.

While the Christian Right is a formidable force in American politics, and one that seeks to advance Christian interests in American political and social life, there are some who are consciously committed to bringing the United States political structure into line with a fundamentalist understanding of biblical law. The Chalcedon Foundation, established in 1965 by the Rev. Rousas John Rushdoony, is devoted to 'proclaiming the Authority of God's Word over every area of life and thought' (Chalcedon Foundation Website n.d.). It describes itself as 'devoted to research, publishing, and promoting Christian reconstruction in all areas of life' ('The Ministry of Chalcedon' n.d.), which is to say that it has as its objective the reconstruction of American society into one which conforms implicitly and explicitly with biblical law as understood by Rushdoony. In contrast with Paul Weyrich, who talks of simply 'spreading the gospel in a political context' (Etzioni 1996: 17), Rushdoony's website proclaims:

> We believe that the whole Word of God must be applied to all of life. It is not only our duty as individuals, families and churches to be Christian, but it is also the duty of the state, the school, the arts and sciences, law, economics, and every other sphere to be under Christ the King. Nothing is exempt from His dominion. We must live by His Word, not our own ('The Ministry of Chalcedon' n.d.).

Thus, this ideology, which calls for political and biblical congruence, has come to be called by its opponents *Reconstructionism* or *Dominionism*. While the movement identifies itself with no single denomination, it has important theological links with the Christian Identity Movement, a movement which most Evangelicals condemn as heretical. However, in a book titled, *The Church Is Israel Now* by Charles D. Provan and published by Rushdoony, the argument is advanced that 'certain select Christians are the "true Jews" or God's chosen people, hence their "identity"'. Reconstructionist thought gives Christian men (not women) 'dominion' over the Earth as articulated in the

Book of Genesis and the responsibility to bring the material world into line with their understanding of biblical expectations.

While the Reconstructionist movement may be considered extreme and of interest only to a minority of Christians, it also maintains a strong postmillennialist position, arguing that the world must be made ready for the return of Christ, which is expected within a generation or two, thus adding a strong note of urgency to the efforts to reform American society in preparation for the event. This serves to contextualize the movement's ideas in a way that make them more attractive to many Evangelical Christians.

Media and American Christianity in the Early Twenty-First Century

According to a March 2002 Pew Research Survey, 58 per cent of Americans surveyed believe that America's strength is based on religion, and 67 per cent believe that the United States is a 'Christian nation'. The same survey reports that in November 2001, one month after the events of 11 September 2001, 78 per cent of Americans surveyed thought that religion's influence on American life was increasing, and 85 per cent felt that this was 'a good thing' ('Religion and the Presidential Vote' 2004).

The Fundamentalist movement that originated in the early decades of the twentieth century generated considerable enthusiasm and stimulated a religious revival the effects of which are readily apparent today. The desire to protect the Fundamentalist Christian way of life from the ravages of secularization, combined with the influences of premillennialist, postmillennialist and dispensationalist ideas, resulted in a strong separatist tendency among those who embraced fundamentalist principles. This Christian separatism has, on occasion, resulted in movements that seek to make American political and social policy conform to biblical law as understood by Fundamentalists.

Such religious fervour exists in direct contradiction to the expectations of secularization theory which sees the decline of religion as a direct result of modernity. This has apparently been true in Western Europe; however, it has not been the case in the United States, despite the efforts of some sociologists to restructure the argument so that it could be made to apply in the United States (Brown 1992). The particular character of American evangelical religion has, however, ensured its survival and good health well into the present, and this trend shows every inclination to continue. Patrick N. Allitt of Emory University gives four possible reasons for this continued religious strength in America:

1) Religion has provided a permissible link with a fading ethnic identity as each new immigrant group began to assimilate; 2) Their sharp detachment

from the state prevented churches from suffering political discredit; 3) In a highly mobile, rootless society, religious organizations have offered a welcome source of community and identity; and 4) Religious organizations have pioneered important social reforms, notably the civil rights movement (2001).

The evolution of American Christianity during the twentieth century from the birth of the ideas of Fundamentalism and millennial dispensationalism in the early part of the century to the political strength of the Religious Right at the end of the century represents a sustained social reaction against the secularizing tendencies of the modern world. It affirms a social need for stability and identity, both of which have become increasingly ephemeral as advances in technology, science and the media have resulted in the development of ideas of a transnational 'global society'.

The Christian message continues to flood the airwaves and the print media. In the 1880s, Dwight L. Moody had used newspapers to advertise his revival meetings, in spite of Christian suspicion of modernity and modern ideas in the wake of the ideas of Charles Darwin. A century later, according to the 1995 *Directory of Religious Media*, the number of full-time evangelical radio stations had increased from 399 in 1972 to 1,328 in 1995 (Hendershot 2004: 56). Clearly, the Christian message is not only heard and seen by millions, but it is also embraced by millions through the media of American radio, television and print; as well as an increasing number of Christian Internet blogs and churches.

Fundamentalist thinking is not by any means limited to American Christianity, as everyone in this post-9/11 world knows. As the world moves more deeply into the twenty-first century, however, it is important to understand the long-standing relationship between American Christian Fundamentalism and the media, which continue to disseminate the Christian political and social agenda to the American public through movies, music, books, magazines, television and radio. Although the Christian Fundamentalist media remain critical of American secular culture, efforts to bring Christian political and social messages to the public continue to proliferate.

Note

1   Ironically, the issue of divorce, which is so often condemned in the Bible, has never become a priority issue among Evangelicals. For more on this, see Balmer 2006.

References

Albanese, C. (1996[1992]), *America: Religions and Religion*. Belmont: Wadsworth.

Allitt, P. (2001), *American Religious History* (audio course). Chantilly, Virginia: The Teaching Company.

Almond, G., Appleby, R. S. and Sivan E. (2003), *Strong Religion: The Rise of Fundamentalism around the World*. Chicago: University of Chicago Press.

Armstrong, K. (2000), *The Battle for God*. New York: Ballantine.

Balmer, R. (2000), *Mine Eyes Have Seen the Glory: A Journey into the Evangelical Subculture in America*. Oxford: Oxford University Press.

Balmer, R. (2006), *Thy Kingdom Come: An Evangelical's Lament*. New York: Basic Books.

Beale, D. O. (1986), *In Pursuit of Purity: American Fundamentalism Since 1850*. Greenville: Unusual Publications.

Bell, J. S. Jr. (ed.) (1977), *The D. L. Moody Collection: The Highlights of His Writings, Sermons, Anecdotes, and Life Story*. Chicago: Moody Press.

Berlet, C. and Lyons, M. (2000), *Right-Wing Populism in America: Too Close for Comfort*. New York: Guilford Press.

Bowden, F. J. and Fairley, C. K. (1996), 'Endemic STDs in the Northern Territory: Estimations of effective rates of partner change', paper presented to the scientific meeting of the Royal Australian College of Physicians, Darwin, 24–25 June.

Brown, C. (1992), 'Revisionist approach to religious change' in S. Bruce (ed.) *Religion and Modernization: Sociologists and Historians Debate the Secularization Thesis*. Oxford: Clarendon Press.

Bulman, R. F. (1999), *The Lure of the Millennium: The Year 2000 and Beyond*. New York: Orbis.

Chalcedon Foundation Website (n.d.), retrieved 10 March 2008 from <http://www.chalcedon.edu>.

Coppa, F. J. (1998), *The Modern Papacy Since 1789*. New York: Longman

'Christian Coalition Leadership Manual' (n.d.), in Christian Coalition special report 'A Campaign of Falsehoods: The Anti-Defamation League's Defamation of Religious Conservatives', 28 July 1994, p. 13.

Christian History (1997), 55, vol. XVI, no. 3, p. 19.

Crutchfield, L. (2002), *The Origins of Dispensationalism: The Darby Factor*. Lanham, MD: University Press of America.

Etzioni, A. (1996), *The New Golden Rule: Morality and Community in a Democratic Society*. New York: Basic Books.

Finke, R. (1992), 'An unsecular America?', in S. Bruce (ed.), *Religion and Modernization: Sociologists and Historians Debate the Secularization Thesis*. Oxford: Clarendon Press, pp. 145–169.

Gaustad, E. S. and M. A. Noll (eds) (2003), *A Documentary History of Religion in America since 1877*. Grand Rapids: Wm. B. Eerdmans Publishing Co.

Heffner, R. D. (2002), *A Documentary History of the United States*. New York: New American Library.

Hendershot, H. (2004), *Shaking the World for Jesus: Media and Conservative Evangelical Culture*. Chicago: University of Chicago Press.

'Jerry Falwell' (n.d.), Answers.com, retrieved 18 June 2008 from <http://www.answers.com/topic/jerry-falwell>.

Kauffman, C. (1992), 'Christopher Columbus and American Catholic Identity: 1880–1900' (lecture), Seton Hall University's Immaculate Conception Seminary, retrieved 21 June 2008 from <http://theology.shu.edu/lectures/columbus.htm>.

Keller, C. (1994), 'De-colonizing Paradise: A Quincentennial Passage' (unpublished paper) in B. C. Strozier, *Apocalypse: On the Psychology of Fundamentalism in America*. Boston: Beacon Press, p. 168.

Lovejoy, D. S. (1985), *Religious Enthusiasm in the New World: Heresy to Revolution*. Cambridge, MA: Harvard University Press.

Mahler, J. (2005), 'With Jesus as our connector: The soul of the new exurb', *The New York Times*, 27 March, 30.

Marsden, G. (1980), *Fundamentalism and American Culture: The Shaping of Twentieth-Century Evangelicalism 1870–1925*. Oxford: Oxford University Press.

Marty, M. E. (1996), *Modern American Religion*, vols 1, 2 and 3. Chicago: University of Chicago Press.

Monteiro, B. G. (2006), ' "Their time has come ..." Evangelicals' Ascendancy in the media: An historical perspective', paper presented to the Conference on Fundamentalism and the Media, University of Colorado at Boulder, 11 October.

'Religion and the Presidential Vote' (2004), Pew Research Center Website, retrieved 15 February 2005 from <http://people-press.org/commentary/display.php3?AnalysisID=103>.

Stout, H. S. (1993), 'Heavenly Comet', *History*, 38 (XII) 2, pp. 9–15.

Strozier, B. (1994), *Apocalypse: On the Psychology of Fundamentalism in America*. Boston: Beacon Press.

'The Ministry of Chalcedon' (n.d.) Chalcedon Foundation Website, retrieved 10 March 2008 from <http://www.chalcedon.edu/minstry.php>.

Torrey, R. A. and Dixon A. C. (eds) (2003[1917]), *The Fundamentals: A Testimony to the Truth*, vols 1 and 2. Los Angeles: Bible Institute of Los Angeles.

Wilcox, C. (2000), *Onward Christian Soldiers? The Religious Right in American Politics*. Boulder, CO: Westview.

Wolfe, A. (2003), *The Transformation of American Religion: How We Actually Live Our Faith*. New York: Free Press.

Part II

Mediations

Chapter 5

Fundamentalism in Arab and Muslim Media

Leon Barkho

Introduction

It can be argued that the divide between a 'Christian' West and an 'Arab' and 'Muslim' East has not been as deep as it is today since the Crusades of the eleventh and twelfth centuries. Western armies are fighting pitched battles in three Muslim countries if we add Israel's ongoing struggle with the Palestinians and some of its neighbours. For many Arabs and Muslims, the military campaigns are nothing but a replication of the Crusades and hence the calls for *jihad* or 'holy war'. This essay focuses on rhetorical and oratory discourse with a fundamentalist, extremist or radical nature that accompanies these military encounters. While guns may not be available to everyone, words, thanks to today's advances in information technology and digitization, are everywhere through television, newspapers, radio and the Internet.

What is Fundamentalism?

Scholars of media texts have no definitive measures to decide which term or phrase is representative of fundamentalism. The reasons are simple: 1) while we agree that fundamentalism is bad, we are still unsure about how to define it or answer it; 2) even if we eventually come up with a definition, fundamentalism as a concept is very subjective as it is interpreted differently by different people and different cultures; 3) even within a seemingly unified religion or culture, one may come across different points of view regarding the concept.

The problem is exacerbated when discussing fundamentalism in Arabic and Islamic cultures. Fundamentalism was once exclusively used to refer to Christians who believed in the inerrancy of the scriptures. Using Christian fundamentalism as a base, the term was later used to designate any religious movement that believed in the inerrancy of its holy books and acted upon them as if they were infallible truth. The online version of *Encyclopedia Britannica* defines fundamentalism as 'the type of militantly conservative religious movement characterized by the advocacy of strict conformity to sacred texts' ('Fundamentalism' n.d.). This definition is useful but falls short of providing a comprehensive picture of modern fundamentalism, particularly the kind prevalent in the Arab and Muslim world. First, Arab and Muslim groups advocating a strict interpretation of the *Sharia*, the revealed or canonical law of Islam, are rarely called 'fundamentalist' in Western ('Christian') or Israeli ('Jewish') media. They are invariably described as 'militants, Islamists, jihadists, extremists, radicals or terrorists' even if their agenda is purely nationalistic aimed at liberating land occupied by foreigners or ridding their peoples of local despots. Second, media in general and political institutions in particular, are in disagreement on how to explain fundamentalism. With the 'War on Terror' in its seventh year, there is no single definition of the term 'terror' and attempts at the United Nations to arrive at one have all but failed. Given the divisive nature of the current rhetorical struggles, a similar difficulty is presented when attempting to distinguish between 'fundamentalism' and 'extremism'. Occasionally, these two concepts are used interchangeably in this essay as well because the media rhetoric uses them in that way.

The data gathered for this essay illustrate that many of the samples, typical of what in the West would be viewed as 'fundamentalist' rhetoric, are not a direct product of strict adherence to Islam's canonical laws or the 'scriptures' in the Western sense. Rather, these examples have gained wide currency in light of specific historical circumstances. For example, the calls for *jihad* were heard across the Arab and Muslim world with the creation of Israel in 1948 and the dispossession of the Palestinians. The former Soviet Union's 1979 occupation of Afghanistan fuelled *jihad* among Arabs and Muslims, with the Western world's blessing. And the occupation of Iraq, which for many Arabs and Muslims is no different than the 'loss' of Palestine to Jews and the Soviet invasion of Afghanistan, is seen by many as one of the main reasons for the current surge in fundamentalist rhetoric in Arab and Muslim media.

This does not mean that the prevalence of fundamentalist oratory and rhetoric has no religious roots. On the contrary, its religious connotations are clearly discernible. But to investigate the religious background of Arab and Muslim fundamentalism, without paying due attention to the causes stimulating it, would be merely a biased, unscientific and to a certain degree futile attempt. One better way to understand fundamentalism in Arab and Muslim media is to look for the constitutive and dialectical relationships it has with the prevalent fundamentalist rhetoric in the West. For the purposes of this essay, *fundamentalism in media includes militant texts illustrating strict advocacy and conformity to Muslim's Holy Book, the Koran, Prophetic tradition and Islamic history as well as the texts Arabs and Muslims use in reaction to current Western ('Christian') and Israeli ('Jewish') practices and rhetoric they see as hostile and a threat to their religion and existence.*

Understanding Fundamentalism

We do not have a model or theory to help us understand the fundamentalist texts cited in this essay. However, if we re-examine our aforementioned definition, we shall see that it has something to do with the past and the present. In the category 'past', we have 'the Koran, Islamic tradition and history' and in the category 'present', we have 'Christian, Arab, Western, Jewish and Israeli'. Thus the world of the fundamentalist texts as used by Arab and Muslim media is extremely wide. It involves: 1) three religions – Judaism, Christianity and Islam; 2) two principal cultures – Muslim and Western; 3) two histories – Arab and Muslim, Jewish and Christian and 4) the events that are shaping the present-day rhetorical struggle as manifested in various media.

In my opinion, any attempt to understand fundamentalist rhetoric, not only among Arabs and Muslims, but everywhere, should be based on the world and context of the texts and expressions reflecting it. To try to understand fundamentalist media with recourse to one or two of the components of its world would definitely provide a twisted picture of the situation in which they thrive. A proper understanding must bear in mind the totality of the world the fundamentalist texts or expressions are found in; otherwise we will only be bending the truth to fit our side of the story. In his classic work, *Covering Islam: How the Media and Experts Determine How We See the Rest of the World*, Edward Said emphasizes the significance of historical and cultural context in interpreting texts:

> Therefore the interpretation of texts, which is what the knowledge of other cultures is principally based on, neither takes place in a clinically secure laboratory nor pretends to objective results. It is a social activity and inextricably tied to the situation out of which it arose in the first place (1981: 156).[1]

Of course the world of fundamentalist media or texts should not be restricted to the four aforementioned elements. Other points such as language, medium, the interpreter's background, conventions, feelings, religion, traditions and values play a role. In order not to impose ourselves on the text, we need to put its world into account. Understanding should involve the parts, in our case the fundamentalist texts selected from the data, and the way they are motivated by their world or whole, in a hermeneutic cycle. Proper understanding will not occur unless the part and whole of a text are integrated.

The approach adopted in this essay to understand Arab and Muslim fundamentalist media, in fact, echoes Hans-Georg Gadamer who also emphasizes the importance of not viewing understanding as, 'an isolated activity of human beings but a basic structure of our experience of life. We are always taking something as something. That is the primordial givenness of our world orientation, and we cannot reduce it to anything simple or more immediate' (1994[1975]: 87).

Method of the Study

The texts cited in the essay as samples of fundamentalist rhetoric are drawn from nearly 200 articles from mainly Arabic print media and more than 100 televised interviews and speeches over a period of four months (June to September 2006). The pieces were selected if the headline and the lead touched upon an issue of fundamentalist connotation in accordance with the definition and scope of fundamentalism presented earlier. Many of the televised pieces come from MEMRI, the Middle East Media Research Institute TV Project Monitor (see http://www.memritv.org). The majority of the samples fall within the opinion or comment category but the impact of ideas, particularly those of clerics, is widely felt across the Arab and Muslim world, far exceeding the influence of hard news.

This study, like many others, is not without limitations. First, it suffers from a certain degree of subjectivity in selecting the articles being discussed. In addition, the large number of articles reviewed may have benefitted from some form of quantitative analysis; such an approach would be worthy of future pursuits. However, this essay's main goal is to present an initial and qualitative exploration into the scope, range, content and themes of present-day fundamentalist rhetoric found in the Arab and Muslim media.

Samples From Print Media

Western 'Duplicity and Hypocrisy'

In one of his daily columns, Jihad Khazen, editor of *al-Hayat*, one of the Arab world's most read newspapers, says he has dedicated his career to exposing Western and particularly American 'hypocrisy, double standard and duplicity' (Khazen 2006a). Writing in both Arabic and English, he has no kind words for groups advocating violence among Muslims and Arabs. But he uses even harsher words to show that fundamentalism is not solely an Arab or Muslim problem. In one of his widely read daily columns *Ayoon Wa Azan* (or 'Eyes and Ears'), Khazen writes:

> Zionist Christians, or the voting base of George Bush, believe that the False Messiah will come and will be followed by most of the people on earth. And then the true Messiah will come and save the believing elite (Christian Zionists) while others, including me and you the reader, because we are not Zionist Christians, will perish (Khazen 2006).

Many writers share Khazen's views. Radhwan al-Saeed, writing in the United Arab Emirates' paper *Al-Ittihad* on 24 July 2006, talks of the 'resurgence' and 'eruption' of the Evangelical brand of Christianity in America. Evangelists, according to the writer, await the 'Second Coming and believe the creation of Israel is a major sign and harbinger' (al-Saeed 2006). But what is 'worrying', Saeed adds, 'is their belief that everyone on earth including Muslims and even Jews, will have to convert to Christianity' (al-Saeed 2006).

To understand Arab and Muslim fundamentalist discourse in isolation will not do justice to the hermeneutic interpretation pursued here. In his oft-cited op-ed of 17 July 2004, Nicholas Kristof of *The New York Times* demonstrates that the kind of rhetoric US evangelicals pursue is no different from that of Muslim and Arab radicals. After quoting a couple of paragraphs of what can be described as 'militant Christian' rhetoric of the *Glorious Appearing*, one of a series of best-seller novels in the United States of which more than 60 million copies have been printed worldwide, Kristof says:

> If a Muslim were to write an Islamic version of 'Glorious Appearing' and publish it in Saudi Arabia, jubilantly describing a massacre of millions of non-Muslims by God, we would have a fit. We have quite properly linked the fundamentalist religious tracts of Islam with the intolerance they nurture, and it's time to remove the motes from our own eyes (Kristof 2004).

Comparisons and Parallels

Muslims, particularly the Arabs, have a great imagination. Their power to draw comparisons and parallels is amazing and for them it is one of the basic tools to discover reality. And it is not important whether the comparison is relevant or not, has a bearing on the present time or not. When a Palestinian group captured Israeli soldier Corporal Gilad Shalit in June 2006, there was condemnation of the seizure from the West but unease and indignation in Arab media most of it vented through comparison and parallel.

In a widely distributed article first published by *Al-Waqt al-Bahraniya* of Bahrain on 27 July 2006, Rashad Abu Dawood addresses Shalit to tell him that if he were a Jew his ancestors had left Palestine (the land of today's Israel) more than 2,000 years ago:

> You are of French origin. Who brought you here? Poor Gilad, how could they convince you to come to Palestine? How could they persuade you that this land is yours, and the house you live in belongs to you and the air and the sea are yours? You come to the so-called Promised Land after 2,000 years while the people who you have replaced still have the dust of their homes on their shoes and keep the keys of their houses in the closet of their new temporary dwellings nearby and are denied the right of return (Dawood 2006).

The aforementioned quotation from Dawood's article may have no meaning or significance for Western readers but it tells Arab and Muslim audiences of their duty to regain a 'lost country' no matter the sacrifices. Dawood's words may not be strictly fundamentalist but they turn many against the West, the creator and supporter of Israel, which in the eyes of many Muslims and Arabs is nothing but a 'usurper'.

Abdulbari Atawan, one of the most outspoken Arab journalists and editor of the influential London-based *Al-Quds al-Arabi* newspaper, in a 6 June 2006 op-ed puts the Shalit saga in the context of the nearly 11,000 Palestinian prisoners languishing in Israeli jails among them more than 1,500 women and children. The Arabs find the comparison and parallel context, whether relevant or irrelevant, easy to grasp:

> We did not know that the Israeli soldier has been elated to the status of a prophet and perhaps surpassing it as we see how the governments of big powers such as the US, France, Britain and most Arab states are calling for his release (Atawan 2006).

The drawing of parallels and comparisons is so vivid and widespread in Arabic media to the extent that if the context or the world of a fundamentalist text is excluded it becomes difficult to understand. For example, the Qatari *Al-Watan* newspaper of 14 June 2006 issues a roster of anti-Muslim actions such as the Guantanamo prison, the deliberate killing of civilians in Haditha in Iraq, the Abu Ghraib prison, the US-supported Israeli attacks on Palestinians, the group rape of a 14-year-old Muslim girl by US marines in Iraq in March 2006, the secret CIA jails, the abuse of the Koran by US guards, the Muhammad cartoons, among others:

> While the Bush administration occasionally reiterates that the American war on terror is not specifically directed against Islam and Muslims, what takes place in reality across the world . . . demonstrates that Islamic peoples are the target and no one else? (Al-Watan 2006)

Texts like these add to the perceived alienation and humiliation many Arabs and Muslims already feel.

History and Fundamentalism

The other important message Arabic media strive to drive home in the campaign to stave off Western rhetoric accusing Arabs and Muslims of violence and radicalism is by digging up historical 'facts'. They tell readers that current Arab and Muslim fundamentalist rhetoric and the violent acts attributed to them dwarf in comparison what used to happen in the West. They say fundamentalist rhetoric and its translation into reality are truly of Western making. They cite 'anti-Semitism' and the 'holocaust' as some of the worst atrocities in the history of mankind of which Muslims and Arabs are innocent. For example, Jihad Khazen of *Al-Hayat* in a column on 6 July 2006 argues that a few decades ago the victims were Jews, but today they have become the Palestinians, Arabs and Muslims. He asserts that instead of burning Jews, witches and gypsies, etc., the West and America are using the Palestinians, the Lebanese and the Iraqis as the new fodder for their cannons. Khazen even invokes the Crusades at the height of the war between Israel and Hezbollah in his column of 14 August 2006:

> Shall I start with the First Crusade in 1095, when blood was shed in Jerusalem, thanks to the European invaders? Or shall I start with the Third Crusade, in which, failing to reach our region, the Christians turned to Christian Constantinople. They killed the people and destroyed the city to such an extent that Christian Greece refuses to forgive them. Greece still demands that the Vatican apologize for what the Crusaders did to the Eastern Christians (Khazen 2006b).

If Western reports say the schism between the two main sects of Islam – the Sunnis and Shiites – is growing, the step to take in the Middle East is for senior Muslim Sunni and Shiite clerics to come together and denounce America and Israel. This is exactly what happened in the 2006 war between Israel and the Shiite Hezbollah party in Lebanon. In the early days of the conflict, there were reports of *fatwas* or religious decrees by top Sunni clerics in Saudi Arabia, condemning Hezbollah and forbidding Muslim Sunnis even from pleading with God to help them dominate in the fighting.

But when the war dragged on, Saudi clergymen, among them top cleric Abdullah Bin Jibrin, went public in their condemnation of Israel and America. In a 9 August 2006 interview aired by one of the Arab world's most influential satellite channels, *al-Arabiya*, he exhorted every Muslim, whether Sunni or Shiite, to back Hizbollah. The centuries-old conflict pitching the Shiites against the Sunnis was no longer there and instead Jenein poured his wrath on:

> Jews (Israelis) and Christians (Americans) who are attacking Muslims in Lebanon, Palestine, Iraq and Afghanistan. We pray to God to have them (Israelis and Americans) suppressed and to thwart the deceits of the enemies of God and foil their covetousness of the lands of Muslims (Bin Jibrin 2006).

'Scapegoats' of 9/11

Since 11 September 2001, many Arabs and Muslims have grown suspicious of whatever the West says or does in regard to their causes, religion and countries.

They feel they are under constant attack from the West. With their weak economies and backward armies, they feel Islam, its tenets, its words, its saints, its *jihad* and its battle cries are the only means left to defend themselves. Verses from the Koran disparaging Jews and Christians and retelling their 'mockery' of the Prophet and 'tricks' to undermine his message, rarely quoted before 11 September 2001, are cited profusely in the media. Israeli policies perceived as hostile and aggressive are blamed on the West. They believe a new breed of 'Crusades' is being unleashed against them.

'Justice is dead, if you're born an Arab', declares Lubna Hussain, in an article in the *Saudi Arab News* of 9 August 2006 (Hussain, L. 2006). It is worth noting that these verbal attacks not only fall into the hands of extremists but undermine the unfortunately diminishing circle and influence of moderate Arab and Muslim writers. A Muslim philosopher and a leading spokesman for Muslims in Europe, Tariq Ramadan, says he fears that the Western media's espousal of anti-Muslim rhetoric and practices is bound to backfire as, 'The (Muslim) extremists argue that, "See, we told you, the West is against Islam" ' (Ramadan 2006). In an interview with *New Perspectives Quarterly* (NPQ) on 8 August 2006, Ramadan argues that the West is wrong to think that it angers the extremists by its anti-Muslim rhetoric only. For example, the Danish cartoons, he says, 'are seen, by average Muslim and not just radicals, as the transgression against something sacred, a provocation against Islam' (Ramadan 2006).

President George W. Bush's gaffes, perceived in the Arab and Muslim world as anti-Islamic, have sparked furious remarks; particularly his statement of 10 August 2006 in which he said, 'This nation is at war with Islamic fascists who will use any means to destroy those of us who love freedom, to hurt our nation' (Bush 2006). Writing in *Pak Tribune* of 30 August 2006, Anwaar Hussain sees the opposite contending that Arabs and Muslims are the ones who are being destroyed by America and its allies.

> The period since 9/11 has seen the Middle Eastern plains continuously being drenched with the blood of innocent Muslims, the supposed perpetrators of the crime. Internationally, during the same period, their coreligionists are increasingly being treated like dogs (Hussain, A. 2006).

Fundamentalism as Counterattack

Western actions and deeds perceived as hostile by Arabs and Muslims have even alienated some of the hitherto most moderate and liberal thinkers whose writings many see as a harbinger of true reforms and revision of strict traditional values. One of Arabs' greatest living literary figures, Ali Ahmad Saeed, better known under his pseudonym Adonis, sees himself drawn into the battle of words pitching the Arab Muslim world against the 'Christian' Western world. Adonis, in a 7 August 2006 article in *Al-Hayat* blames the West for the surge in fundamentalism among Muslims and Arabs.

> Look at these (Western) countries and how they see terror as if it grows naturally and voluntarily as if it were an abstract point or one of the forms of metaphysical existence, without reasons or causes or if there are reasons they are confined to a cheap 'will' among the Arabs to destroy the West and its ally Israel. As for how this 'will' has come into being and the reasons behind it, the answer is with Israel and the United States through which they do not stop reiterating the stupid and unjustified mixture between terror, liberation and a tendency towards independence (Adonis 2006).

What brings a writer of Adonis's stature to the rhetorical clash between the East and the West? It is the deep sense of alienation, humiliation and estrangement Arabs and Muslims feel in today's world, Adonis explains (2006). But not everyone has Adonis' common sense and careful use of words. Many writers are less cautious, more fiery and inciting. In a vitriolic directed at the West and Israel, Subhi Ghandour of *Al-Bayan*, a United Arab Emirates newspaper, says:

> Once we realize the extent of efforts the media steered by the rancorous and racist Zionist outlets have implanted in the hearts and minds of their audiences, it becomes easy to comprehend the reasons behind the massive volume of Arab and Muslim fury (Ghandour 2006).

The Saudi *Al-Riyadh* of 9 August 2006, says it is the duty of Arabs and Muslims to stand up to the fundamentalist onslaught from the West which aims at disparaging and insulting the symbols of their religion in what it sees a harbinger or revisit of the Crusader campaigns of the Middle Ages:

> All Islamic peoples must move alongside the Kingdom (of Saudi Arabia) to defeat the idea of Islamic fascism that is being promulgated through media and politics. The mobilization of Muslim peoples and Muslim governments and Islamic organizations to confront these statements is a confrontation of plans that want to make Islam the enemy of the non-Muslim peoples (el-Jar Allah 2006).

No matter how bitterly scathing the Arab and Muslim fundamentalist rhetoric is, it does not amount to the ferocity of that directed at them from the 'Christian West', according to Ayda Qanat of the UAE's *Al-Khaleej*. The way Arabs and Muslims are being described in the Western media and the labels given to them by Western political and religious leaders 'have never been employed by any Western official since the Crusades', says Qanat in a 17 September 2006 article (Qanat 2006). The war, whether of words or bullets, Qanat says, has been raging against Islam since the fall of the former Soviet Union. He adds, 'It is an open war which is being developed and transformed, assuming a different title at every different stage' (Qanat 2006).

Same Form but Different 'Hermeneutics'

What the West and particularly America and Israel see as 'terrorists', 'militants', 'Islamists', 'extremists', 'fundamentalists' and 'jihadists' are 'freedom fighters', 'peace lovers' and 'defenders of the faith' in Arabic and Islamic media. No matter what Israel and the US may say, many of these groups are not 'terrorist' organizations, writes the renowned British journalist Patrick Seale in the English version of al-Hayat on 11 August 2006. 'They are popular movements which represent the longing of their respective communities', Seale (2006) adds. The newspaper's editor Khazen dubs the neocons in Washington 'the evil clique' and a 'kind of cancer' and calls a Shiite Lebanese suicide bomber who in 1982 killed 76 Israeli occupation troops in Lebanon 'the prince of martyrs' (Khazen 2006c). In fact, Arab and Muslim media often borrow Western fundamentalist terms such as 'terrorists or extremists' to designate their adversaries. Neocons and Israelis are invariably called 'terrorists' or 'extremists'. Appellations like 'Zionists' or 'Christian Zionists' are also common. Even words like 'Nazism' and 'fascism' are being used to refer to Israeli Jews and their leaders as well as US neocons.

Western 'atrocities' targeting Arabs and Muslims are said to be as horrific for them as Hitler's Holocaust. The Holocaust for them is what Israel and America do in Palestine, Lebanon, Iraq and Afghanistan. Khazen in a column published in al-Hayat on 6 August 2006, calls Israeli Prime Minister Ehud Olmert the 'small Fuher' in reference to Adolf Hitler and likens US and Israeli wars in Lebanon, Iraq and Palestine to 'pure Nazi terrorism . . . similar to that committed against the Jews in the ghettos of Warsaw and elsewhere' (Khazen 2006d). Al-Hayat generally talks of two Holocausts: the one the Nazis committed against the Jews and the other being committed by the Jews against the Palestinians. 'Today's Jew has turned from a victim to a killer', it declares (Khazen 2006d).

Other respected newspapers with large circulation across the Arab world, hammer the same message home. Egypt's al-Ahram, in a 12 September 2006 article titled 'Who are the Nazis' writes:

> The Jews who escaped (the Nazi) oppression persecuted the Palestinians by having them expelled from their land. [. . .] Thus the old victims of Nazism have become new Nazis, killing children and fracturing their bones and leveling houses on their occupants (Hajazi 2006).

As we conclude this survey of several Arabic newspapers and their view of the current fundamentalist verbal struggle, it is important to highlight here that almost all national and pan-Arab newspapers quoted in this study do not condone violence and are critical of Muslim extremist groups practicing it. However, they immediately draw parallels and comparisons in which such acts are interpreted within a wider context and explained in relation to the acts and fundamentalist rhetoric emanating from what they regard as their main adversary, the 'Christian' West and its ally the Jewish state of Israel.

Samples from Television and the Internet

More 'Ferocious' Rhetoric

Arab and Muslim fundamentalist rhetoric escalates and assumes tones bordering on aggression, bigotry and hatred vis-à-vis Western policies as one moves to television[2] broadcasting where technology has made controls and censorship rather difficult. Radical Islamists, using the Internet and satellite television as carriers of their messages, constantly invoke religion and history in their rhetoric. The new al-Qaeda leader in Iraq, Abu Hamza al-Muhajer, in a tape recording that was broadcast by *Aljazeera* on 9 September 2006, calls Bush 'the liar crusader', 'the dog of the Romans' and 'the worshipper of the cross' (Aljazeera 2006) – silly appellations to a Western ear, but full of emotions and meanings in an Arab and Muslim context.

Muhajer's master and Osama Bin Laden's deputy, Ayman al-Dhawahiri, calls Bush, in a video statement posted on the Internet on 30 September 2006, '[a] deceitful charlatan' currently bent on conceiving yet another invasion of Muslim territories. 'There is a Crusader plan to send Crusader forces to Darfur that is about to become a new field of the Crusader war', the Associated Press quoted him as saying (Gardiner 2006).

The parallels and comparisons highlighted in print media are given more prominence in the fundamentalist rhetoric of Muslim clerics who today command a large following across the Arab and Muslim world. Arabic print media are usually reluctant to carry sermons and speeches these clerics give and would normally shun publishing them. But now they rely on an even more powerful media, namely television which is the main source of information in the Arab and Muslim world mainly due to high illiteracy rates.[3]

Many of these clerics may not openly side with radical organizations like those of al-Qaeda but it is not difficult to see how the essential concepts of al-Qaeda rhetoric have crept into their sermons and *fatwas*, or religious decrees. The interviews and sermons by senior Arab and Muslim clerics examined for the purposes of this research highlight a central theme in the speeches of Bin Laden and his deputy al-Dhawahiri. Both of them strive to persuade Arabs and Muslims that they are under attack from Western 'Crusaders'. Both justify the use of violence and fundamentalist rhetoric because in their eyes it is an act of self-defense, or *jihad*. Al-Qaeda always has a litany of grievances in the speeches it makes to justify an act of violence or terror. Even Bin Laden had a 'justification' for 11 September 2001. In a tape issued nearly a month later, he said, 'What the United States tastes today is a very small thing compared to what we have tasted for tens of years' (BBC 2001).

Clerical Fundamentalism

Clerical fundamentalist rhetoric differs from secular fundamentalist discourse in its ferocity. It is so loud and forceful that it buries any moderating tones in Arab and Muslim media. It is not that the moderates are scared to speak their mind, but they have apparently run out of logic to advance their conciliatory tones as the dangerous turn of events in Muslim lands and the surge in fundamentalist texts makes them sound very unconvincing to the majority of Arab and Muslim populations. These clerics, unlike moderate writers and reporters, are not very much concerned to have Western audiences on their side. Their primary priority is how to deliver their message to Arab and Muslim masses. Hence their invocation of historic and religious figures and events with tremendous sentimental and psychological impact on Arab and Muslim life as the following excerpt from a speech by Iraq's al-Qaeda leader, Abu Hamza al-Muhajer, shows:

> You, the worshiper of the cross [US President George Bush], you, the dog of the Romans, are on your way to meet defeat. [. . .] You, infidels and tyrants [America and the West] your good news is the bad news as we are proceeding ahead with our *Jihad* and will not stop . . . until *Sharia* [Islamic jurisdiction] rules the land and the people (Aljazeera 2006).

Arabic television is dominated by religious programs and the number of Arabic satellite channels which are wholly devoted to Islam and Islamic issues outstrips those dedicated to entertainment and news. Even the most influential all-news channels rely on their religious programs to garner and sustain wide viewership. *Aljazeera*, for example, has propelled Sheikh Yousif Qaradhawi to a star status in the Arab and Muslim world for his weekly phone-in program *al-Sharia wal-Hayat*, (or 'Islamic Law and Life'). The majority of religious television channels are sponsored by Saudi Arabia, a Western and US ally in the region, and that some of the fiercest fundamentalist rhetoric comes from Saudi clerics. One of these channels is *Iqra* (or 'Read'), in which Saudi clerics and intellectuals dominate the screen. On 16 March 2006, Saudi intellectual Awadh al-Qarni drew parallels between the Nazis and what he described as 'the Likud Jews . . . Zionist gangs and neo-cons. . . . They are the closest thing there to Nazism. The neo-cons are identical to Nazis' (MEMRI 2006b).

Rarely are tapes and speeches by radical groups carried out in their entirety, even by *Aljazeera* which seems to have access to the majority of them. I went through the 53 speeches which *Aljazeera* has aired, 25 for Bin Laden and 28 for al-Dhawahiri, for the period September 2001 to September 2006 along with related stories the network has posted on its widely read website and found that the majority of them quote what has become almost the rallying cry of Arabs and Muslims worldwide. The statements in paraphrase say that once the West and America leave Arabs and Muslims in peace, the group and its followers will reciprocate and stop fighting. But so long as America and the West are fighting Muslims (through Israel), in Palestine and Lebanon and invading their territory in Iraq and Afghanistan, there will be no letup in their *jihad*. 'If you guarantee our security, you will for sure have your own security guaranteed. You shall not obtain peace unless we have it, too' reads the phrase which is mentioned in almost all the speeches (Aljazeera 2001).

Televised radical clerics' rhetoric is more forceful and perhaps more convincing for the average person than that of the print and official media. Senior clerics, particularly those delivering their sermons and speeches in Arabic, utilize their immense rhetorical and linguistic repertoire to sway and electrify audiences. One such cleric, Iraqi born Ahmad al-Kubeisi, is of immense influence among Sunni Muslims in the Gulf and Iraq. His media tool is Al-Risala television of Saudi prince Walid bin Tala. Kubeisi's sermons and speeches are thought to be persuasive as they are directed at the minds of average Muslims, keen to put in context the chaotic world they find themselves in. Speaking on 15 March 2006, Kubeisi urges his audiences to rally for *jihad* because it is Islam which the West has as a target in what he sees as 'the third [world] Crusader war':

> How can you talk to me about *Jihad* under these conditions? Sir, *Jihad* is an individual duty. . . . The West's conflict with Islam and the Muslims is eternal, a preordained destiny that cannot be avoided until Judgment Day (MEMRI 2006c).

The longer this so-called 'war on terror' drags on and so long as the causes leading to it are not addressed, the ferociousness of the current rhetoric belching from the Arab and Muslim world is bound to escalate and attain closer affinity to that of al-Qaeda and its lieutenants. Many of the earlier citations, particularly those from senior Muslim clerics, are a rehearsal of al-Qaeda rhetoric and echo one of its main platforms. The following excerpt from a video address by Ayman al-Dhawahiri presents the same justification for *jihad* as the one promulgated by Kubeisi earlier. The difference is Kubeisi's remarks are slightly 'watered down' in comparison:

> The Jews and Crusaders everywhere should pay the price for killing Muslim brothers in Lebanon, Palestine, and other Islamic countries . . . You (Jews

and Crusaders) have given us the Islamic legal and logical reasons to fight and punish you, because you have committed heinous crimes (MEMRI 2006a).

Scrambling for Fundamentalist Terms

Muslim clerics and officials running ministries of religious affairs and endowments now scour their holy books, particularly the Koran, to disparage and condemn their enemies and mobilize the masses. The Koran, like any other holy book, can be used to heal or harm. Muslim theologians recognize that the verses of the Koran, perceived by Muslims as words of God, may not be easy for a human being to interpret and hence one verse may have several aspects. This is quite obvious when two Muslim nations fight each other, as it happened in the 1980–1988 Iraq–Iran war. Each country's propaganda machine never tired of quoting Koranic verses to prove it was in the right.

Some Arabs and Muslims are surprised to hear clerics quoting the Koran as lashing out at the Jews and describing them as the descendants of 'apes and pigs'. Dr. Muhammad Abed al-Sattar of the Syrian Ministry of Religious Endowments chooses some of the most disparaging terms the Koran uses to describe the Jews. In a 12 July 2006 televised interview at the height of the war in Lebanon, the minister says:

> The Koran depicts the people of Israel in a very sinister and dark way. [. . .] The only ones who were cursed are those murderous criminals. [. . .] They were also likened to apes and pigs. [. . .] Look at the bestiality they demonstrate in the destruction of the Arab, Lebanese, and Palestinian people (MEMRI 2006d).

Adding Fuel to Fire

The examples, as mentioned earlier, are illustrative of almost all the televised pieces examined for this study and their message in one way or another can be gleaned from most of the 200 print articles. And almost all were issued before Pope Benedict made his 12 September 2006 speech quoting a fourteenth-century Christian emperor criticizing the Prophet Muhammad and Islam. According to the BBC, which published key excerpts of the speech on 15 September 2006, the Pope quoted the emperor as saying, 'Show me just what Muhammad brought that was new and there you will find things only evil and inhuman, such as his command to spread by the sword the faith he preached' (BBC 2006). The Roman Pontiff's speech added more fuel to the raging fundamentalist fire.

Muslim clerics utilized the Pope's remarks to illustrate what they have been warning of all the way through that Islam is under threat and that the 'Christian' West, and its 'puppet' Israel, are determined to press ahead with their 'Crusades'. Senior clerics like Qaradhawi led the counter rhetorical attack against the Pope. In a 24 September 2006 sermon in Cairo – reported by http://www.islamonline.net/arabic and cited widely in Arabic media and aired over several satellite stations – Qaradhawi quotes from the Biblical book of Joshua and the instructions ancient Jews were given before entering a battle to put to death by the sword all the males in the conquered cities in ancient Palestine or finish off their inhabitants:

> This is what the Christian peoples have bequeathed and applied in the lands they conquered. It derives from Jewish Torah . . . which you [Pope] and all Christians believe in because its part of the Holy Bible. The Jews applied it on the Palestinians. [. . .] As for Islam, it rejects the extermination of people. It in fact rejects the extermination of animals (Islamonline.net 2006).

Qaradhawi quotes excessively from the Bible to smear the other side and cites Koranic verses to glorify his own. Thus, Muslim conquests for Qaradhawi were 'for the liberation of colonized peoples . . . and Islam was not a new form of colonialism as some think' in those days (Islamonline.net 2006). Qaradhawi is as skillful as the Pope in quoting out of context from Christian and Jewish holy books and historical events to prove his point and rally Arab and Muslim masses.

Qaradhawi's texts, despite their aggressive nature, are a watered down version in comparison to texts produced by al-Qaeda in response to the Pope. Qaradhawi has to deal within the limits and constraints of his sponsors, the royal family in Qatar; however, al-Qaeda's No. 2, Ayman al-Dhawahiri, is under no such restrictions. In his 30 September 2006 online speech, and according to the Associated Press, Dhawahiri drew parallels between Benedict and Pope Urban II, who in 1095 ordered the First Crusade to establish Christian rule in Palestine:

> This charlatan Benedict brings back to our memories the speech of his predecessor charlatan Urban II in the 11th century . . . in which he instigated Europeans to fight Muslims and launch the Crusades because he [Urban] claimed 'atheist Muslims, the enemies of Christ' are attacking the tomb of Jesus Christ, peace be upon him (Associated Press 2006).

The Last Word

John Kenneth Galbraith in his *The Economics of Innocent Fraud* talks of the impact television and conventional oratory have on audiences. They have the power of 'mass persuasion', he says, and the huge sums of money they deploy are used to lure customers to buy corporations' products or services. Aside from their economic interests, the media today employ their massive financial resources to win hearts and minds of audiences and lure them not only to buy products but also ideas. Selling fundamentalist oratory is slowly but steadily turning into an industry with far greater consequences than the 'innocent' fraudulent practices of governments, management and corporations, which Galbraith brilliantly outlines in his book.

As audiences we seem to have lost our independence since we have grown to believe in the deluge of texts whether fundamentalist or otherwise media flood us with. The way consumers of today have little say in the manufacture and sale of goods and services, so are the audiences who have almost no say in the selection and presentation of the fundamentalist texts they are exposed to. True, they have the choice to 'switch the channel' but even that choice is apparently hard to make. It is like telling a chain smoker or a drug addict that they have the choice to stop. Fundamentalist media are mushrooming in the Arab and Muslim world. But it is wrong to restrict fundamentalism to Arabs and Muslims, though their current world and context are very tempting for this kind of media which they use as a weapon to encounter what they perceive as an onslaught by the 'Christian' West.

It is time researchers develop new models to help audiences interpret the fundamentalist texts they come across by other than their own restricted backgrounds and contexts. Understanding fundamentalist media, whether among Arabs and Muslims or in other societies, requires an investigation of the causes and reasons spewing it. We cannot understand the resurgence of fundamentalist rhetoric in Arab and Muslim world without first coming to grips with an attempt to answer the why's and how's of the texts we study. The parts and pieces of our texts must be placed within their world and context or whole if we want to understand the fundamentalist rhetoric of religions and cultures other than our own.

Notes

1   Said suggests that hermeneutics, as outlined by Gadamer, is among the best interpretive tools to understand the gulf separating cultures, particularly that between Islam and the West.
2   According to Arab Advisors Group (http://www.arabadvisors.com), an independent research, analysis and consulting group, there are currently more than 200 Arabic satellite broadcasting stations beaming to the 22 Arab states. Television is a major source of information for the Arabs due to high illiteracy rates (see Note 3).
3   Adult illiteracy rates among the nearly 300 million Arabs are among the highest in the world. According to the United Nations Development Program Arab Human Development Report of 2002 an estimated 43 per cent of Arabs are illiterate (UNDP 2002).

References

Adonis (2006), 'Madarat' [Orbits], *Al-Hayat* website, retrieved 7 September 2006 from <http://drkalam.maktoobblog.com.

Aljazeera (2001), 'Nas Hadeed Osaman Bin Laden' [Text of Bin Laden's speech], retrieved 26 June 2006 from <http://www.aljazeera.net/NR/exeres/E052B608-8D21-4DD8-9A3B-281491B9FC11.htm#L1>.

Aljazeera (2006), 'Zaaeem Alqaida Wathiq Min Alnaser Aala Alamrikiyeen' [Iraq's al-Qaeda leader is confident of victory over Americans], retrieved 8 September 2006 from <http://www.aljazeera.net/News/>.

Al-Saeed, Radhwan (2006), 'Althawran Aldinin Fi Alwilayat Almutahida' [The religious flare-up in the United States], *Al-Ittihad* website, retrieved 28 June 2006 from <http://www.elaph.com/ElaphWeb/NewsPapers/2006/6/158120.htm?sectionarchive=NewsPapers>.

Al-Watan (2006), 'Nuzalaa Ghantanamo Kulohom Muslimoon. Hal Hiya Musadafa' [Guantanamo inmates are all Muslims! Is that a coincidence?] (editorial), *Al-Watan* website, retrieved 29 June 2006 from <http://www.al-watan.com/data/20080625/index.asp>.

Associated Press (2006), 'Bin Laden deputy blasts Bush', retrieved 30 September 2006 from <http://findarticles.com/p/articles/mi_qn4188/is_20060930/ai_n 16762235>.

Atawan, A. (2006), 'Ghaza Alsamida Tasaal Ayna Alarab?' [The steadfast Gaza wonders where are the Arabs?], *Al-Qudus al-Arabi* website, retrieved 29 June 2006 from <http://www.arabrenewal.net/index.php?rd=AI&AI0= 15172>.

BBC (2001), 'Bin Laden's warning: full text', BBC website, retrieved 15 July 2006 from <http://news.bbc.co.uk/2/low/south_asia/1585636.stm>.

BBC (2006), 'Muslim anger grown at Pope speech', BBC website, retrieved 25 September 2006 from <http://news.bbc.co.uk/2/hi/europe/5347876.stm>.

Bin Jibrin, A. (2006), 'Bin Jibrin Yooakedu Anna Fatwahoo Lam Takun Aan Hizbollah' [Bin Jibrin confirms his fatwa was not related to Hizbollah], *al-Arabiya* website, retrieved 9 August 2006 from <http://www.alarabiya.net/articles/2006/08/08/26443.html>.

Bush, G. W. (2006), 'President Bush discusses terror plot upon arrival in Wisconsin' (speech), White House website, retrieved 25 June 2008 from <http://www.whitehouse.gov/news/releases/2006/08/20060810-3.html>.

Dawood, R. A. (2006), 'Jalaat . . . Ayoha Ljundi Almiskeen' [Gilad . . . you the poor soldier!], *Al-Waqt* website, retrieved 28 July 2006 from <http://www.alwaqt.com/blog_art.php?baid=301>.

El-Jar Allah, A. el-A. (2006), 'Muslims must unite against "fascist" label', *Watching America* website, retrieved 27 August 2006 from <http://www.watchingamerica.com/alriyadh000005.shtml>.

'Fundamentalism' (n.d.), Encyclopedia Britannica Website, retrieved 27 September 2006 from <http://search.eb.com/eb/article-9390025>.

Gadamer, H. G. (1994[1975]), *Truth and Method*. New York: Continuum.

Galbraith, J. K. (2004), *The Economics of Innocent Fraud*. Boston/New York: Houghton Mifflin Company.

Gardiner, B. (2006), 'Al-Qaeda's second in command, Ayman al-Zawahri appears in new videotape', retrieved 5 October 2006 from <http://qnewsupdates.blogspot.com/2006_10_01_archive.html>.

Ghandour, S. (2006), 'Khames Sanawat Ala Kaboos Alarab Fi Amrika' [Arabs' five-year long nightmare in America], *Al-Bayan* website, retrieved 7 September 2006 from <http://www.elaph.com/ElaphWeb/NewsPapers/2006/9/174976.htm?sectionarchive=NewsPapers>.

Hajazi, A. (2006), 'Man Howa Al-nazi Al-aan?' [Who's the Nazi now?], *al-Ahram* website, retrieved 13 September 2006 from <http://www.elaph.com/ElaphWeb/NewsPapers/2006/9/176360.htm?sectionarchive=NewsPapers>.

Hussain, A. (2006), 'Oh what tangled webs we weave', *Pak Tribune* website, retrieved 4 September 2006 from <http://www.paktribune.com/news/index.shtml?152862>.

Hussain, L. (2006), 'Justice is dead, if you're born an Arab', *Arab News* website, retrieved 25 September 2006 from <http://www.arabnews.com/?page=7&section=0&article=77354&d=4&m=8&y=2006>.

Islamonline.net (2006), [Text of Qaradhawi's sermon], retrieved 29 September 2006 from <http://www.islamonline.net/Arabic/index.shtml>.

Khazen, J. (2006a), 'Ayoon Wa Azan' [Eyes and Ears], *Al-Hayat* website, retrieved 15 June 2006 from <http://uaesm.maktoob.com/vb/uae68616>.

Khazen, J. (2006b), 'Ayoon Wa Azan' [Eyes and Ears], retrieved 14 July 2006 from <http://www.arabinfocenter.net/index.php?d=42&id=16651>.

Khazen, J. (2006c), 'Ayoon Wa Azan' [Eyes and Ears], retrieved 14 July 2006 from <http://www.alnahdah.org/Art126.htm>.

Khazen, J. (2006d), 'Ayoon Wa Azan' [Eyes and Ears], retrieved 2 July 2006 from <http://www.elaph.com/ElaphWeb/NewsPapers/2006/7/160728.htm?sectionarchive=NewsPapers>.

Kristof, N. D. (2004), 'Jesus and *jihad*', *The New York Times* website, retrieved 23 November 2006 from <http://query.nytimes.com//gst/fullpage.html?res=9C06E5D7153AF934A25754C0A96>.

MEMRI (2006a), 'Al-Qaeda leader Ayman Al-Zawahiri: *Jihad* should strive to liberate any land that was once Islamic', retrieved 28 September 2006 from <http://www.memritv.org/clip_transcript/en/1269.htm>.

MEMRI (2006b), 'Bin Laden's former mufti Saudi cleric Musa Al-Qarni', retrieved 30 March 2006 from <http://memri.org/bin/articles.cgi?Page=archives&Area=sd&ID=SP112406>.

MEMRI (2006c), 'Iraqi cleric Ahmad Al-Kubeisi promotes *jihad*', retrieved 21 September 2006 from <http://www.memritv.org/search.asp?ACT=S9&P1=1075>.

MEMRI (2006d), 'Syrian Deputy Minister of Religious Endowment Muhammad 'Abd Al-Sattar calls for *jihad* and says Jews are descendants of apes and pigs', retrieved 9 September 2006 from <http://www.memri.org/bin/articles.cgi?Page=archives&Area=sd&ID=SP121706>.

Qanat, A. (2006), 'Al-anwan Al-jadeed Lilislam Walmuslimeen' [The new identification of Islam and Muslims], *al-Khaleej* website, retrieved 3 December 2006 from <http://www.elaph.com/ElaphWeb/NewsPapers/2006/9/173980.htm?sectionarchive=NewsPapers>.

Ramadan, T. (2006), 'The Danish cartoons, free speech and civic responsibility', NPQ website, retrieved 8 August 2006 from <http://www.digitalnpq.org/archive/2006_spring/04_ramadan.html>.

Said, E. W. (1981), *Covering Islam: How the Media and Experts Determine How We See the Rest of the World*. New York: Pantheon Books, p. 156.

Seale, P. (2006), 'The ball is in Israel's court', *Al-Hayat* website, retrieved 11 August 2006 from <http://english.daralhayat.com/opinion/OPED/08-2006/Article-20060811-fcca6f43-c0a8-10ed-019d-d97b9356ffb5/story.html>.

UNDP (2002), *Arab Human Development Report 2002*, United Nations Development Programme.

Chapter 6

Conservative Christian Spokespeople in Mainstream US News Media

Kirsten Isgro

Introduction

When Concerned Women for America's (CWA) founder, Beverly LaHaye, spoke at the organization's 1985 convention, she reportedly urged her audience of 2,000 'to "speak softly, but with clout" in order to help restore traditional family values' (Cordray 1985: 2A). According to *The Washington Times* news stories of this annual convention, LaHaye was particularly concerned about the amount of attention the feminist National Organization of Women (NOW) was receiving from US media: 'There are many thousands of women who have never heard of us [CWA]. When the media wants women's reactions on any given issue, they always call NOW. Hopefully that will change' (Cordray 1985: 2A). Twenty years later, LaHaye and her conservative Christian women's public policy organization have undeniably captured the attention of mainstream media. As a case in point, in 2005, during the media coverage surrounding Terri Schindler Schiavo and the coverage of Pope John Paul II's death, CWA staffers were sought out for quotes by news outlets such as National Public Radio, *The Washington Times*, and *The New York Times*.[1] Likewise, organizations such as the Family Research Council (FRC) have been sought to comment in media such as *USA Today* on topics relating to embryonic stem cell research and the now infamous 2004 Super Bowl halftime show where Janet Jackson's wardrobe 'malfunctioned' (Oldenburg 2004, Stone 2006). In the following study, I ask if the number of media citations of conservative Christian organizations, such as CWA and FRC as authoritative sources increased between 1995 and 2005. Such an increase would suggest the growing normalization of a dogmatic Christian standpoint as representative of American political and cultural life. Additionally, I ask if such organizations have an increased prominence in news stories in this same span of time. Taking this empirical approach allows me to give some concrete evidence that there is an increase in citations of conservative Christian organizations in mainstream media. This quantitative approach allows me to show real evidence of this trend that has only been suspected or suggested until now.

Historically, conservative Christians in the United States have focused attention on non-Christian media arguing that mainstream news outlets operate without regard for biblical principles. This presumption has led to the proclamation from many conservative Christian leaders that the mainstream media do not report or reflect the average American citizen.

In their book *A Nation Without a Conscience*, Beverly LaHaye and her husband Timothy LaHaye point to mainstream media as one of the central sites of a contemporary culture war:

> All one has to do is read the daily newspapers or watch network television newscasts to understand their heavy leanings toward liberal politics. Some are more liberal than others, but most media leaders are liberal and much of their programming reflects anti-Christian sentiment (LaHaye and LaHaye 1994: 181).

As a result, many conservative Christians respond to what they perceive to be a hostile mass culture by becoming media savvy and producing and/or consuming alternative media that represents conservative Christians as both resistors and manufacturers of popular culture (see Hendershot 2004).

A number of conservative Christian institutional structures have been created for evangelistic and fundamentalist ends.[2] Media scholar Julia Lesage (1998) notes that in their origins, contemporary Christian media are entrepreneurial where each communications outlet is used not only for message diffusion but also to direct the reader, listener or computer user to other Christian information media. This Christian media production uses multiple modes of communication, creating a synergy that ultimately has political effects: suggesting directions for prayer, sending money to conservative Christian organizations or causes, contacting a Congress member or signing a petition. Such a Christian media synergy has cultural effects, argues Lesage (1998), creating a common vernacular amongst consumers that provides a coherent view of society and the world, weaving around the audience a sense of community that ties together individuals who share a specific moral, social, and religious worldview. CWA and FRC produce their own publications and issue papers, send out regular emails regarding legislative issues to their constituents, and generate a plethora of online materials for their respective organizational web pages.

Political scientist Cynthia Burack (2003) notes, however, that since the mid-1990s, conservative Christian right leaders have honed their media messaging more effectively so that their political statements are now regularly published in the mainstream press and heard on mainstream radio. The central argument of this paper is that mainstream US print news media increasingly rely on spokespeople from predominantly conservative Christian organizations such as CWA and FRC to comment on a wide range of political, cultural and economic topics without consistently identifying their religious and political affiliations. In part, this trend of citing conservative Christian organizations may be due to news editors' attempts at 'balancing' news stories (for an added example of this with a non-Christian conservative women's organization, see Spindel 2003). Another explanation is that there have been explicit endorsements by three US Presidents (Ronald Reagan, George H. W. Bush and George W. Bush) of the activities of groups such as CWA, Focus on the Family, and the FRC on both the domestic and international level. These well-known conservative think tanks have become a permanent part of the nation's political infrastructure. Having US Presidents sympathetic to such organizations has helped merge religious orthodoxy with politics, creating a theocratic climate in the United States.

It is an underlying premise of this research that the ways in which these conservative Christian organizations are included in mainstream US media is representative of a more disquieting tendency to include an ideology that is dogmatically organized around four main platforms: pro-American, pro-life, pro-moral and pro-family, with the heteronormative family as the foundation (see Petchesky 1981). More savvy media production, in conjunction with the more explicit convergence of politics with religion, means spokespeople from these organizations are increasingly making an impact on mainstream media by being invited for interviews and generating truth claims about national moral, social and political issues. This phenomenon is the basis for this study, focusing specifically on how CWA and the FRC are referenced as credible news sources over the last several years in *The New York Times*, *Los Angles Times*, and *The Christian Science Monitor*. I measure the prominence of these organizations in mainstream media coverage and evaluate the type and range of issues where this source is employed. In these two organizations' own language, they operate as Christian evangelical organizations: those who believe that the Word of God is to be taken literally and that it is important to spread the faith and convert others. The findings suggest that conservative Christian authorities, such as these two organizations, have received more media attention and references over time. I argue for the need to continually monitor religious right discourses in the mainstream media in order to understand how moralist truth claims are generated and distributed, making extreme religious views more palatable to those outside a fundamentalist framework.

Theoretical Foundations

Communication scholars have focused extensively on culture, examining the symbolic forms and exchanges that occur within specific contexts between particular actors/producers of culture at certain times and places and with particular effects. Yet an analysis of culture cannot ignore questions of religion

(Carrette 2000, Hoover 2002). According to communication scholar Stewart Hoover (2002: 29), studying the convergence of media and religion requires 'an interdisciplinarity where the social-scientific sensibilities of communication and media studies encounter cultural studies . . . where systems of representation, meaning, and exchange are critically analyzed and interpreted'. Hoover in particular has been instrumental in calling for research on media and religion that takes into account questions of lived culture and actual practices as well as the discursive constructions of religion in media (Clark and Hoover 1997, Hoover 1997, Hoover 2002, Hoover and Lundby 1997). Aside from studies of televangelism, Hoover argues that religion has been a 'blind spot' or the 'unpopular popular culture' for communication scholars (Hoover 1997). This anthology is an attempt to rectify such an oversight by deepening our understanding of the complex role media play in the rise and spread of conservative religiosity.

A working definition of religious fundamentalism is offered by Minoo Moallem (1999: 323) that I have found fruitful for my own work: 'a regime of truth based on discourses identified with, or ordained by, God (taken metaphorically or literally) and binding its observants'. My study of media discourses confirms that CWA and FRC are important conduits for fundamentalist ideals. For instance, within such groups, the terms 'pro-family' and 'pro-marriage' refer to values and beliefs that promote a singular understanding of family founded on the legal marriage between one man and one woman as the most suitable place to raise children (heteronormative family). Many scholars of fundamentalism have pointed out that prescribing appropriate gender and sexual norms and behaviours and maintaining a central role in defining the family (as biologically natural, patriarchal and self-sufficient) is critical for the religious right (Burack and Josephson 2003, Lehr 2003, Moallem 1999). CWA and FRC position themselves against those who have a more expansive or inclusive notion of family, gender and sexual norms. For example, in a 2000 article in *The Christian Science Monitor*, FRC's then-director of cultural studies, Robert Knight, commented on controversies over gay rights:

> To place domestic partner relationships on a par with marriage denigrates the marital imperative. Call it what you will – fairness, political correctness, tolerance – but it won't change the fact that what is happening in Vermont [same-sex civil unions] is an enormous tragedy, and an assault on the very foundations of our civilization (Knickerbocker 2000: 2).

In 2001, CWA launched the Culture and Family Institute, and in 2003, FRC established the Family Research Council's Center for Marriage and Family Studies. Both were formed as alternatives to more liberal research and policy groups that address social issues and positioned these organizations as key players in the so-called 'culture wars'.

CWA was founded in the United States in 1979 as a Christian women's alternative to the feminist NOW and claims over 500,000 members in its organization, with over 400 regional Prayer/Action chapters across the country. Throughout its history, CWA's charismatic visionary, founder and chairman, Beverly LaHaye, has situated herself as someone whose mission is to instruct women 'in the delicate blend of the calling to be wives, mothers and leaders' (CWA 2007). Likewise, FRC – with a current membership of 455,000 – was founded in 1983 in order to promote 'the Judeo-Christian worldview as the basis for a just, free, and stable society' (FRC n.d.). Closely affiliated with Focus on the Family, FRC's first two presidents worked with Ronald Reagan in the White House. CWA and FRC have patterned their operations on what political scientist David Callahan (1999) calls 'an activist think tank model' common among conservative policy institutions whose political project is guided by specific moral precepts. While clearly different organizations, their strategies to shape US culture in its favour include recruiting and training grassroots activists, targeting policymakers, and producing and influencing media.

Both of these organizations have been central in redirecting the nation's cultural agenda to a particular Christian fundamentalism. This redirection involves bolstering capitalism, patriotism and militarism – strategies which are made apparent in CWA's and FRC's public discourses. These activist think tanks also encourage certain religious views of morality and culture in secular society while still operating within the electoral system (Berlet 1998, Diamond 1995). As a case in point, in a 2003 article on anti-pornography legislation, CWA (identified as a 'pro-family lobby') reportedly sent letters to 'scores of US attorneys' offices around the country to see what they were doing about porn' (Schmitt 2003: A34). While state laws and policies may be informed by a singular interpretation of one religion, these cultural, economic and policy decisions may not always be coded as 'religious' by judges, military personnel, media or others in elite positions of decision-making.

The Christian right vernacular in the United States over the last decade has been able to harness certain widespread discontents which cut across various divisions in society, tapping into people's common lived experiences (Hardisty 1999). By arousing a populist sentiment around family and nation, identifying with the authority of God, values of traditionalism and firm leadership, these organizations have created what Stuart Hall (1988a, 1988b) terms 'authoritarian populism'. They explicitly see the heterosexual ('natural') family as the stabilizing and foundational unit of society, a basic tenet of many pro-family – what are often self-described as 'traditionalist' – groups. According to its web page, 'CWA believes the traditional family consists of one man and one woman joined in marriage, along with any children they may have. We seek to protect traditional values that support the Biblical design of the family' (CWA 2007). CWA's discourses echo other conservative women's groups in their constructions of self/other, motherhood and the family, with technologically and politically sophisticated methods and socially conservative objectives (Bacchetta and Power 2002, Petchesky 2003). FRC also 'champions marriage and family as the foundation of civilization, the seedbed of virtue, and the wellspring of society' (FRC n.d.). As other cultural critics have pointed out, the public debates and lobbying efforts of conservative organizations have concrete implications for people's daily lives, working at the intersections of politics, everyday life, and popular culture (Grossberg 1992, Schreiber 2002).

Key to cultural studies scholars is an understanding of hegemony – what can be identified as the 'war of position' – a struggle that is ongoing across many fronts. As part of the formation of hegemony, the structures and institutions of civil society become the sites of these struggles. The structures of civil society – media, judicial systems, police forces, as examples – serve as varying fronts of struggle in the positioning of ruling ideas, as shown in Stuart Hall's (1988a, 1988b) work on Thatcherism in Britain, Larry Grossberg's (1992) study of US popular conservatism, and Jean Hardisty's (1999) examination of US conservative resurgences.

To study these struggles from an ideological perspective opens the possibility for media researchers and theorists to ask 'how does the ideological process work and what are its mechanisms? How is "the ideological" to be conceived in relation to other practices within a social formation?' (Hall 1982: 65). As Hall argues in much of his work, the media help shape, educate and legitimize what we come to understand about the world, thus creating a 'politics of signification'. In addition to Hall's, Grossberg's and Hardisty's research, there are other excellent demonstrations of the role media play in securing consent, particularly of the new conservative right. These media studies include analyses of Jerry Falwell (Harding 2000), the Independent Women's Forum (Spindel 2003), Timothy LaHaye's popular *Left Behind* series (McAlister 2003a, 2003b), James Dobson's *Focus on the Family* radio program (Apostolidis 2000), and Jerry Falwell's comments on Pat Robertson's *700 Club* (Burack 2003). The following analysis contributes to this body of literature; anecdotal evidence indicates that conservative Christian spokespeople are often quoted in media and being cited as authoritative sources. This study is an attempt to substantiate this impression by testing the following hypotheses:

H1: Media citations of CWA and FRC as authoritative sources have increased between 1995 and 2005.

H2: Prominence of these two organizations in news stories as authoritative sources has increased.

Method

This current study is primarily a content analysis of newspaper stories that mention CWA and FRC in three major US newspapers between January 1995 and December 2005. The dates were chosen to encompass an 11-year period in which speculation about the increased religious right's involvement in electoral politics and popular culture could be quantified. A number of scholars note that the mid-1990s mark a moment in which an extensive Christian right network, in alliance with Republican administrations, have shaped a terrain on which economic, political, scientific and cultural agendas have been established (Buss and Herman 2003, Martin 1996, Kaplan 2004). Political scientists (Rozell and Wilcox 1996, Rozell et. al. 1998) note that the Christian right movement has attained an unparalleled degree of legitimacy and influence in American politics since the 1994 Republican Congress. *The New York Times*, *LA Times* and *The Christian Science Monitor* were each selected for their geographic location and wide circulation. Together, the three newspapers arguably represent a cross section of print coverage of current US news and events.

On a more utilitarian note, each of these newspapers was selected based on the full text availability from the ProQuest historical newspaper database. All articles containing the name of each organization, respectively, were retrieved. Of the 554 articles available, 434 were analysed; duplicate articles, commentary and letters to the editor were discarded. Letters to the editor were eliminated in the final count for two reasons: 1) being personal commentary, the valence was often (positively or negatively) stronger than news stories; and 2) these letters were commentary generated directly from CWA or FRC staffers aiming to promote their organizations' positions, made apparent by their organizational affiliation noted in these letters.

Between 1 January 1995 and 31 December 2005 a total of 132 articles ran in *The New York Times*, 349 articles were published in *Los Angels Times* and 73 stories ran in *The Christian Science Monitor*. In contrast, between 1979 and 1994, less than 200 articles total ($n = 196$) were found in the entire ProQuest historical database (which contains 62 national or local newspapers) that cited these two organizations. In order to underscore the relatively low level of representation in mainstream media reflected in these numbers one should note that the National Organization for Women (NOW) was cited over 400 times ($n = 416$) in *The New York Times* alone between 1980 and 1995; this number drops considerably in the next decade ($n = 101$). Articles were chosen if they explicitly quoted a spokesperson from the organization or made mention of the organization. Each article was coded for date, total word length, topic, placement of article and the length of quote from source. The majority of the articles analysed were located prominently in the publications studied. Of the articles coded, 24.1 per cent ($n = 114$) were front page cover stories; 62.4 per cent ($n = 296$) were found elsewhere in Section A of the newspaper. The terms on which the organization was described or inferred were coded using a four-point scale (ultra conservative Christian, conservative Christian, conservative and nondescript/apolitical). In order to measure the valence of the news story toward CWA, a five-point scale was employed (very positive, somewhat positive, neutral, somewhat negative, very negative). A second coder was used for 15 per cent of the sample for coder reliability. The primary coder was not informed of the research questions or coding key so that evaluations were not influenced by the principle investigator's expectations.

Findings of the Current Study

The distribution of news stories in which the organizations were either referenced or directly quoted indicates that between 1995 and 2005, there was a marked increase (see Figure 6.1). Most notable was between 2000 and 2005 when the visibility and mention of conservative Christian organizations in the three newspapers analysed witnessed a ten-fold increase in CWA citations and a three-fold increase in FRC references. In 1998 there was a marked although temporary increase of FRC references, primarily due to FRC's president, Gary Bauer, running in the presidential Republican primaries.

The results indicate the increasing prominence of CWA and FRC in news stories as authoritative sources, comparing 1995 to 2005. Prominence is measured by the ratio of the number of words included in quotes by CWA authorities to the total article word count. For example, if the total word count of a *New York Times* article is 574 and 16 of these words are from a spokesperson identified as a CWA staffer, this ratio is 2.79 per cent. Overall, these organizations were cited 2.45 per cent of average word count in all three newspapers, with *The Christian Science Monitor* citing both CWA and FRC the most frequent.

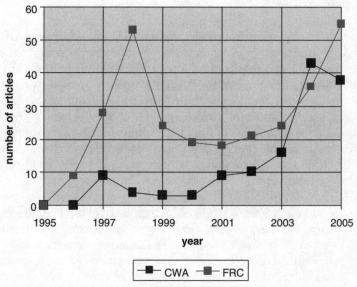

Figure 6.1 Number of Articles Citing CWA & FRC

Figure 6.2 summarizes the key topic of the news stories in which CWA or FRC are drawn upon as an authoritative source. Notably these organizations were sought to comment on a large range of social and political issues that presumably had some level of controversy. The overall picture of this study indicates that government conduct and policy (e.g., elections, legislative and judicial hearings, and political appointments) was the number one topic wherein CWA and FRC appear. The second most overall pertinent topic that elicited comment from CWA and FRC was issues pertaining to gay men and lesbians, including same-sex marriage, parenting and adoption. Same-sex relations and reproductive health issues (e.g., abortion and the FDA approval of Plan-B) were chief topics on which these organizations were consulted. The additional top topic pertained to a wide range of current popular culture subjects (e.g., gambling, pornography, Victoria's Secret fashion show, internet, Harry Potter). The 'other' category hereafter includes miscellaneous stories that could not be appropriately categorized in the other three topics (e.g., stem cell research, right to die issues, women in the military, press releases of new leadership in organization and holiday greetings in retail stores). Whereas both organizations' stated mission is to support Judeo-Christian values within the public sphere, the topics on which they were consulted by the media were variable. Whereas FRC is quoted in more of the 'hard news' stories considered to be more politically-oriented, CWA tends to be quoted more in 'soft news' stories presumed to be related primarily to women, such as reproductive health issues and political appointments of women (e.g., the debate over Harriet Miers for the US Supreme Court).

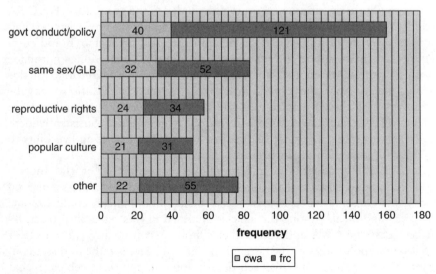

Figure 6.2 Topics of Articles

Discussion and Implications

The fact that organizations such as CWA and FRC are being quoted with more frequency in mainstream media, but not identified as religious, enables their discourses to become normalized as 'American' rather than as 'fundamentalist Christian'. The focus of this essay has been an exploration of the increased reliance on these organizations, as credible sources on an array of issues ranging from US presidential primaries, the Abu Ghraib scandal, same-sex marriage, FCC cable television legislation, stem cell research and emergency contraception to the blockbuster movies such as *Broke Back Mountain*. A quantitative content analysis of 434 news stories provides evidence that over time, CWA and FRC have increasingly been cited. As Linda Kintz (1998) points out in her assessment of culture and the religious right, it is not the activities and organization of conservative Christians that is surprising but their increased visibility. These organizations are the cornerstone for much conservative religious activism in the United States. They also are important actors in the positioning of a particular theocratic perspective within mainstream media.

A cultural studies approach to media, religion and culture offers a way for scholars to investigate the importance of symbolic meanings and cultural activities that help determine what counts as fact. Additionally, as political scientist Paul Apostolidis (2000) notes in his study of Focus on the Family – the parent company from which FRC originated – 'culture can be politically consequential even when it does not directly address public policy issues or align itself with specific party leaders' (6). The results of this media content analysis substantiate Apostolidis' claim; regardless of the topic discussed in each newspaper, there are political overtones in the quotes included in the given story. For CWA and FRC leadership and their allies, the central importance of Christian religiosity may very well influence their electoral politics, their church and community participation, and their moral beliefs. Yet this connection is not made obvious in the news content analysed in this study. An implication of this phenomenon is that the general readership of these publications may be unfamiliar with these organizations and their ideologies. Those staffers from CWA and FRC sought to comment on various issues are not consistently identified thus generating a normative discourse that gives credence and visibility to ideologically conservative Christians.

Through the production, circulation and consumption of the sources reviewed in this study, one can conclude that with more media messaging and placement, conservative Christian ideas, beliefs and policies could become viewed as apolitical. Among the articles analysed in this research project, 89 per cent describe CWA and FRC either simply as conservative ($n = 183$) or nondescript/apolitical ($n = 202$) organizations. This seems to be in direct contrast to these organizations' own self-description found in their web pages that explicitly state a commitment to protecting and promoting Judeo-Christian Biblical values. While these groups often scorn the secular world, declaring that the world is polluted and vile, they also identify a life that is worthy of pursuing; their traditionalist discourses are a form of cultural criticism. There is undoubtedly some powerful confirmation in the messages that CWA and FRC produce and circulate that appeal to many people's lived experiences and that cannot be dismissed. These two organizations are part of a larger community of self-identified Christian conservatives, exchanging and producing ideas and attempting to put these ideas into practice, while at the same time being malleable enough to modify their ideas to new circumstances and changing audiences (see Ammerman 1994, Irvine 2002, Wuthnow and Lawson 1994).

These organizations have helped shape the boundaries with which one can make sense of the role of religion in public life. Within their faith, the comments from CWA and FRC leadership invoke a moral outrage which shores up its vision for a Christian nation and have positioned themselves on multiple fronts where such righteous messages may be posited. Given the ways that CWA and FRC produce and influence media, educate their grassroots constituents with populist appeals, and target local, national and international public policymakers, the faith which drives these organizations cannot be underestimated or trivialized. If the dream of democratic life – at least one that includes and values a plurality of voices on these issues – is to persist in the twenty-first century, it is of utmost importance to closely and perceptively monitor those movements that aim to reduce these real and dynamic debates to moralistic tautologies.

Notes

1   The case of Schiavo – the 41-year old Florida woman, who due to complications from an eating disorder, had existed in a persistent vegetative state for the last 15 years – became a rallying point in Spring 2005 for legislatures, disability rights groups, the medical community, conservative Christian organizations and Jeb Bush, brother of the US President and the governor of Florida, to raise questions of end-of-life decisions, euthanasia and government intervention in one's personal life. On 29 March 2005, Wendy Wright, CWA former Senior Policy Director (now President), spoke on NPR's *Talk of the Nation* regarding 'the culture of life', arguing for 'the very innocent, the most vulnerable [the unborn and the disabled] that are having their very right to live taken away from them'. Wright also argued that the sanctity of marriage was undermined by Terri Schiavo's husband, Michael, and offered multiple examples of how he 'made a mockery' of his marriage (2005). In *The New York Times*, Beverly LaHaye is quoted: 'In terms of the goals of our organization, this Pope was a vital force on two different fronts: he was a peerless

defender of life, marriage and the family, and his leadership helped bring about the collapse of communism' (Banerjee 2005).

2   Martin Marty and Scott Appleby (1994) offer a concise explanation for the deliberate use of the term 'fundamentalism' in scholarship, including the urgent need to have terms that 'do justice to the particularities of separate realities' (9). For a basic understanding of Christian fundamentalists, I draw on William Martin's definition as those who believe in an inerrant Bible, 'meaning not only that the Bible is the sole and infallible rule of faith and practice, but also that it is scientifically and historically reliable' (Martin 1996: 11).

References

'About FRC' (n.d.), Family Research Council Website, retrieved 25 November 2007 from <http://www.frc.org/get.cfm?c=ABOUT_FRC>.

Ammerman, N. (1994), 'The dynamics of Christian fundamentalism: An introduction', in M. E. Marty and R. S. Appleby (eds), *Accounting for Fundamentalisms: The Dynamic Character of Movements*, vol. 4. Chicago: University of Chicago Press, pp. 13–17.

Apostolidis, P. (2000), *Stations of the Cross: Adorno and the Christian Right Radio*, Durham, NC: Duke University Press.

Bacchetta, P. and Power, M. (2002), 'Introduction', in P. Bacchetta and M. Power (eds), *Right-Wing Women: From Conservatives to Extremists Around the World*. New York: Routledge, pp. 1–15.

Banerjee, N. (2005), 'People of all faiths recall pope with fondness', *New York Times*, 4 April.

Berlet, C. (1998), 'Who is mediating the storm? Right-wing alternative information networks', in L. Kintz and J. Lesage (eds), *Media, Culture, and the Religious Right*. Minneapolis: University of Minnesota Press, pp. 249–273.

Burack, C. (2003), 'Getting what "we" deserve: Terrorism, tolerance, sexuality, and the Christian right', *New Political Science*, 25, pp. 329–349.

Burack, C. and Josephson, J. J. (2003), 'Introduction', in C. Burack and J. J. Josephson (eds), *Fundamental Differences: Feminists Talk Back to Social Conservatives*. Lanham, MD: Rowman & Littlefield, pp. 1–8.

Buss, D. and Herman, D. (2003), *Globalizing Family Values: The Christian Right in International Politics*, Minneapolis, MN: University of Minnesota Press.

Butler, J. (2000), 'The Christian right coalition and the UN special session on children: Prospects and strategies', *The International Journal of Children's Rights*, 8, 351–371.

Callahan, D. (1999), *$1 Billion for Ideas: Conservative Think Tanks in the 1990s*. Washington, DC: National Committee for Responsive Philanthropy.

Carrette, J. R. (2000), *Foucault and Religion: Spiritual Corporality and Political Spirituality*. New York: Routledge.

Clark, L. S. and Hoover, S. M. (1997), 'At the intersection of media, culture and religion', in S. M. Hoover and K. Lundby (eds), *Rethinking Media, Religion, and Culture*. Thousand Oaks, CA: Sage Publications.

Cordray, R. (1985), 'Women urged to speak softly, but with clout', *The Washington Times*, 27 September.

Diamond, S. (1995), *Roads to Dominion: Right-Wing Movements and Political Power in the United States*. New York: Guilford Press.

Grossberg, L. (1992), *We Gotta Get Out of This Place: Popular Conservatism and Postmodern Culture*. New York: Routledge.

Hall, S. (1982), 'The rediscovery of "ideology": Return of the repressed in media studies', in M. Gurevitch, T. Bennett, J. Curran and S. Woollacott (eds), *Culture, Society, and the Media*. New York: Methuen, pp. 26–90.

Hall, S. (1988a), *The Hard Road to Renewal: Thatcherism and the Crisis of the Left*, London/New York: Verso.

Hall, S. (1988b), 'The toad in the garden: Thatcherism amongst the theorists', in C. Nelson and L. Grossberg (eds), *Marxism and the Interpretation of Culture*. Urbana: University of Illinois Press, pp. 35–73.

Harging, S. F. (2000), *The Book of Jerry Falwell: Fundamentalist Language and Politics*. Princeton, NJ: Princeton University Press.

Hardisty, J. (1999), *Mobilizing Resentment: Conservative Resurgence From the John Birch Society to the Promise Keepers*. Boston: Beacon Press.

Hardisty, J. and Bhargava, D. (2005), 'Wrong about the right: Let's not misunderstand the tactics that propelled conservatives to power', *The Nation*, 281, 22–6.

Henvershot, H. (2004), *Shaking the World for Jesus: Media and Conservative Evangelical Culture*. Chicago: University of Chicago Press.

Hoover, S. M. (1997), 'Media and the construction of the religious public sphere', in S. M. Hoover and K. Lundby (eds), *Rethinking Media, Religion, and Culture*. Thousand Oaks, CA: Sage Publications, pp. 283–297.

Hoover, S. M. (2002), 'The culturalist turn in scholarship on media and religion', *Journal of Media and Religion*, 1, 25–36.

Hoover, S. M. and K. Lundby (1997), 'Introduction: Setting the agenda', in S. M. Hoover and K. Lundby (eds), *Rethinking Media, Religion, and Culture*. Thousand Oaks, CA: Sage Publications, pp. 3–14.

Irvine, J. M. (2002), *Talk About Sex: The Battles Over Sex Education in the United States*. Berkeley: University of California Press.

Kaplan, E. (2004), *With God on their side: How Christian fundamentalists trampled science, policy, and democracy in George W. Bush's White House*. New York: New Press.

Kintz, L. (1998), 'Culture and the religious right', in L. Kintz and J. Lesage (eds), *Media, Culture, and the Religious Right*. Minneapolis: University of Minnesota Press, pp. 3–20.

Knickerbocker, B. (2000) 'Election spotlights battle over gay rights', *The Christian Science Monitor*, 11 September.

LaHaye, T. and LaHaye, B. (1994), *A Nation Without a Conscience*. Wheaton, IL: Tyndale House Publishers Inc.

Lehr, V. (2003), 'Family values: Social conservative power in diverse rhetorics', in C. Burack and J. Josephson (eds), *Fundamental Differences: Feminists Talk Back to Social Conservatives*. Lanham, MD: Rowman & Littlefield, pp. 127–142.

Lesage, J. (1998), 'Christian media', in L. Kintz and J. Lesage (eds), *Media, Culture, and the Religious Right*. Minneapolis: University of Minnesota Press, pp. 21–54.

Martin, W. C. (1996), *With God on our Side: The Rise of the Religious Right in America*. New York: Broadway Books.

Marty, M. E. and Appleby, R. S. (1994), 'Introduction', in M. E. Marty and R. S. Appleby (eds), *Accounting for Fundamentalisms: The Dynamic Character of Movements*. Chicago: University of Chicago Press.

McAlister, M. (2003a), 'An Empire of their own: How born-again Christians turned biblical prophecy into big-time profit', *The Nation*, 277, 31–36.

McAlister, M. (2003b), 'Prophecy, politics, and the popular: The *Left Behind* series and Christian fundamentalism's new world order', *South Atlantic Quarterly*, 102, 773–798.

Moallem, M. (1999), 'Transationalism, feminism, and fundamentalism', in C. Kaplan, N. Alarcón and M. Moallem (eds), *Between Women and Nation: Nationalisms, Transnational Feminisms, and the State*. Durham, NC: Duke University Press, pp. 320–348.

'Mrs. Beverly LaHaye: Founder and chairman' (2007), Concerned Women for America Website, retrieved 11 October 2007 from <http://gideon.cwfa.org/articledisplay.asp?id=2114&department=CWA&categoryid=>.

Oldenburg, A. (2004), 'A cultural class . . . in a nation a flutter; with a flash, Super Bowl's halftime show pushes indecency debate to a new level', *USA Today*, 3 February.

'Our Core Issues' (2004), Concerned Women for America Website, retrieved 29 August 2007 from <http://www.cwfa.org/coreissues.asp>.

Petchesky, R. (1981), 'Antiabortion, antifeminism, and the rise of the new right', *Feminist Studies*, 7, 206–246.

Petchesky, R. (2003), *Global Prescriptions: Gendering Health and Human Rights*. London: Zed Books/United Nations Research Institute for Social Development.

Rozell, M. and Wilcox, C. (1996), 'Second coming: The strategies of the new Christian right', *Political Science Quarterly*, 11(2), 271–294.

Rozell, M., Wilcox, C. and Green, J. (1998), 'Religious constituencies and support for the Christian right in the 1990s', *Social Science Quarterly*, 79, 815–827.

Schmitt, R. (2003), 'US anti-porn effort in found wanting: Obscenity foes say their support for Attorney General John Ashcroft hasn't translated into the aggressive crackdown they expected', *Los Angeles Times*, 23 November.

Schreiber, R. (2002), 'Injecting a woman's voice: Conservative women's organizations, gender consciousness, and the expression of women's policy preferences', *Sex Roles*, 47, pp. 331–342.

Spindel, B. (2003), 'Conservatism as the "sensible middle": The independent women's forum, politics, and the media', *Social Text*, 21, 99–125.

Stone, A. (2006), 'States stepping in to underwrite stem cell science; Maryland is the latest to authorize money for work limited on the federal level', *USA Today*, 7 April.

Talk of the Nation (2005), 'Conservatives and the culture of life', National Public Radio Website, retrieved 30 October 2007 from <http://www.npr.org/templates/story/story.php?storyId=4565929>.

Wuthnow, R. and Lawson, M. (1994), 'Sources of Christian fundamentalism in the United States', in M. E. Marty and R. S. Appleby (eds), *Accounting for Fundamentalisms: The Dynamic Character of Movements*, vol. 4. Chicago: University of Chicago Press, pp. 18–56.

Chapter 7

Use of the Term 'Fundamentalist Christian' in Canadian National Television News

David Haskell

Introduction

Social construction theorists, proponents of structural linguistics, and other scholars have shown that language shapes our perception of reality (Berger and Luckman 1966, Fishman 1980, Hacking 1999, Kay and Kempton 1984, Sapir 1985[1949], Whorf 1956). They explain that words are not neutral arbiters of meaning; how we think about something is influenced by the connotations associated with the word or words used to describe it (Carey 1989, Fleras 2003). Members of religious, racial, ethnic and other minorities concur that words, specifically those words used to demarcate them as a group or community, have the power to shape how others view them. In many cases, first-hand experience has shown these minorities the effect referential monikers have on their societal status and advancement.

For example, in the 1960s and early 1970s African Americans, conscious that words play a role in the political distribution of power, began to dissociate themselves from the term Negro – up to that point the self-referential term of choice – because they felt the word called forth an accommodationist, or 'Uncle Tomish' perception. The term Negro was also viewed disfavourably because it had been conferred upon the group by whites. By the late 1980s Afro-American and African American were becoming the favoured group identifiers. It was a term that celebrated the group's historical and cultural ties with the African continent and it was in keeping with linguistic precedent; that is, historically other ethnic groups in American society had adopted names descriptive of their families' geographical points of origin (such as Italian American, Irish American and Polish American) (Baugh 1991, Hine et al. 2005, Philogene 1999).

More recently, Canadian evangelical Christians – a denominationally mixed religious community comprising about 12 per cent of the country's popula-tion and linked by an overarching doctrine of conservative Protestantism

(VanGinkel 2003) – launched an offensive to control the referential monikers applied to them. Leading the charge was Brian Stiller, at the time the executive director of the Evangelical Fellowship of Canada (EFC). It was in the fall of 1993. A federal election campaign was in full swing and a new political entity, the Reform Party of Canada led by well-known evangelical Preston Manning, was poised to substantially increase its number of seats in parliament. Stiller observed that over the course of the campaign rival politicians and media personnel became 'mean spirited, unfair and nasty' in their comments about Manning and his faith calling him 'a "fundamentalist", implying all sorts of negative images' (Stiller 2002: 1). Furthermore, he saw the negative treatment of Manning as emblematic of a more pervasive problem when it came to the media's categorization of conservative Protestants. In response, Stiller – on behalf of the over 140 evangelical denominations, ministry organizations and educational institutions represented by the EFC – sent an open letter to Canada's major media outlets, political parties and government organizations (Stiller 2002). In the letter he asked 'that people call us "evangelicals" and not to resort to unfair names and innuendoes which the term "fundamentalist" triggers' (Stiller 2002: 1). Fundamentalist, he conceded, was once used synonymously with evangelical as a religious term to denote practitioners of conservative Protestantism, but it now stood for 'bigoted, narrow, dogmatic and war-like people and is used to convey contempt and ridicule' (Stiller cited in McAteer 1993: K17). Driving home the point as strongly as possible, Stiller concluded the letter saying, 'For you to label an evangelical a "fundamentalist" is like calling an Afro-Canadian a "nigger" or a Canadian aboriginal with mixed ancestry a "half-breed". "Fundamentalism" is a code word, signifying [to] people that the media elite have judged you to be less than legitimate, and view you as having no place in the public mainstream of our culture' (Stiller cited in McAteer 1993: K17).

As a direct response to Stiller's letter, two major news outlets, CBC Radio (the radio division of Canada's public broadcaster and the country's most extensive provider of radio news) and Canadian Press (Canada's largest print news wire service) instituted policies whereby their journalists were not to use the word 'fundamentalist' to describe Christians unless the Christians themselves used that term self-referentially (Stiller 2002). Given the national attention it garnered, it is likely that journalists in other newsrooms across Canada were aware of Stiller's campaign; however, if other newsrooms changed their policies to ensure accurate use of the term fundamentalist Christian none issued statements to that effect (Stiller, Brian. Personal communication, 11 May 2006).

Purpose, Scope and Limits of This Study

As a researcher, Stiller's open letter to the media piqued my curiosity and convinced me it would be worthwhile to explore how journalists have employed the term fundamentalist Christian. Peripherally, I wondered if media outlets other than the two that had publicly acknowledged their change in policy, were influenced by Stiller's invective. To proceed I examined the reports of Canada's top three national television news programmes in the years following Stiller's campaign for correct nomenclature observing *how* and *when* journalists used the term 'fundamentalist Christian'. I chose national television news for two reasons. First, it was clear that Stiller's letter had resonated with national radio and print journalists – two key players in these communities had acknowledged changes to their policies – but there had been no public reaction from national television journalists to delineate whether their usage of the term Fundamentalist Christian had changed. Second, out of all the news sources available, national television news is most influential; its audience is the greatest and thus, it has the greatest potential for shaping public opinion (cf. Bureau of Broadcast Measurement 2006, Mazzuca 2001, Miljan and Cooper 2003, Nielson Media Research 2006).

While national television news' extensive ability to affect perceptions made it the superior candidate for examination, choosing it as the focus of my analysis came with its own particular drawback. Ideally, a study of this nature should be designed as a before and after comparison. That is, TV news reports that aired prior to Stiller's letter and those that aired after should both be examined and then compared in order to assess whether a change in the use of the term fundamentalist (as it applied to Christians) took place. However, with Canadian national television news such a comparison is virtually impossible. It was not until late 1993 and early 1994 that Canada's national television newsrooms began regularly archiving, via computer database, the full-text transcripts of their news reports. The advantage of the database system is that stored transcripts can be searched according to any word in the text. Conversely, prior to the installation of the database system only the videotaped versions of stories were archived. In some cases where the story was deemed of minor importance even the videotaped version was not kept. Those that were saved were catalogued by just three or four key words related to the main subject of the report (e.g., anti-abortion rally in Ottawa; Ontario government same-sex legislation). Because fundamentalist Christians would most often have been peripheral players and not the focus of most stories, the chance that a pre-1993 videotaped report would be catalogued using the specific term fundamentalist Christian is very unlikely. To track down pre-1993 news reports in which the term fundamentalist Christian was specifically referenced in the body of the story, one would need to view all a station's videotapes – literally thousands – that had been catalogued using key words that *hinted* at the presence of fundamentalist Christians (Ashurst, Carol [Director of Research and Archives – CTV National News]. Personal communication, 29 September 2006).

Thus, while Stiller's 1993 letter to the media is a crucial reference point for this research, for the reasons outlined above, this study's data lack the empirical standing to conclusively argue for or against the efficacy of his missive.

Therefore, in relation to the term fundamentalist Christian in national television news, this study must be content to explain 'what has happened' without categorically arguing 'why' it has occurred. However, that is not to say that inferences cannot be drawn. To be sure, the descriptive findings of this study do allow postulations to be made as to whether Stiller's campaign for correct nomenclature was successful and these are found in the concluding section of this paper.

To guide the analysis of the television news reports the following specific research questions were used:

1   What monikers were used to describe practitioners of conservative Protestantism featured in the television news reports and what was their frequency of use?
2   When the practitioners of conservative Protestantism featured in a news report were described as fundamentalist Christians was the term used correctly or incorrectly?
3   Who used the term fundamentalist Christian to describe the practitioners of conservative Protestantism featured in the news report: the reporter, non-evangelical interviewees/sources, or the conservative Protestant interviewees/sources themselves?

As is obvious from the second research question, this study veers somewhat from the implied definitional parameters of Stiller's 1993 open letter. Stiller suggested the term fundamentalist should never be applied to a conservative Protestant (regardless of the stridency of his or her beliefs). Instead, he said 'evangelical' was to be the titular designation of choice. However, I posit that *there are* certain individuals and groups for whom the moniker fundamentalist Christian, and not the more moderate descriptor evangelical, is the correct titular designation (the operational definitions this study employed are explained in detail in the next section of this paper).

Defining 'Fundamentalist Christian'

While this research is interested in how often the fundamentalist Christian moniker was employed in news stories, it is primarily concerned with whether the term was employed correctly. To that end, it is important that the terms fundamentalist Christian and evangelical Christian be operationally defined for this study – we must be able to distinguish one from another.

Because fundamentalist Christians are a subgroup of evangelical Christians – possessing the evangelicals' key traits though in a more extreme fashion – it makes sense to define the characteristics of the larger group first. Evangelicals are conservative Protestants – conservative in the sense that they tend to hold to the traditional beliefs of the Christian church. While certain Protestant denominations in Canada are known for their large number of evangelical members – Baptists, Christian and Missionary Alliance, Nazarene, Pentecostal and the Salvation Army denominations just to name a few – evangelicals are found in all Protestant churches. Indeed, it is what one believes and not where one worships that makes one an evangelical (Bibby 1987, Rawlyk 1996, Reimer 2003, Schultze 1996).

Four core beliefs qualify one as an evangelical. First, evangelicals have a very high view of scripture; they see the Bible as divinely inspired and true. That is not to say that evangelicals take everything in the Bible literally; many evangelicals are willing to accept that certain scripture is metaphor or poetry.[1] However, they would consider the metaphor and poetry to be divinely inspired and true in its *implied* message. Second, evangelicals believe one must make a conscious decision to give one's life over to following Christ. Third, they believe one must actively practise one's faith through witnessing (telling others about Christ and his message) and through volunteer and charity work. Fourth, Christ's 'work' on the cross is emphasized over other aspects of his life and teachings (Marsden 1991, Rawlyk 1996, Reimer 2003). That is, incorporated into most theological discussion inside and outside of church is the belief that Christ died on the cross, rose physically from the dead and that through the enactment of that process is now able to expunge the sins of those who believe in him and offer them eternal life.

As noted above, fundamentalist Christians are a subgroup of evangelicals – the most religiously rigid of the bunch. In Canada, this subgroup is extremely small. While 12 per cent of Canadians are evangelicals (VanGinkel 2003), it is estimated that only one to 2 per cent of those religious believers hold the austere traits and beliefs necessary to be categorized as a fundamentalist Christian (Harvey 2003).

To say that the religious traits and beliefs of fundamentalist Christians are austere is one thing; to classify those specific traits and beliefs is another. Some scholars have posited very elaborate descriptions. Writing of religious fundamentalists and fundamentalism in general, Marty and Appleby (1991) were able to distinguish more than a dozen defining characteristics. For this study, I have chosen to use a more straightforward description of fundamentalist Christians; it is widely accepted by scholars and, in all likelihood, resembles the mental image the 'person-on-the-street' would have of this group.

Fundamentalist Christians are, first and foremost, defined by their Biblical literalism. Unlike their more moderate evangelical cousins who are willing to accept some scripture metaphorically, fundamentalists, for the most part, take accounts in scripture as accurate records of actual events (Kellstedt and Smidt 1996, Marsden 1991, Reimer 2003, cf. Stackhouse 1993: 12).

Militancy and separatism are the two other defining characteristics of fundamentalist Christians (Kellstedt and Smidt 1996, Marsden 1991, Rawlyk 1996, Stackhouse 1993, 1994, 1995). Regarding their militancy, Stackhouse states that fundamentalists see confrontation as the proper response to an unbelieving culture; they are 'glad to be known as Protestant Christians who are "willing to do battle royal" for the fundamentals of their faith' (cf. Stackhouse 1993, 1995: 28). Marsden (1991: 1) says of fundamentalist Christians that 'militancy is crucial to their outlook . . . they are conservatives who are willing to take a stand and to fight'. Conversely, most Canadian evangelicals reject the aggressive, adversarial 'my way or the highway' style of debate employed by fundamentalists and instead choose to advocate their various positions calmly, responsibly and with decorum (Stiller 1997, 2006).

Of their separatism, Stackhouse (1995: 28) says, 'they dissociate themselves not only from those who compromise the faith [i.e., sinners, secularists, liberal Christian believers and people of non-Christian faiths], but also from anyone who does not keep all of his or her associations equally pure'. That is to say, fundamentalists criticize other evangelicals for their lack of concern over doctrinal purity and for their willingness to work cooperatively with other Christians of differing doctrinal views.

Furthermore, in their quest to remain ideologically pure, fundamentalists withdraw from/reject many aspects of mainstream culture. Contemporary music, movies, books and magazines that are not overtly Christian are carefully vetted before consumption, those deemed too 'worldly' are avoided. Prohib-itions against dancing, drinking, smoking and certain types of clothing are also common. Some fundamentalist Christians see the public education system and other government run institutions as corrupted by secular values and as such try to diminish reliance on those bodies by creating parallel, 'Christ-focused' structures of their own (Kellstedt and Smidt 1996, Marsden 1991, Reimer 2003, Stackhouse 1994, 1995).

Evangelicals, on the other hand, are not separatist but actively engage contemporary culture (Stackhouse 1994). While they endeavour to remain sep-arate from *worldliness*, they actively engage the *world* (Kellstedt and Smidt 1996, Marsden 1991, Smith 1998). Evangelicals commonly use elements and references from popular culture as 'springboards' or 'bridges' when communi-cating the Gospel message to the uninitiated or 'under-initiated' (Mackey 1995, Pinsky 2006, Smith 1998, cf. Hendershot 2006). They are willing to cross denominational lines to cooperate with fellow believers, with whom they may not agree doctrinally, for the greater cause of evangelizing and bringing people to Christ (Marsden 1991, Stackhouse 1993, 1994, 1995). This tendency among evangelicals to overlook the minutia of doctrine to achieve a greater good has historically been stronger in Canada than in the United States (Clarke 1996, Murphy 1996). Some think that Canadian evangelicals' willingness to reach pragmatic compromises on doctrine has muted the growth of funda-mentalist Christianity in that country; that is, for fundamentalism to thrive believers must subscribe to precise and specific theological formulas (Reimer 2003, Stackhouse 1993). Others say Christian fundamentalism is weak in Canada because there is no charismatic leader to marshal followers (Rawlyk 1996, Stackhouse 1994). Still others suggest that the absence in Canada of a systemic fundamentalist-modern debate (as was witnessed in the USA in the 1920s and 1930s) meant the forces of fundamentalism had no cause around which to rally, coalesce and, ultimately, grow (Stackhouse 1994).

Method

This research involved a secondary analysis of data collected for a study on the framing of evangelical Christians in Canadian television news (Haskell 2007). Previously, 119 full-text print transcripts of nightly, national television news reports from Canada's three largest networks – CBC TV, CTV and Global TV[2] – had been gathered.[3] Those scripts served as the artifacts of examination for this study. Each of those news reports had aired between 1 January 1994 and 1 January 2005 and contained one of the following key words (or its close variant): evangelical, fundamentalist Christian, conservative Christian, Christian right, Baptist, Pentecostal, or born-again. Scripts referencing Baptists and Pentecostals were included because those two denominations house Canada's largest number of evangelical members (Bibby 1987, Reimer 2003, cf. Statistics Canada 2003). Conservative Christian, Christian right and born-again were included because all are commonly used to describe evangelical Christians (Rawlyk 1996, Reimer 2003). However, reports that described an individual or group as conservative Christian, Christian right or born-again and also as Catholic were not included in the sample. At 58 reports, CTV aired the most reports about members from this broad religious community; Global was second with 33 and CBC third with 28 reports over the 11-year period.

The study involved two stages of analysis. The first stage of analysis was conducted by the researcher alone. Each news report was scanned for the monikers it used to designate conservative Protestants. The frequency of each descriptor was logged and tabulated. Those reports that employed the moniker 'fundamentalist Christian' (or its close variant) were set aside for the second stage of analysis.

The second stage of analysis was conducted by two coders: the researcher and a trained undergraduate student. Only those reports that used the term fundamentalist Christian were examined. Because our primary interest was to determine whether the fundamentalist moniker was used correctly in the new reports, we content analysed the text of the reports for manifested evidence of the three core fundamentalist traits: Biblical literalism, militancy and separatism.

According to the coder's guidebook used for this study, a conservative Protestant featured in a news report was deemed to have demonstrated Biblical literalism if he/she stated (either directly in a quote or through a paraphrase relayed by the reporter) that all scripture is to be 'taken literally', 'at face value', 'accepted word-for-word' or some such similar phrase.

For a conservative Protestant featured in a report to be coded as demonstrating militancy he/she must have used (or have been reported to have used) hostile or intimidating words or deeds. Name calling, slurs, acts of violence or coercion were clear examples of militancy.

A conservative Protestant in a report was coded as demonstrating separatism if he/she was shown or was cited as disparaging or criticizing other religions – or the faith of other Christians – as wrong or inadequate. Separatism was also to be coded if the subjects were engaged in some type of activity or behaviour specifically designed to isolate or 'protect' them from people, systems or cultural forces outside their own religious community.

In certain instances a report was coded as using the fundamentalist Christian moniker correctly even if the conservative Protestant featured in a report did not exhibit Biblical literalism, militancy or separatism. When it was the case that the featured subject(s) used the term fundamentalist Christian self-referentially the moniker was deemed to have been correctly employed even in the absence of the defining traits. Reports were also coded as using the moniker correctly – in the absence of the defining traits – when the conservative Protestant(s) was famous (i.e., very well-known nationally and internationally) for his/her fundamentalist Christianity and for using the fundamentalist moniker self-referentially in the past.

Results

Scripts by Moniker

It was not uncommon for a conservative Protestant featured in a news report to be referred to by more than one religious descriptor. For example, on first reference a report might describe the conservative Protestant as a Baptist and then in subsequent references call him/her an evangelical. Because multiple descriptors were employed in some news reports, the total number of descriptors used in the reports is greater than the total number of reports in the sample.

The most popular moniker to be applied to conservative Protestants was the title evangelical. Fifty-four news reports (14 from Global; 19 from CBC and 21 from CTV) used this term when referring to members of this faith group. The more specific denominational moniker, Baptist, appeared in 27 reports (10 from Global; 1 from CBC and 16 from CTV) and the moniker Pentecostal appeared in 11 (2 from Global; 0 from CBC and 9 from CTV). Conservative Protestants were referred to as 'born-again' Christians in nine reports (0 from Global; 4 from CBC and 5 from CTV) and, collectively, as conservative Christians or members of the Christian right in nine reports (3 from Global; 4 from CBC and 2 from CTV). In a total of 25 news reports, conservative Protestants were referred to as fundamentalist Christians (6 from Global; 6 from CBC and 13 from CTV).

Use of the Fundamentalist Christian Moniker

The fundamentalist moniker was seldom used in conjunction with other monikers. Only 4 of the 25 reports referred to their featured conservative Protestants as fundamentalist Christians and then by another descriptor. Specifically, three used the term fundamentalist and evangelical interchangeably to describe their featured Christians; one used fundamentalist and Pentecostal Christian interchangeably.

In 21 of the 25 reports it was the reporter who used 'fundamentalist Christian' as an identifying term for the conservative Protestants in his/her story. In 3 of the 25 reports, the conservative Protestants self-identified as fundamentalists and in just one report the conservative Protestants were labelled fundamentalists by a non-evangelical source/interviewee featured in the same report.

Five of the 25 reports employing the moniker fundamentalist Christian used the term incorrectly (all from CTV). That is to say, in those reports there was no evidence manifested in the text to suggest the featured Christians were fundamentalists, nor were the featured Christians self-identifying as fundamentalists, nor were they well-known ('celebrity') practitioners of the faith. As such, a different descriptor, such as 'evangelical', should have been applied. Conversely, 20 of the reports in which the fundamentalist descriptor was used met the evidentiary criteria of this study (8 from CTV; 6 from Global and 6 from CBC).

In 10 of the 19 news reports that employed the term correctly, evidence of separatism was found, though usually in combination with another fundamentalist trait. Specifically, three reports contained evidence of separatism alone, while four contained evidence of separatism and Biblical literalism, two contained evidence of separatism and militancy, and one contained evidence of separatism, Biblical literalism and militancy.

As noted in the Method section of this paper, conservative Protestants in a report could be coded as demonstrating separatism if they were shown disparaging other religions or the faith of other Christians. Only 1 of the 10 reports evidencing separatism contained proof of that nature: in it, one of the featured Christians stated that her beliefs 'were the only right way of thinking' while others in her group were cited as ridiculing the Islamic faith calling it false (Newton 1995).

The other nine reports that evidenced separatism all showed their Christian subjects engaged in some type of activity or behaviour specifically designed to isolate or 'protect' them from people, systems or cultural forces outside their own religious community. For example, in a few reports the featured Christians had formed their own communal society in an effort to retain their spiritual purity. In one report where the trait of militancy was evidenced in conjunction with separatism, the 'communal' Christians were reported to have sabotaged the equipment of an oil company that had encroached upon their land. In other reports evidencing separatism, the featured Christians were shown to have rejected the public school system, which they felt taught secular values and humanistic doctrines; instead, they enrolled their children in religiously orthodox, Christ-focus educational institutions they themselves had created. One report that evidenced separatism and Biblical literalism was particularly quirky: the Christian farmer it featured refused to participate in any government system or process that involved picture identification. The man, a Biblical literalist, was convinced that prophecy in the Book of Revelation insisted 'anyone who allows their image to be archived by an outside agency bears the mark of the beast and will drink the wine of the wrath of God' (O'Hara-Byrne 2003). The reporter noted that the farmer's refusal to be photographed by government agencies meant he had been without a driver's licence for years and that, in turn, was causing his farming business to fail.

In 2 of the 19 reports that employed the moniker correctly, Biblical literalism was the sole fundamentalist trait evidenced. The same Christian interviewee was featured in both reports. In each he cited his belief in Biblical literalism as the reason for his rejection of Darwin's theory of evolution.

One report of the 19, a particularly long piece exploring the eschatological beliefs of certain communities of conservative Protestants, evidenced militancy and strongly hinted at Biblical literacy. For example, at one point in the report the featured Christians insisted that the Muslim mosque situated at the Dome of the Rock had to be destroyed because God's Word prophesized that the destruction had to come to pass.

One report of the 19 evidenced militancy alone. In it the featured Christians were shown fomenting dissention and inciting violence in the Israeli West Bank by meeting with, encouraging, and giving financial support to, a group of extreme right-wing Jewish settlers illegally occupying Palestinian land. The Christians were described as willing to use financial and other means to replace established Palestinian occupants with new Jewish settlers.

Three of the 19 reports contained no evidence of fundamentalist traits but were deemed to have correctly employed the moniker as they featured people known for their fundamentalist beliefs. Two featured self-proclaimed fundamentalist, Reverend Jerry Falwell. As founder and leader of the Moral Majority, by the mid-1980s Falwell had established himself as the 'king' of American Fundamentalism. His political activities and his religious TV shows led to his name becoming a household word. *Time Magazine* called Falwell 'the truest and bravest voice in the whole Fundamentalist movement' (Ajemian 1985: 58, cf. Falwell 1984). The third report featured Canadian politician Stockwell Day. Over the years, in multiple interviews and public appearances, Day has expressed his firm belief in Biblical literalism. The non-evangelical source who applied the fundamentalist moniker to Day did so during the course of a political debate. In the report, the non-evangelical accused Day of allowing his 'Christian fundamentalist principles' to influence his stand on governmental policies related to Israel (Moscovitz 2000). Finally, as mentioned above, in 3 of the 19 reports the featured conservative Protestants referred to themselves as fundamentalist Christians; these reports contained no evidence of fundamentalist traits.

In the five reports that employed the fundamentalist moniker incorrectly, it was the journalist narrating the news story who was responsible for misuse of the term.

Three of the reports in which journalists used the term incorrectly aired during the mid-1990s and focused on government legislation meant to grant homosexual couples the same family benefits as heterosexual couples. In each of those three reports, Christians who were lobbying against the legislation were referred to as fundamentalists; however, their behaviour was polite and decorous not militant, they made no mention of the Bible, and they did not self-identify as fundamentalist. Neither could their behaviour be considered separatist. In opposing legislation meant to put homosexual relationships on par with heterosexual ones, the Christians featured in the reports were not on the far-fringe of mainstream culture but were, as polling data from those years demonstrates, reflecting a view shared by about a third of Canadians at the time (Bibby 2002).

The other two reports in which journalists misused the moniker focused on the activities of the para-church organizations Focus on the Family Canada and Promise Keepers International, respectively. Lower-level administrators of these organizations were featured in the reports and while they occasionally referred to passages of scripture, they did not avow Biblical literalism, nor did they exhibit militancy or separatism. In fact, the Christians featured in the report on the Promise Keepers were shown to be self-consciously non-judgemental and pleased to accept believers from all denominational traditions. This behaviour was in keeping with the Promise Keepers' inclusive statement of faith which states, 'All believers in the Lord Jesus Christ are members of His one international, multi-ethnic and transcultural body called the universal church. Its unity is displayed when we reach beyond racial and denominational lines to demonstrate the Gospel's reconciling power' ('Statement of Faith' 1994: para. 7). Regarding the identification of Focus on the Family personnel as fundamentalists, some sympathy can be extended to the journalist who had to accurately apply a titular designation. The founder, chairperson, and virtual face of the organization, James Dobson, has been characterized as a fundamentalist for his hard-ball political tactics (militancy?), harsh cultural criticism (separatism?) and ultra-orthodox interpretation of some passages of scripture (Biblical literalism?) (Alexander-Moegerle 1997, Blaker 2003, Boston 2000). In light of such appraisals, one can understand why the term fundamentalist might be mistakenly applied to those associated with Dobson's organization. However, Dobson does not consider himself, or his organization – which works collaboratively with Protestants, Catholics and Jews – fundamentalist. 'Evangelical', or the more generic 'Christian', are the only monikers that he and his organization use self-descriptively (Alexander-Moegerle 1997, 'Our guiding principals', n.d., 'Who we are', n.d.).

Conclusions

The primary conclusion we can draw from this analysis is that the term fundamentalist Christian was, in large measure, used judiciously and sagaciously in Canadian national television news reports airing between 1994 and 2005. During this 11-year period, only 5 times out of 25 was the moniker incorrectly applied to a conservative Protestant of moderate religious tendencies.

As stated at the outset, without access to pre-1993 national television news it is difficult to tender incontrovertible conclusions regarding the efficacy of Stiller's open letter to the media. However, findings from the post-1993 data do allow inferences to be made. We know that prior to the issuing of his letter Stiller saw the media's misuse of the term fundamentalist Christian as endemic – it was so pervasive he felt forced to raise a public complaint. In contrast, the findings of this study show that in the months and years following Stiller's reprimand, news reports (at least those aired nationally on television) would have given him little reason to complain. The use of the term fundamentalist Christian was infrequent at about two references per year; when it was employed by reporters it was with 80 per cent accuracy.[4] It is probable, therefore, that the public relations campaign carried out by Stiller in the fall of 1993, led, in subsequent years, to greater accuracy among Canadian television journalists in their application of the fundamentalist Christian moniker. Confidence in this assertion is significantly reinforced by the fact that other national media outlets – CBC radio and Canadian Press – *did* change their practices on account of Stiller. That is to say, precedent supports that such a change is well within the realm of the possible.

However, an opposing hypothesis deserves mention. Because a comparison cannot be made of television reports airing before Stiller's campaign and those airing after, there are those who might question whether Stiller had reason to complain in the first place. They might argue that just as people who own a particular make and model of car are more apt to notice other vehicles like their own – thus acquiring a false sense that their car is more popular than other types – Stiller, as an evangelical Christian himself, may have had a heightened sense of the media's coverage of his religious constituency. Specifically, in the months leading up to the release of his letter, Stiller's strong religious faith may have led to an exaggerated sense of the media's use and abuse of the term fundamentalist Christian. In short, some might propose that what Stiller 'saw' as an endemic problem was, in fact, no more than a few isolated incidents. Certainly, studies have shown that ardent members of any group, faith groups included, are more likely than others to feel that the news media provide a distorted view of them and their fellow constituents (Vallone et al. 1985).

While also possible, this second hypothesis is unlikely in light of Stiller's own observations following his campaign for correct nomenclature. Post campaign, Stiller detected a significant positive change in the way all major Canadian news organizations used the term fundamentalist; where he had previously noted problems on a daily basis, after his public letter he found problems surrounding the use of the term Christian fundamentalist were virtually absent from news content. Furthermore, he observed that the change was lasting. In fact, Stiller suggests that the Canadian news media's careful application of the term fundamentalist when writing about Muslims following the events of 11 September 2001 can be directly accredited to the turn in attitude media professionals experienced following his public chastisement of their practices back in 1993 (Stiller, Brian. Personal communication, 1 March 2008). In sum, if Stiller had continued to insist that the media's misuse of the fundamentalist moniker remained pervasive even after his campaign, then the case could be made that his religious faith played a factor in exaggerating his sense of the problem. That he was able to recognize a dramatic shift in the media's practice gives credibility to his pre-campaign perceptions.

The specific fundamentalist traits that were evidenced in the news reports warrant some discussion. Ultra-conservative Protestants demonstrated separatism, alone or in combination with another defining fundamentalist trait, in 10 of 25 reports employing the fundamentalist moniker. Biblical literalism was evidenced conclusively in seven reports and was strongly suggested in one. Militancy, on the other hand, was demonstrated, on its own or in combination with another trait, in just five reports. That militancy was evidenced half as often as separatism, may have something to do with the nature of Canadian conservative Protestants in general. Research by sociologist Sam Reimer (2000, 2003) has determined that Canadian conservative Protestants (of all types) tend to shy away from militancy; when presented with situations in which they are at odds with others, Canadian conservative Protestants would rather 'agree to disagree' than fight over an issue. In comparison with American conservative Protestants, Reimer states, 'regardless of whether one looks at racial, political, religious, or moral tolerance, Canadian evangelicals are more tolerant' (Reimer 2000: 235, cf. 2003). In Canada, specific government measures – federal sponsorship of multi-culturalism since the 1960s and the enshrining of minority rights in the Canadian Charter in 1982 – have helped to establish tolerance, or in a broader sense pluralism, as the dominant ideology of its citizens (even, to a certain extent, the fundamentalist ones) (Adams 2003, Reimer 2003). Conversely, the greater militancy and intolerance found in American society – and among conservative Protestants, particularly fundamentalist Christians in that country – is thought to find its roots in the historical tendency towards individualism, revolution and dissent (Adams 2003, Reimer 2003). Interestingly, two of the five Canadian national television news reports that evidenced militancy featured fundamentalist Christians who hailed from the United States.

Finally, a brief mention of the implications this study might have for evangelical Christians themselves. Today in Canada the battle between the media and evangelicals over referential monikers is but part of a larger war over perceptions of balance and fairness: the news media think they are balanced and fair in their treatment of evangelicals; evangelicals do not (VanGinkel 2003). This study, therefore, may provide some insights and encouragement to those conservative Protestants who long for greater understanding between themselves and the media. While we cannot say with complete empirical certainty that Brian Stiller's public relations campaign affected the way television journalists write about evangelicals, the findings of this study – viewed in conjunction with the identified reactive changes at CBC radio and Canadian Press – lend significant weight to that argument. What, then, does that tell us about evangelicals? It tells us that through tenacity, diplomacy and clarity of message they *can* get their opinion heard in the public square and have their recommendations heeded. And what does that tell us about journalists? It tells us that journalists long to be fair and, when offered a logical and reasonable means, will be so.

Notes

1   Typically, scripture from the New Testament that reads as rules, edicts or direct instructions to believers is interpreted and followed literally by evangelicals – especially the words of Jesus and the letters of the Apostle Paul. The claims made in early church creedal statements – such as the Apostles' Creed and the Nicene Creed – are also taken as fact (e.g., that Jesus was born of a virgin). Those scriptures that follow a simple narrative structure, particularly Old Testament passages like the story of creation and the fall of Adam and Eve found in the Book of Genesis, are often interpreted more symbolically. For example, an overwhelming majority of Canadian evangelicals do not believe that God literally created the world in six 24-hour days (Reimer 2003).

2   For the purposes of this study nightly, national news is that which has typically been aired at 6:30 p.m. on Global, 10:00 p.m. on CBC TV and 11:00 p.m. on CTV. Briefly, during the mid-1990s CBC TV changed the time of its national news programme from 10:00 p.m. to 9:00 p.m. Former Global News producer Carmen Harvey (Personal communication, 17 October 2005) states that prior to 2001, Global's national newscast was not available in the provinces of Alberta and British Columbia.

3   The transcripts from CTV's news reports were obtained through the Proquest CBCA Current Events Database. Full-text transcripts from Global and CBC TV were obtained from the news archivist-librarians at those networks.

4   As Stiller was of the opinion that the term fundamentalist Christians

33333333333333

should never be used to describe a conservative Protestant – regardless of his or her religious rigour – he would likely dispute this figure of 80 per cent accuracy.

References

Adams, M. (2003), *Fire and Ice: The United States, Canada and the Myth of Converging Values*. Toronto: Penguin.

Ajemian, R. (1985), 'Jerry Falwell spreads the word: The fundamentalist leader wages political war on immorality', *Time Magazine*, 126(9), September, 58–61.

Alexander-Moegerle, G. (1997), *James Dobson's War on America*. Amherst, NY: Prometheus.

Baugh, J. (1991), 'The politicization of changing terms of self reference among American slave descendants', *American Speech*, 66(2), 133–146.

Berger, P. L. and Luckman, T. (1966), *The Social Construction of Reality*. New York: Anchor Books.

Bibby, R. W. (2002), 'Homosexuality in Canada: A national reading' [press release]. Lethbridge, AB: Project Canada Survey Series, 13 May.

Bibby R. W. (1987), *Fragmented Gods: The Poverty and Potential of Religion in Canada*. Toronto: Irwin.

Blaker, K. (2003), *The Fundamentals of Extremism: The Christian Right in America*. New Boston, MI: New Boston.

Boston, R. (2000), *Close Encounters with the Religious Right: Journeys into the Twilight Zone of Religion and Politics*. Amherst, NY: Prometheus.

Bureau of Broadcast Measurement (2006), *Programs – Total Canada, 12 September 2005 to 26 May 2006*. Toronto: Bureau of Broadcast Measurement.

Carey, J. (1989), *Communication as Culture*. Boston: Unwin Hyman.

Clarke, B. (1996), 'English speaking Canada from 1854', in T. Murphy and R. Perin (eds), *A Concise History of Christianity in Canada*. Toronto: Oxford University Press, pp. 261–359.

Falwell, J. (1984), 'Foreword', in L. R. Keylock (ed.), *Fundamentalism Today: What Makes it so Attractive?* Elgin, IL: Bretheren, pp. 7–8.

Fleras, A. (2003), *Mass Media Communication in Canada: Power, Persuasion, and Politics*. Scarborough, ON: Nelson.

Fishman, J. A. (1980), 'The Whorfian hypothesis: Varieties of valuation, confirmation, and disconfirmation', *International Journal of the Sociology of Language*, 26, 25–40.

Hacking, I. (1999), *The Social Construction of What?* Boston: Harvard University Press.

Harvey, B. (2003), 'Word battles show media problems with religious stereotypes', *Faith Today*, May/June, p. 17.

Haskell, D. M. (2007), 'Evangelical Christians in Canadian national television news, 1994–2004: A frame analysis', *Journal of Communication and Religion*, 30(1), 118–152.

Hendershot, H. (2006), *Shaking the World for Jesus: Media and Conservative Evangelical Culture*. Chicago: University of Chicago Press.

Hine, D. C., Harrold, S. C. and Hine, W. C. (2005), *African Americans: A concise history*. Upper Saddle River, NJ: Prentice Hall.

Kay, P. and Kempton, W. (1984), 'What is the Sapir-Whorf hypothesis?', *American Anthropologist*, 86, 65–79.

Kellstedt, L. A. and Smidt, C. E. (1996), 'Measuring fundamentalism: An analysis of different operational strategies', in J. C. Green, J. L. Guth, C. E. Smidt and L. A. Kellstedt (eds), *Religion and Culture Wars: Dispatches from the Front*. Lanhan, ML: Rowman and Littlefield, pp. 119–218.

Mackey, L. (1995), *These Evangelical Churches of Ours*. Winfield, BC: Wood Lake.

Marsden, G. M. (1991), *Understanding Fundamentalism and Evangelicalism*. Grand Rapids, MI: Eerdmans.

Marty, M. E. and Appleby, R. S. (1991), 'The fundamentalism project: A users guide', in M. E. Marty and R. S. Appleby (eds), *Fundamentalisms Observed: The Fundamentalism Project, Volume 1*. Chicago: University of Chicago Press, pp. vii–xiv.

Mazzuca, J. (2001), 'Network and local TV news sources remain most popular', *The Gallup Poll*, 61(9).

McAteer, M. (1993), ' "Fundamentalist" dirty word, evangelical Christians say', *Toronto Star*, 6 November, K17.

Miljan, L. and Cooper, B. (2003). *Hidden Agendas: How Journalists Influence the News*. Vancouver, BC: UBC Press.

Moscovitz, J. (2000), *The National* [television broadcast]. Toronto: CBC Television Network, 10 October.

Murphy, T. (1996), 'The English speaking colonies to 1854', in T. Murphy and R. Perin (eds), *A Concise History of Christianity in Canada*. Toronto: Oxford University Press, pp. 108–189.

Newton, P. (1995), *CTV National News* [television broadcast]. Scarborough, ON: CTV Television Network, 18 April.

Nielson Media Research (2006), *National Program Reports, 6–9 February*. Markham, ON: Nielson Media Research.

O'Hara-Byrne, B. (2003), *Global National* [television broadcast]. Toronto: Global Television Network, 4 October.

'Our guiding principles' (n.d.), Focus on the Family Website, retrieved 2 September 2006 from <http://www.family.org/welcome/aboutfof/a0000078.cfm>.

Philogene, G. (1999), *From Black to African American: A New Social Representation*. Westport, CT: Praeger.

Pinsky, M. I. (2006), *A Jew Among the Evangelicals: A Guide for the Perplexed*. Louisville, KY: Westminster John Knox.

Rawlyk, G. A. (1996), *Is Jesus Your Personal Saviour? In Search of Canadian Evangelicalism in the 1990s*. Montreal: McGill-Queens University Press.

Reimer, S. (2003), *Evangelicals and the Continental Divide: The Conservative Protestant Subculture in Canada and the United States*. Montreal: McGill-Queens University Press.

Reimer, S. (2000), 'A generic evangelicalism? Comparing evangelical subcultures in Canada and the United States', in D. Lyon and M. Van Die (eds), *Rethinking Church, State, and Modernity*. Toronto: University of Toronto Press, pp. 211–248.

Sapir, E. (1985[1949]), 'The status of linguistics as a science', in D. Mandelbaum (ed.), *Selected Writings of Edward Sapir in Language, Culture and Personality*. Berkley, CA: University of California Press, pp. 160–167.

Schultze, Q. J. (1996), 'Evangelicals uneasy alliance with the media', in J. Buddenbaum and D. Stout (eds), *Religion and Mass Media: Audiences and Adaptations*. Thousand Oaks, CA: Sage, pp. 61–73.

Smith, C. (1998), *American Evangelicalism: Embattled and Thriving*. Chicago: University of Chicago Press.

Stackhouse, J. G. (1995), 'Three myths about evangelicals', *Faith Today*, May/June, p. 28.

Stackhouse, J. G. (1994), 'More than a hyphen: Twentieth century Canadian evangelicalism in Anglo-American context', in G. A. Rawlyk and M. A. Noll (eds), *Amazing Grace: Evangelicalism in Australia, Britain, Canada and the United States*. Montreal, QC: McGill-Queen's University Press, pp. 375–400.

Stackhouse, J. G. (1993), *Canadian Evangelicalism in the Twentieth Century: An Introduction to its Character*. Toronto: University of Toronto Press.

'Statement of Faith' (1994), Promise Keepers Website, retrieved 2 September 2006 from <http://www.promisekeepers.org/about/statementoffaith>.

Statistics Canada (2003), *2001 Census: Analysis Series. Religions in Canada*. Ottawa: Queen's Printer for Canada.

Stiller, B. (2006), *Jesus and Caesar: Christians in the Public Square*. Pickering, ON: Bayridge.

Stiller, B. (2002), 'I, too, remember Peter', *Christian Week*, 19 February, p. 1.

Stiller, B. (1997), *From the Tower of Babel to Parliament Hill: How to be a Christian in Canada Today*. Toronto: Harper Collins.

Vallone, R., Ross, L. and Lepper, M. (1985), 'The hostile media phenomenon: Biased perception and perception of media bias in coverage of the Beirut massacre', *Journal of Personality and Social Psychology*, 49, 577–585.

VanGinkel, A. (2003), *Church and Faith Trends, Evangelical Beliefs and Practices: A Summary of the 2003 Ipsos-Reid Survey Results*. Markham, ON: Evangelical Fellowship of Canada.

'Who we are' (n.d.), Focus on the Family Canada Website, retrieved 2 September 2006 from <http://www.fotf.ca/b_01aboutus/who/index.html>.

Whorf, B. L. (1956), *Language, Thought, and Reality*. Boston: MIT Press.

Chapter 8

The Vernacular Ideology of Christian Fundamentalism on the World Wide Web

Robert Glenn Howard

Introduction

Since the emergence of mass-produced vernacular Bibles, communication technologies have given individuals a growing responsibility for interpreting the Christian message. With the rise of secular governments, individual choice came to be the primary guide for religious expression. More recently, new communication technologies have allowed individuals to express and consume a greater diversity of religious ideas. Meanwhile, religious commitment in the United States seems to be growing more individualized and fluid (Ammerman 1997, Campbell 2005, Lindlof 2002). Today, personal religious expression emerges side-by-side with mundane talk in a vast public web of vernacular discourse made possible by computer networks (Howard 2005c, 2008). In this situation, individuals are empowered to transcend the institutions of religion and enact their own vision of 'the church' or 'the faith community', referred to by many of my informants as the 'ekklesia' online.

This article documents one such virtual ekklesia as it emerges from a network of websites where individuals express a specific set of conservative evangelical beliefs. Not unified by any institutional ties, this web of belief exists only in individual expressive behaviours. I have termed this web 'vernacular Christian fundamentalism'. To document this phenomenon, ethnographic data were collected and examined to locate specific defining traits of the interactions on the sites within this web. Four traits: Biblical literalism, evangelicalism, spiritual rebirth and apocalypticism were identified and will be discussed in detail later in the paper. Based on these four traits, data from 40 websites were collected and two specific website examples were selected for analysis in this essay. These two linked examples – Acts17-11.com and the Watcher Website – contextualize and contain the four traits. Besides containing these traits, the two examples also represent the diversity in communication styles, topics and level of connection to other websites found in the sample. While the two sites' individual online performances differ, they nonetheless resolve towards a commonality that appears like one link out of a vast web of vernacular fundamentalism I am interested in. Because this link results from the four inter-locking traits described above, the structuring of their content functions to reinforce belief.

Methods

To locate 'vernacular fundamentalism' in online communication, specific examples of websites have been collected and compared. For purposes of the research, a definitive textual mark was identified that would locate a particular online communication as likely to be involved in this ideology. Interview data that were collected previously to the 1990s surge in internet-use were also consulted. The four traits of Christian fundamentalism were enumerated in those data. Because the first three traits (Biblical literalism, evangelicalism and spiritual rebirth) mark conservative evangelism more generally, an interest in the 'end times' was taken to be the definitive marker for fundamentalism (Strozier 1994).

For this article, the two linked websites exemplify the way that very different individuals can choose to create connections based on the vernacular ideology of Christian fundamentalism. The first of these two sites was the amateur 'Bible study' site titled *Acts17-11.com* and maintained by Laura and Dean VanDruff. This site represents a low-profile example, that is, it had a relatively low num-ber of links to other sites.

The second site represents a high-profile example, i.e., a high number of links to other sites. This was David and Brenda Flynn's *Watcher Website*. Often referring to themselves by the collective pseudonym 'the Watcher', the Flynns are a middleclass married couple in Helena, Montana. A mix of Biblical literal-ism, conspiracy theory and UFO beliefs, their site has been one of the most popular sites about the end times since the late 1990s. It had 29 incoming links from 14 different external sites.

The Vernacular Ideology of Christian Fundamentalism

Sociologists of religion have argued that modern religious expression is increas-ingly the product of individual choice instead of institutional doctrine (Ammerman 1997). As a result of individuals' growing ability to pick among a diverse range of religions, religious media scholar Thomas R. Lindlof has suggested, 'researchers will need to become more sensitive to the multiple ver-naculars' (Lindlof 2002: 71–72). The rise in individualized religious expression suggests the need for an examination of *vernacular religion*.

Based on the work of Don Yoder (1974) and Leonard Norman Primiano (1995), the term 'vernacular religion' refers to those beliefs and practices that emerge from the bottom up. Because no central agent imposes them from the top down, vernacular religion is recognized as distinct from (though it may or may not coincide with) religious institutions (Yoder 1974). Even a religious leader's prayer is vernacular insofar as it is the product of emergent personal belief and not imposed by doctrine (Primiano 1995).

In this situation, religious institutions are losing their ability to assert central authority. As a result, there is less standardization. This process began in Christianity as early as the tumultuous Protestant Reformation of sixteenth-century Europe. Before the Reformation, individuals exhibited a wide range of regional and local beliefs. However, the ideology of the Catholic Church attempted to overlay that diversity. Expressed by priestly elites in a language that everyday people could not understand, the doctrines of the Catholic Church could not be engaged by the vast majority of adherents. The emphasis by Luther and his followers on individual religious experience and, in particular, access to and familiarity with printed vernacular translations of the Bible began to break down that centralization (Howard 2005d).

With the withdrawal of centrally imposed and organized ideas promoted by institutional authority, diffuse and often vague ideologies can emerge. While they may not be legitimated by centralized authorities, they can and do nevertheless exhibit specific continuities and consistencies that mark their presence. In this sense, they are not necessarily *emic* genres but, instead, analytic categories that can be located in discourse based on specific recurring features. As an analytic category, I have termed the system of ideas this chapter locates among conservative evangelicals the 'vernacular ideology of Christian fundamentalism'.

Though vernacular fundamentalism is different from the historical movement of Protestant Fundamentalism of the 1920s, using the term locates the ideology in both its historical antecedents and as a topic of significant previous research (see Marty and Appleby 1995: 6–7, Harris 1998: 1ff). Vernacular fundamentalism refers to an ideology with traits that are recognizable in discourse but not necessarily so named by the actors in that discourse. This analytic or *etic* perspective on fundamentalism goes at least as far back as the work of James Barr starting in the mid-1960s (Barr 1966, 1978, Kellstedt and Smidt 1991, Perkin 2000). For Barr, fundamentalism denoted a way of thinking. In historical and discursive terms, Barr's 'cognitive' fundamentalism is better understood as 'ideological'. Here, ideology refers to a set of interrelated ideas that function as the symbolic apparatus through which a social group understands its world (Althusser 1984, Eagleton 1991). As a way of thinking based on shared beliefs, ideology emerges in discourse when it exhibits specific observable traits.

Based in ethnographic data, a systematic catalogue of four observable traits that indicate the existence of ideological fundamentalism can be found in the work of the sociologist of religion Charles B. Strozier: 1) an 'orientation toward biblical literalism', 2) 'evangelicalism (or the obligation to convert others)', 3) 'the experience of being reborn in faith' and 4) 'an apocalypticism in its specific-ally end time form' (Strozier 1994: 5). By my definition, when these four traits appear in a non-institutional communication, that communication is an expression of the 'vernacular ideology of Christian fundamentalism'.

As the first trait of the ideology, an emphasis on literalism holds the four together. After this first trait, the other three represent degrees of conservatism in approaching Biblical understanding. Going back to the beginnings of the Reformation itself, Martin Luther's claim that there was a 'simple' and 'literal' meaning in the biblical texts became an institutional mechanism that gave more power to vernacular interpretations of the Bible than had the Catholic Church (Howard 2005b). This situation allowed lay people to serve as important actors in spreading Protestantism. This practice was itself grounded in a literal reading of the Bible. Often termed 'The Great Commission', the final lines of the Gospel of Mathew depict Jesus commanding his disciples to evangelize (28: 18–19). This is the scriptural basis for the second trait: 'the obligation to convert others'.

The two remaining traits are also easily located in the King James version of the New Testament. The belief in spiritual rebirth is a literal interpretation of Jesus' words to the Pharisee Nicodemus in the Gospel of John: 'Verily, verily, I say unto thee, except a man be born again, he cannot see the kingdom of God' (3: 3). Sometimes understood more metaphorically, various manifestations of this idea are also common among less conservative evangelicals. The more distinctively fundamentalist trait emerges, however, from an insistence on a literal reading of biblical prophecy as describing the 'end times'.

Throughout the New Testament, there are descriptions of the return of 'The Kingdom' (see Mathew 24: 29–30). When the literal interpretation of these passages is emphasized, apocalypticism becomes a distinctive marker for the vernacular fundamentalist ideology. However, all four traits reinforce each other. If Christ literally commanded his disciples to spread a literal message of the Bible, then they are compelled to attempt to induce spiritual rebirth in others before a rapidly approaching end times renders it too late.

Most historians consider Christian fundamentalism in the United States dis-tinct from the more conciliatory neo-evangelicalism. While neo-evangelicalism is characterized by openness to contemporary culture, more conservative evan-gelicals seek to hold themselves separate from what they consider modernist secularism. Though opposed to secularism, Christian fundamentalism is not opposed to the use of modern technology (Balmer 2002: 232ff). The set of ideas that came together as the historical movement of Christian fundamentalism emerged in communication technologies starting at the beginning of the twen-tieth century (Balmer and Winner 2002: 81–82, Marsden 1980: 4ff, Harris 1998: 3ff).

The early twentieth century was a time of upheaval for institutional

Protestantism in the United States. Reacting to a perceived growth of secular influence both inside and outside religious institutions, Protestant leaders began to split on the proper Christian understanding of Charles Darwin's theory of evolution. For liberals, the Bible's description of creation in the Book of Genesis was figurative and hence compatible with Darwin's theory. For conservatives who emphasized a literal interpretation of the Bible, Darwin's ideas were replacing a belief in God's divine plan with a belief in random chance and human will. When John Scopes, a small town schoolteacher, was charged with breaking a Tennessee state law against teaching evolution, he was prosecuted in 1925. Though the conservatives won the trial, their leadership was publicly ridiculed. Disgraced in the glare of media attention, radical conservatives receded and disappeared from Protestant institutions (Howard 2006a).

As historian of American religion Karen Armstrong (2000) has noted, however: 'Fundamentalists had not gone away. Indeed, after the trial their views became more extreme. They felt embittered and nursed a deep grievance against mainstream culture' (177–178). Rejected by both more liberal Christians and most Christian institutions, the term 'fundamentalism' largely fell out of use, except by adherents. However, the ideas persisted at the vernacular level. From that vernacular bedding, fundamentalists would later begin to reemerge in mass media.

In what media historian Quentin J. Schultze has termed a 'rhetoric of conversion', conservative evangelical radio broadcasts in the 1920s and 1930s were characterized by simple moral messages of personal devotion presented in emotional tones by charismatic preachers (Schultze 2003: 139ff). They deployed strategies to arouse a sense of emotional connection to a personal divine. Funded primarily by audience donations, evangelical radio was wedded to the market of its consumers. As a result, it could not overly challenge its audience with too specific or difficult claims (Moore 1994, Schultze 2003). Emphasizing a simple, literal and emotional understanding of the Bible, it appealed to a wide variety of individuals from diverse denominational backgrounds and garnered a large audience. Creating a wide consumer base for these non-denominational Protestant media, the market expanded from radio to television and to popular press books.

In the 1970s, a series of these books drove a resurgence of 'end times' speculation. Hal Lindsey's dispensational interpretation of biblical prophecy as foretelling Cold War politics sold 7.5 million copies in 1970, becoming the best-selling non-fiction book of the decade (excluding the Bible itself). During the 1980s, television-based evangelical ventures like The Trinity Broadcasting Network, The PTL Club and The 700 Club expanded the consumer market for evangelical media products. Meanwhile, Lindsey published more successful books, hosted his own television show and developed a significant following. Noting his success, Baptist minister Tim LaHaye updated Lindsey's ideas in the form of evangelical fiction. With his co-writer Jerry Jenkins, LaHaye published the first in a twelve-novel series called *Left Behind* in 1995. In 2001, Tim LaHaye was named the most influential leader in the evangelical movement by Wheaton College. By May of 2004 (when the *Left Behind* series was completed), LaHaye appeared on the cover of Newsweek proclaiming that the combined sales of the 12 books had topped 62 million – excluding 'prequels', spin-offs, study editions, companion guides and children's editions (Hendershot 2004).

Conservative Protestant mass media placed an emphasis on a simple and literal interpretation of the biblical texts and an overtly emotional personal relationship with the divine. This simplified message appealed across a variety of denominational boundaries. As a result, the mass media audience of conservative Protestant Christians could be large enough to support a growing industry of media evangelism. As a byproduct, the conservative evangelical media spread a coherent set of basic values across institutional lines. Using the internet, an emphasis on the 'end times' allowed the most conservative Christians to locate each other among more liberal evangelicals.

Laura and Dean Meet 'The Watcher'

In the 1990s, the four traits marking the vernacular ideology of Christian fundamentalism began to emerge in virtual communities formed by amateur website builders. Today, they can be seen as virtual *ekklesia* enacted on amateur websites engaged in discourse about the 'end times'. This section locates the four traits as they manifested on two very different websites that were, literally, linked based on their shared ideology.

Though all four individuals associated with these two sites identified themselves as Christians, the couples are very different. David and Brenda Flynn are adult converts. David was raised Catholic but had abandoned it as an adult. When they met, Brenda was practising Wicca. Later, they both experienced spiritual rebirths that led them to consider themselves Christian converts. Unlike David and Brenda, Laura and Dean VanDruff were both raised as Baptists. Later, they joined a series of Bible Churches, Assemblies of God, and independent charismatic churches. In addition to these different religious histories, the two couples are separated by over 1,500 miles geographically. These differences seem to manifest in the style and content of their sites. Where Laura and Dean's site offers a simple, serious and family-oriented series of topical Bible studies, David and Brenda's site offers a busy, playful and sometimes darkly humourous pastiche of conspiracy theory, UFOlogy, and 'end times' speculation.

Despite these differences, the four individuals share an interest in the 'end times'. On a page articulating their basic belief about the impending approach of the 'end times', David and Brenda placed a long quote from one of Laura and Dean's sub-pages. Underneath the quote, they placed a link directly to the page on *Acts17-11.com*. Despite the fact that the *Acts17-11.com* site is not focused on the end times, the Flynns labeled their link to it: 'End Time Bible study website'. This is a telling detail because it demonstrates that David and Brenda imagined their linkage to Laura and Dean in terms of that definitive trait of vernacular Christian fundamentalism. Recognizing their participation in end times discourse, a closer examination reveals that both couples exhibit all four of the definitive traits of the ideology of vernacular Christian fundamentalism.

Self-identifying as 'born again' when asked directly during an interview, Brenda and David's use of those terms established that they are conversant with the typical evangelical Protestant emphasis on spiritual rebirth. As would be expected, this emphasis on spiritual rebirth was accompanied by evangelism in the form of an interest in spreading the word about the availability of this experience for others. Presented on their website in the form of a variety of scriptural interpretations or 'studies', this second of the four traits of vernacular fundamentalism is clearly evident.

Since 1993, the couple has slowly expanded their site by periodically adding new studies and making new links to other sites that relate to their interests. Deploying a mix of pop culture, humour and links to a wide variety of controversial and often-sinister material from all over the web, the site garners a wide audience for its message about the UFO presence. However, one of its most prominent pages is bluntly evangelistic. At the top of that page, a brightly coloured graphic flashes: 'The most important page of all!'. Below the graphic, they invite their audience to perform a Sinner's Prayer by asking, 'Salvation is only a prayer of faith away, so what are you waiting for?' ('Why doesn't God just show up now?' n.d.). The inclusion of this traditional evangelical prayer is the marker of a commitment to the second trait of the ideology: evangelism (see Howard 2005a).

During an interview, we directly discussed the meaning of the term 'fundamentalism' and their feelings about it. David specifically stated that they are not 'Christian fundamentalists'. For David, to align themselves with such a movement would, 'entail that we would buy into some of the Christian tradition'. Instead, they self identified as 'scriptural fundamentalists' who 'focus on just the Bible, *scripture sola* [stet], nothing else but the Bible' (Personal interview 17 October 1999, Helena, MT). This statement marks a third trait of the ideology: an orientation towards biblical literalism.

A popular slogan among evangelicals, the phrase '*sola scriptura*' or 'by biblical texts only' refers to one of the Reformation's 'five *solas*' or 'slogans'. These doctrines directly challenged the authority of priests to interpret the Bible. *Sola scriptura* suggests that the Bible is written clearly by the divine so that anyone can understand it and, as a result, individuals have no need to rely on interpretative methods or authorities beyond their own reading of the texts. Without other methods or authorities, the meaning of the Bible is thought to be understandable when taken at face value even in vernacular translations. As a

result of this literal orientation, interpretations that render the more problematic biblical accounts figurative are unacceptable. In addition to overtly stating
their commitment to a literal meaning, the Flynns manifest it in the way they
make claims on their website.

When incorporating ideas about UFOs, conspiracy theory and the Bible, they
locate ultimate authority in biblical quotes. For example, making the claim that
'UFO's and alien abduction are nothing new', they begin by quoting the Bible
without explanation: 'Matthew 24: 37 but as the days of Noah, so also will be
the coming of the Son of Man. For as they were in the days before the flood . . .'
('Seraphim, cherubim and Ezekiel's wheels . . .' n.d.). Then they raise the
rhetorical question, 'Just what was going on in the "days before the flood"?'
('Seraphim, cherubim and Ezekiel's wheels . . .' n.d.) Describing a pre-Flood
world where demons 'hybridized' with humans, they use 27 citations containing some 1,137 of their words and 691 words of quoted text from the Bible
('Seraphim, cherubim and Ezekiel's wheels . . .' n.d.). With nearly a biblical
quote for every two of their own words, this style of arguing demonstrates their
commitment to a literal interpretation of the Bible because they offer no
interpretive method and expand little if any on the quotes they cite.

The Flynns demonstrate a commitment to literalism, evangelism and spiritual rebirth. While those three traits alone might only indicate an adherence to
less conservative evangelicalism, the primary topical focus of their website is
the definitive trait of the vernacular ideology of Christian fundamentalism: an
interest in apocalypticism in its end times form. Specifically using the term
'End Time', the Flynns imagine a rapidly approaching apocalyptic scenario that
climaxes with a destructive world war in Jerusalem and the return of Jesus
Christ. On their website, they express belief in the basic components that comprise the prophetic end times narrative. Those include: the rise of anti-Christ to
power, a bodily 'rapture' of Christians, the Tribulation Period, the building of
the 'Third Temple' in Jerusalem and the final triumphant establishment of the
Millennial Reign of Christ (Howard 2006b).

The Flynns connect this narrative to their belief in UFOs saying, 'Our studies
of scripture have lead us to the controversial view that civilizations of pre-
rebellion angels lived on the planets of our solar system before the creation
of Adam'. For them, these demons founded a civilization on Mars called
'Cydonia' ('Invasion from Mars?' n.d.). Calling it 'The End Time Delusion,' the
Flynns claim that the anti-Christ will come to power partially based on her or
his false-revelation that supposed space-aliens are the ancient progenitors of
the human race. The anti-Christ will offer scientific proof by unveiling the
'discovery' of an ancient civilization on Mars. In this scenario, the aliens
are actually fallen angels acting in league with the anti-Christ (specifically the
'nephilim' mentioned in the Old Testament).

Seeming to contradict the biblical account of creation with the suggestion
that there were pre-Adamic space-aliens who helped 'create' the human race,
'would deceive even the elect [Christians already born-again] and will lead to

the setting up of antichrist on the world throne' ('UFOs and Conspiracy in Popular Culture' n.d.). As is typical of this discourse, they ground their claims in references to the Bible:

> Proof of artificially built structures on Cydonia Mars will lead to the conclusion that the entities responsible not only designed and guided our species through history, they also qualify as our gods . . . that the beings from Mars, and in UFOs, are the God of the Bible. This is THE strong delusion allowed for 'those dwelling on the earth to believe the lie' II Thess 2: 11 ('Invasion from Mars?' n.d.).

Though the topic and style of David and Brenda Flynn's *Watcher Website* is radically different than that of Laura and Dean VanDruff's *Acts17-11.com*, the Flynns demonstrate a shared ideology when they name Laura and Dean's site an 'End Time Bible study website'. Though they justify their linkage between the two sites on this basis, only one page of Laura and Dean's site is focused on the end times and only a few comments touch upon it at all.

In 1993, while working in the computer industry in Dallas, Texas, Laura and Dean both felt dissatisfied with their face-to-face church communities. Often simplifying difficult questions into 'legalistic' answers, the couple felt that their experiences with organized evangelical churches were not fully serving their spiritual needs (Personal correspondence 21 July 1999). Both of them stated that they had been 'born again' in the 1970s. In 1990, Dean experienced 'a powerful conveyance of the Holy Spirit'. He described it on the website saying, 'It was real . . . Submission to God in this event was one of the most terrifying and difficult experiences of my life, but has resulted in a crop of righteousness, peace and joy in the Holy Spirit' ('History, influences, background, etc.' n.d.). Both stating they were 'born again', they exhibited their first trait of the vernacular ideology of Christian fundamentalism: the experience of being reborn in Christ.

Based on their revelatory experiences, Dean and Laura began to believe that the Holy Spirit was pushing them to make changes in their lives. To try to enact such change, they began to invite their Christian friends to their home to read and discuss the Bible over simple dinners. Soon, this practice became a Saturday night tradition. Dean: 'We had a sense during that time that we had gotten swept into or caught up in something. I had been a Christian at that point for 13 years and gone to church and had a little bit of a sense of knowing God' (Personal interview 28 August 1999, San Jose, CA). Unlike their institutional church experiences, this informal group of friends gave Laura and Dean a renewed sense of spiritual presence.

Seldom bringing any particular topic to their meetings, they found that each evening the particular combination of individuals would (under the guidance of the Holy Spirit) give rise to important insights into biblical verses. Often friends-of-friends or acquaintances travelling through town would unexpectedly show up at these meetings with particular problems or ideas that yielded new insights. After a while, Dean began to carefully document the informal group's discussions. Soon he was writing them up and filing them away; often handing them around to other participants after the meeting and co-writing full discussions of the topics that had emerged.

In 1993, after a year or more of these meetings, Dean's job took the couple to San Jose, California. At that time, the Worldwide Web was exploding as a popular medium. So Dean decided to make his group's Bible studies available to his friends in both California and Texas by putting them online.

> When we wrote those studies – given what we have told you – we had in mind that there would be maybe fifteen people who would come; and it was for them. We had absolutely no idea of what I have just told you . . . that they would get spread around later. Ya know, read by thousands of people a day on the internet. [Laughs] It just seemed kinda funny. The limit of what we were doing was simply to serve the brothers and sisters in Christ that we knew (Personal correspondence 21 July 1999).

Inspired by the correspondence generated by their new web-presence, Laura and Dean felt that the spiritual lack in their church institutions was abated. They discovered an internet-based community of likeminded Christians who could share in discussions about their beliefs and values in more specific and intimate ways than they were finding through their real world churches. By actively seeking to share their understanding of the Bible, Laura and Dean were clearly evangelical. In this way, they exhibited a second trait of vernacular fundamentalism.

The satisfaction they gained through their virtual community was powerful and, in the case of Dean at least, surprising. As he put it, 'We find a life and fellowship on the internet that is embarrassing to admit! Who would have thought? Who would have believed it? [. . . that] the [Holy] Spirit is able to pierce through beyond mere characters floating on a screen' (Personal correspondence 21 July 1999). Not only did Dean and Laura suddenly start receiving inspiring emails from likeminded Christians, they were also brought into the virtual community of individuals engaged in fundamentalist discourse.

Their Biblical literalism emerges as a third trait of vernacular Christian fundamentalism. As with the Flynns, this literalism also emerges in their deployment of biblical quotes as authoritative. On an introductory page titled 'Doctrinal Statement', they group 69 quotations from the Bible under 19 single word or phrase heads like 'The Trinity', 'Inspiration of Scripture', 'Satan', 'The Fundamentals' and 'The End of The Age'. Even more strongly exhibiting a reliance on the 'Bible only' than did David and Brenda in the example above, these quotes are offered with no other explanatory material at all ('Principles on content, emphasis and doctrine' n.d.). On another page, they state that:

The Scripture should speak for itself to make every major point ... A fundamental requirement of each study is that it must accurately depict what Scripture teaches on the subject, as opposed to what is currently popular or would tickle the ears ('Doctrinal statement' n.d.).

With this emphasis on literalism, Laura and Dean exhibit a third trait of vernacular fundamentalism. However, it was their expression of the final definitive trait that most significantly linked them to the virtual Christian community. Analysing access logs for Dean and Laura's website, it was clear that there were hundreds of individuals looking at their website every day. Based on those logs, the few pages that had sections dealing with end times topics were the most often visited. While the end times may have both marked them as participants in fundamentalism and connected them with the most other believers, Dean expressed ambivalence about this aspect of his and Laura's site.

As early as 1999, Dean no longer paid much attention to end times discourse. However, he left up the End Time Study page at least as late as the writing of this article in the Fall of 2007. When asked about the page during an interview, he stated: 'Most eschatological teaching is shameful! Embarrassing. All these ideas distract and bring shame to the cause and name of Christ' (Personal interview 28 August 1999, San Jose, CA). Laura, at first quiet, spoke up. She stated that she was still interested in the topic and discussed it with some of her friends. A brief discussion ensued between them. Then Dean expanded on why he considered the topic 'shameful':

> We should be like virgins waiting to be consummated with our husbands! So we shouldn't be distracted. If our husband comes and we have our room all coated with charts about when he's gonna come, ya know, I don't think he's gonna say: 'Way to go!' It's like ... He would say: 'You have no idea what my coming means. It's *not* to see these charts!' [laughs] (Personal interview 28 August 1999, San Jose, CA).

Despite ambivalence for apocalyptic prophecy, the VanDruffs have become caught up with thousands of likeminded Christians into a new kind of virtual community based on a vernacular ideology. The use of internet media created the opportunity for a relatively small group to forge a new kind of fellowship based on the four definitive traits of vernacular fundamentalism. It seems that the 'Holy Spirit', as Dean put it, does indeed have the capacity to 'pierce beyond' the 'mere characters floating on a screen' (Personal interview 28 August 1999, San Jose, CA). Unmediated by institutional documents, religious leaders or community-based churches, those individuals touched by that Spirit enact a sort of virtual church. However, the individuals who can locate this church among the vast expanse of network media are an exclusive and exclusionary group.

The Problem of Geography-Free Community

Believing that they were acting in a way much like 'first century Christians', David specifically told me that they used the internet to enact their *ekklesia*. For David, 'any time people are together – two or more are gathered in His name: there you are! You're the *ekklesia*!' (Personal interview 17 October 1999, Helena, MT). Rejecting the need for institutional religion, David stated clearly that Brenda and his communication online functioned as a 'church'.

> There is no real reason you have to show up at a denomination or every Sunday show up at this certain location in the city or else you're a reprobate. And I think it's absolutely viable for the 'church', if you understand what I mean by that: the *ekklesia*; to meet on the internet. And I have seen it happen a lot. And that's pretty much where we hold our church (Personal interview 17 October 1999, Helena, MO).

In classical Greek, *ekklesia* referred to an assembly of important persons. In New Testament Greek, it came to refer to the congregation associated with a particular synagogue. When the Apostle Paul brought the Christian message to non-Jews, he made it clear that a shared knowledge of Christ's message (instead of Jewish heritage) was the prerequisite to membership in the Christian *ekklesia* (Colossians 1: 1–24). Both the Catholic and Eastern Churches emphasize the importance of institutional leaders having interpretative and doctrinal authority. In this sense, 'church' came to refer to the institutions of Christianity.

David, however, emphasizes the older meaning of 'church': the people who comprise a congregation. While individuals may not have always needed an overarching institution to be a 'church' in this sense, such institutions function to spread shared knowledge through institutional documents, religious leaders and community-based organizations. As those ideas are shared, they become the glue that holds the congregation together. When Brenda and David 'hold church' online however, the integration of network media into their daily spiritual lives gives them a new means to share ideas without any recourse to religious institutions. So doing, they enact a new kind of *ekklesia*.

Unlike most real-world communities, this virtual *ekklesia* is comprised of weakly linked individuals in the sense that they generally share no resources and seek no action beyond the sharing of ideas itself (Csermely 2006, Wellman and Guilia 1999). As a result, virtual communities such as these can exist freed of many geographic and social forces. With few conditions pressed upon them from the outside environment, these individuals can choose their beliefs (and the ways they express those beliefs) without confronting the obstacles normally associated with community organization, institutional structures and the need to share resources. As Heidi Campbell has argued, individuals involved in religion online can choose to engage in 'self-regulated forms of socialization' (2005: 188).

In the case of the virtual *ekklesia* that emerges from vernacular fundamentalism, the expression of the four definitive traits of the ideology enables like-minded believers to locate each other online when they already know the key terms. At the same time, individuals uninterested or unable to engage in this ideologically driven discourse can simply move through the web unaware. As a result, those who choose to participate in the discourse are primarily individuals who already share in its beliefs. They locate this virtual *ekklesia* as they seek out the specific topics cued by phrases like 'the Antichrist' or 'predicted in The Bible', and it is these topics that are the shared beliefs that define this church (Howard 1997, 2000).

The ability to pick and choose with whom to share religious information allows individuals to bypass the forces of 'civil society'. As Harris Breslow has described, 'civil society' can be imagined as a discursive space in which 'all may congregate where subjective identity and social membership are made palpably obvious' (1997: 254). When individuals choose to use new media to bypass broader publics to engage a public that is already in agreement with the fundamental literalism of their belief system, challenges to their literalism are unlikely to occur. Because literalism itself suggests that here is a single correct understanding to the biblical texts, the virtual *ekklesia* amplifies a tendency to discount alternate interpretations. The findings of this research suggest that in cases where civil society's normative force is not brought to bear on individuals' fundamentalist beliefs, those individuals are less likely to accommodate new or divergent ideas.

In this way, the internet offers a very particular benefit unavailable from a traditional church organization. Without recourse to institutional forms of power or any more public forum to offer alternate interpretations, the virtual *ekklesia* can link virtual community members with a very specific interest across vast amounts of space. Because virtual community members often have few if any local or real-world obligations, their primary function can be community building itself. Since these communities exist only virtually, they only exist in so far as the members are communicating. That communication, then, is enacted primarily so that the community itself can come into being. This individual empowerment made possible by network communication comes at a significant price. If individuals are able to filter out opposition to their views, those views go unchallenged. When the mechanisms for challenging widely held opinions are diminished, so too are the social processes by which a pluralistic society keeps a majority from silencing the voices of the minority.

References

Althusser, L. (1984[1976]), *Essays on Ideology*. London: Verso Press.

Ammerman, N. T. (1997), 'Organized religion in a voluntaristic society', *Sociology of Religion*, 58, 203–215.

Armstrong, K. (2000), *The Battle for God*. New York: Alfred A. Knopf.

Balmer, R. (2002), *Encyclopedia of Evangelicalism*. London: Westminster John Knox Press.

Balmer, R. and Winner, L. F. (2002), *Protestantism in America*. New York: Columbia University Press.

Barr, J. (1966), *Old and New in Interpretation: A Study of the Two Testaments*. London: SCM Press.

Barr, J. (1978), *Fundamentalism*. Philadelphia: Westminster Press.

Breslow, H. (1997), 'Civil society, political economy, and the internet', in S. G. Jones (ed.), *Virtual Culture: Identity and Communication in Cybersociety*. London: Sage Publications, pp. 236–257.

Campbell, H. (2005), *Exploring Religious Community Online: We are One in the Network*. New York: Peter Lang Publishing.

Csermely, P. (2006), *Weak Links: Stabilizers of Complex Systems from Proteins to Social Networks*. New York: Springer Verlag Publishers.

'Doctrinal statement' (n.d.), *Acts17-11.com*, retrieved 30 September 2006 from <http://www.acts17-11.com/doctrinal.html>.

Eagleton, T. (1991), *Ideology: An Introduction*. London: Verso Press.

Harris, H. A. (1998), *Fundamentalism and Evangelicals*. Oxford: Clarendon Press.

Hendershot, H. (2004), *Shaking the World for Jesus: Media and Conservative Evangelical Culture*. Chicago, Illinois: University of Chicago Press.

'History, influences, background, etc.' (n.d.), *Acts17-11.com*, retrieved 30 September 2006 from <http://www.acts17-11.com/mission_history.html>.

Howard, R. G. (2008), 'Electronic hybridity: The persistent processes of the vernacular web', *Journal of American Folklore*, 121(480), 192–218.

Howard, R. G. (2006a), 'Fundamentalism', in D. A. Stout (ed.), *Encyclopedia of Religion, Communication, and Media*. New York: Routledge, pp. 155–160.

Howard, R. G. (2006b), 'Sustainability and narrative plasticity in online apocalyptic discourse after September 11, 2001', *Journal of Media and Religion*, 5(1), 25–47.

Howard, R. G. (2005a), 'A theory of vernacular rhetoric: The case of the "Sinner's Prayer" online', *Folklore*, 116(3), 175–191.

Howard, R. G. (2005b), 'Sustainability and radical rhetorical closure: The case of the 1996 "Heaven's Gate" newsgroup campaign', *Journal of Communication and Religion*, 28(1), 99–130.

Howard, R. G. (2005c), 'Toward a theory of the Worldwide Web vernacular: The case for pet cloning', *Journal of Folklore Research*, 42(3), 323–360.

Howard, R. G. (2005d), 'The double bind of the Protestant Reformation: The birth of fundamentalism and the necessity of pluralism', *Journal of Church and State*, 47, 91–108.

Howard, R. G. (2000), 'On-line ethnography of dispensationalist discourse: Revealed versus negotiated truth', in D. Cowan and J. K. Hadden (eds), *Religion on the Internet*. New York: Elsevier Press, pp. 225–246.

Howard, R. G. (1997), 'Apocalypse in your in-box: End-times communication on the internet', *Western Folklore*, 56(3/4), 295–315.

Kellstedt, L. and Smidt, C. (1991), 'Measuring fundamentalism: An analysis of different operational strategies', *Journal for the Scientific Study of Religion*, 30, 259–278.

Lindlof, T. R. (2002), 'Interpretive community: An approach to media and religion', *Journal of Media and Religion*, 1(1), 61–74.

Marsden, G. (1980), *Fundamentalism and American Culture: The Shaping of Twentieth Century Evangelicalism, 1870–1925*. New York: Oxford University Press.

Marty, M. and Appleby, R. S. (eds) (1995), *Fundamentalisms Comprehended. The Fundamentalism Project*, vol. 5. Chicago: University of Chicago Press.

Moore, R. L. (1994), *Selling God: American Religion in the Marketplace of Culture*. Oxford: Oxford University Press.

Perkin, H. (2000), 'American fundamentalism and the selling of god', *The Political Quarterly*, 71(1), 79–89.

Primiano, L. N. (1995), 'Vernacular religion and the search for method in religious folklife', *Western Folklore*, 54(1), 37–56.

'Principles on content, emphasis and doctrine' (n.d.), *Acts17-11.com*, retrieved 30 September 2006 from <http://www.acts17-11.com/mission_emphasis.html>.

Schultze, Q. J. (2003), *Christianity and the Mass Media in America: Toward a Democratic Accommodation*. East Lansing, MI: Michigan State University Press.

Strozier, C. B. (1994), *Apocalypse: On the Psychology of Fundamentalism in America*. Boston: Beacon Press.

'Why doesn't God just show up now?' (n.d.), Watcher Website, retrieved 1 April 2000 from <http://www.mt.net/~watcher/most.html>.

'Seraphim, cherubim & Ezekiel's wheels, aliens, nephilim & the days of Noah' (n.d.), Watcher Website, retrieved 5 June 2007 from <http://www.mt.net/%7Ewatcher/noah.html>.

'Invasion from Mars?' (n.d.), Watcher Website, retrieved 5 June 2007 from <http://www.mt.net/%7Ewatcher/antimars.html>.

'UFOs & Conspiracy in Popular Culture' (n.d.), Watcher Website, retrieved 5 June 2007 from <http://www.mt.net/%7Ewatcher/endtimedelusion.html>.

Wellman, B. and Gulia, M. (1999), 'Virtual communities as communities: Net surfers don't ride alone', in M. A. Smith and P. Kollock (eds), *Communities in Cyberspace*. New York: Routledge, pp. 167–194.

Yoder, D. (1974), 'Toward a definition of folk religion', *Western Folklore*, 33(1), 2–15.

Chapter 9

Opus Dei *and the Role of the Media in Constructing Fundamentalist Identity*

Claire Hoertz Badaracco

Introduction

When media frame religious identity questions through cultural artifacts, using cartoons, films or popular books, and in doing so offend fundamentalist groups by ridicule or irony, they 'confiscate' historical memory in favour of social commentary, provoking mass audiences to react violently out of a religious conviction that the mass media undermine their identity – as Muslim audiences did in the Danish cartoon controversy. The media both construct the identity conflict and negotiate its meaning through mediation of the conflict, serving both as cause and effect by storytelling about groups on the margin of mass culture, who they are and what their beliefs mean to public culture. By contrast, yet similar in terms of its demonstration of both fundamentalisms in popular culture and how mass media are perceived to usurp the collective identity of religious groups by offering a challenge to their position as 'outsiders' or 'strangers', the resistance offered by *Opus Dei*, a fundamentalist Catholic sect defamed in *The DaVinci Code*, demonstrates how employing multimedia to resist the false cultural identity within the narrative of the 'global blockbuster' could be opposed and capitalized upon by collective cultural resistance. While condemning its depiction in the story as false, *Opus Dei* used both notoriety and increased visibility to expand membership in the once clandestine sect. According to the Prelature of *Opus Dei* in the United States, the film insulted Catholic identity:

'*Opus Dei* members are falsely depicted as murdering, lying, drugging people, and otherwise acting unethically, thinking that it is justified for the sake of God, the Church, or *Opus Dei* [. . .] Besides attributing criminal activity to *Opus Dei*, *The DaVinci Code* also falsely depicted *Opus Dei* as being focused on gaining wealth and power [. . .] [The film] makes it appear that members practice bloody mortifications. In fact, though history indicates that some Catholic saints have done so, *Opus Dei* members do not do this [. . .] Some members also make limited use of the cilice, [. . .] [but] *The Da Vinci Code*'s description [. . .] is greatly exaggerated and distorted ('The *Da Vinci Code*, the Catholic Church and *Opus Dei*' 2006).

Perhaps the conservative Christian lay worker group took a page from the manual of Mel Gibson, who had been accused of being anti-Semitic in his film *The Passion*, and had employed an affinity marketing grassroots approach in *The Passion*'s release. Gibson silenced those he anticipated as critics by an embargo; only those who could be counted on to praise the film were allowed to see it in previews. Beyond the fence were media and other denominations. Tyndale, the religious publisher, and Icon, the religious marketing specialists, packaged biblical lessons for the pulpit and disseminated them through the evangelical parish structure.

Opus Dei Catholics used similar affinity marketing tactics to oppose *The DaVinci Code* film, based on the only global best-selling religious fiction book to outpace sales of the *Left Behind* series as a cult classic about biblical fundamentalism, blending the search for the historical Jesus in a slick murder–romance genre. The *Left Behind* series is a fundamentalist narrative written by a cleric and ghostwritten by a screenwriter, interpreting the *Book of Revelation* literally, in the context of the extreme beliefs in Millennialism (Badaracco 1998, 2006).

Given the profitability of contemporary religious fiction produced as books with film rights and multimedia product lines that embed prejudice against 'the Other' in entertainment commodities, one rightly expects a repeat performance, while analysing how groups best manage the media assaults on their religious identity. Embedded in the controversies of the cartoons or films are dubious crossover messages re-contextualizing biblical history as a basis upon which to build fictional identities. While there are several recent comparable cases, almost enough to constitute a type of fundamentalism, where mediation of religious prejudice resulted in contested meaning or in conflict throughout the world and web today, this chapter describes the role media played in both disseminating prejudice and responding to positioning on the fringe on the part of the offended group – processes through which negative images contextualized religious prejudice against fundamentalists as out of step with mainstream culture.

Fundamentalism and Popular Culture

Rhetorically speaking, fundamentalists need the margins to define themselves against the commodities offered through mediation, the 'irreligious' forces of the mainstream media that are in opposition not only to the philosophical principles of the fringe, but to their literalism, to their logo-centrism. While fundamentalists caricatured in media productions might protest, they want to be careful not to protest too much. Their *habitus* is on the margin of mediated culture. Fundamentalist thinking characterizes the media as 'the opposition' as much as the media frame the fundamentalists as characters in a secular drama that opposes dark and light, past and present, centre and edge in popular culture. Fundamentalists take pride in being not of the media world, but that does not mean that they hesitate to use media to defend their identity or to evangelize.

Hypothetically, a fundamentalist sect treats the power of the Word as something transformational, transcending ethnic, geographic and cultural borders, and the text is given primacy over the image, as something that achieves identity for the self and attributes identity to believers (Hoover 2006). The difference between logo-centric versus ethnocentric fundamentalisms is that the first group are believers who tend to achieve their identity as 'People of the Book', conserving as extreme the literal interpretation of ancient, sacred texts, while the second category of believers tend to construct their identity through mediated interpretation of the imagined community, the ethnic inheritance that positions ideas about authority residing with hierarchical patriarchs – clergy, family, church, mosque, synagogue – categories articulated as masculine and read as primary. In this world, the feminine is personified as both Mystery and as corruptive in its ability to overthrow the primacy of patriarchy. In terms of mediated popular cultural paradigms, the woman is the quintessential audience, the observer of God's action in the world, and a witness to male primacy (Jeffrey 2003, Nord 2004, Anderson 1983, Lannstrom 2004). One could write a separate chapter about the role of women in the fundamentalist fiction of LaHaye, Gibson, Dan Brown and best-selling evangelical romance fiction tracts. The focus of this chapter, however, is on the mediation of collective fundamentalist identity both caused and reified by and through mass media.

The role of media in fundamentalist identity can transform images of 'the enemy', legitimize leaders or groups, increase public fear or intensify conflict. As Wolfsfeld (2001: 4) observed in relation to violence in the Middle East and in Ireland, 'a high level of sensationalism in a media environment . . . invariably worsens a situation'. Using political conflict as a metaphor about how religion is transformed into fundamentalist ideology, it is fair to state that narrative borders attribute identity through characterization, alleging who belongs to the mainstream, who inhabits the fringe and whether or not resistance is legitimate. Yet the first ethical responsibility of the media is not to establish borders but to build bridges (Wolfsfeld 2001). For example, the political violence in Islamic states in response to the cartoons depicting the Prophet Mohammed in *Jyllands-Posten* is a study in media ethics (Norby Bonde 2007: 33–48). The subject of this chapter is another case with a rather different outcome: Dan Brown's global best-seller *The DaVinci Code* defamed *Opus Dei*, the fundamentalist Catholic organization, and caricatured the divinity of Christ. *Opus*

Dei used savvy public relations and strategic media management to spin the insulting caricature into a positive, creating new affinity groups and recruiting new members among sympathizers who heard about the group through the fictional storyline in book and film.

Opus Dei and The DaVinci Code

The premise of *The Code* is, briefly, that the Papacy kept in its Vatican library secret documents that would reveal a line of descendents from the offspring of Christ and Mary Magdalene, and that the fourth-century Roman emperor Constantine invented and enforced the doctrine of the divinity of Christ for political reasons. From a critical standpoint, the argument might be made about how the plot adapts *James Bond* and the *Thomas Crowne Affair*, starting with a murder in the Louvre. An albino *Opus Dei* monk murders people as he searches for the Holy Grail in a fast-paced thriller where men are capable of action, women of reaction. Prior to the film, *Opus Dei* had very low recognition among Catholics. After the film, the growth in membership resulting from its increased visibility served to normalize the sect's image in the world Church, moving it from extreme marginality slightly closer to Catholic cultural centrality.

Yet *Opus Dei* is a fundamentalist organization that uses its fundamentalism to achieve group identity, set against secular culture: opposition is part of its story. Further, *Opus Dei* enjoys the distance from so-called 'cafeteria' Catholicism (those Americans who pick and choose among doctrines), and from 'cultural' Catholicism, the type common in Italy, where there continues to be a strong loyalty to the ethnic traditions implied by claiming membership in the Church, as distinct from church attendance and behaviours consistent with dogma. *Opus Dei* thrives as a group that wants to occupy the *liminal* space between 'clergy' and 'lay' groups, emphasizing good works over beliefs. In comparison to the Muslims who were offended by mediated portrayals of the Prophet Muhammad and whose violent protests set them in opposition to 'The West', the *Opus Dei* group is a fundamentalist sect even within the Roman Catholic church, which itself is 'fundamentalist' in the sense that the historical Jesus and the organizational identity as the 'one true church' based on that history is rooted in a logo-centric reading of Biblical scripture.

There was nothing transcendental about how the sect responded to the film. *Opus Dei*'s campaign used reputation management techniques from the contemporary practice of Madison Avenue professionals to counter the negative portrayal of its organization in the film version of *The Code*. Inherent in the strategy of cultural resistance was the use of global media to create an impression that the fringe group was mainstream, by projecting an image of normalcy by a barrage of historical data about itself, its members and its ideals, rather than confrontation or denying the negative images contained in the production itself, which they dismissed as 'ludicrous'. But ludicrous in popular culture is the first threshold of credibility in opposing the arcane. Among the allegations about the sect were that they mistreated women, forcing them to clean the men's living quarters without pay, and that *Opus Dei* bailed out the Vatican Bank and as a result the founder of the organization was put on the fast track to sainthood bending the rules of canonization. Among the other charges were that the group engaged in 'brainwashing', 'coercion' and 'aggressive recruiting', according to the organization, 'tarring' them with the same epithets used to describe cults (Hoover 2006: 33).

The media 'lesson' learned, according to *Opus Dei* media relations workers in a report available on their website, was that by using communication rather than confrontation, the group actually established an image before an American if not a global public where there had been mystery and suspicion before (Carroggio et al. 2006). *Opus Dei* constructed a strategic response that both communicated with the sources of production and appealed to *The DaVinci Code* audience as two separate objectives in its overall strategy. While *Opus Dei* failed to exert control over the original source, the book on which the film was based, and failed to diminish the popularity of the negative portrayal among anti-Christians or the unchurched, the sect's response did raise its media visibility, receiving positive press coverage as a result of proactive media relations.

As the book and film about a murder in the Louvre demonstrated, religious conspiracy is a profitable genre. Examined from a marketing perspective, Mel Gibson's *The Passion* was less about religion than it was about violence, and the dramatization of 'end-times' by Timothy LaHaye is similarly violent. With an increasing number of media productions blurring the distinction between biblical history and fiction, or between superstition and religious belief, spinning the spin-offs may be a proactive strategy that could be more widely adapted in the future, rather than violent responses to insult by the offended parties.[1]

In this case, Michael Baigent lost his copyright violation lawsuit in the U.K. against *The DaVinci Code* author Daniel Brown. In the lawsuit he had claimed that Brown's book plagiarized Baigent's idea of a married Jesus from his 1982 book *Holy Blood, Holy Grail*. The lawsuit coincided with Baigent's 2007 release of *The Jesus Papers* in the US bookstores.[2] Baigent's legal action achieved the pre-publication notoriety that advanced sales of the book.

Curiously, the blasphemy in Baigent's work was met with little resistance from the worldwide Christian community. More surprising was the seriousness with which presumably 'objective' American news media treated Baigent's ideas about the Vatican's suppression of 'lost documents'. As the central axis of mediatization is that the fictional storyline or framed cause itself becomes reality through repetition and widespread dissemination, the success of *The Code* as entertainment can be seen as having influenced the reality of the perceptions about religion.

The image of the Vatican as clandestine fit the stereotype of Catholics as both loyalists to authoritarian models of power, obedient to a fault and dogmatic about their interpretation of biblical principles. Yet the image of fundamentalists in entertainment media makes a virtue of their ambiguous quirkiness (the albino monk is both ominous and pathetic) engaging audiences through an idiosyncratic appeal that uses religion as a backdrop for the dark side. Seen through the lens of popular culture, the pious Christians who regard highly the view they have of themselves as fundamentalists, savour their distance from the values embraced by mass media. *Opus Dei* wrote, in defence of celibate members:

'Numerary members' – a minority – choose a vocation of celibacy in order to be available to organize the activities of *Opus Dei*. They do not, however, take vows, wear robes, sleep on straw mats, spend all their time in prayer and corporal mortification, or in any other way live like *The Da Vinci Code's* depiction of its monk character . . . [N]umeraries have regular secular professional work' ('*The Da Vinci Code*, the Catholic Church and *Opus Dei*' 2006).

Yet this expression of 'truth' masks resistance to the formula beneath: the idea of the historic conspiracy and lost documents has been replayed time and again in media and with success. The idea of the 'oddball' group on the social margin, in league with both the international art market at the Louvre and the Pope, hiding the sexuality of Jesus Christ (imagine the furor if it had been a movie about the Prophet Muhammad) became contagious. Its anachronistic or 'spooky' image was precisely the point of fascination by the media. Even the *National Geographic* got the fever, featuring the alleged *Gospel of Judas* in its May 2006 issue and turning a television special into a DVD.

The grave professional tone used by 'investigative journalists' who followed this story imitated another style of a 'search for the historical Jesus', demonstrating the dilemma religion news writers have when reporting on sacred history, differentiating between fact as stereotype and prejudice embedded in fiction. The media frenzy, as it turned out, was over a document of questionable provenance rejected by Yale University's Beinecke division of rare books and manuscripts. Despite the dubious claim for authenticity in its provenance, the individual who claimed to be the archeological discoverer of the manuscript reaped $2.5 million for the 'find'. When *The New York Times* (2006) reported on the $2.5 million *Gospel of Judas*, it did so not on the business or entertainment pages but on page one, centre, above the fold – the place where Americans usually read about the War in Iraq. Notably, the story appeared during the Easter-Passover holiday. In offering its readers this vignette about 'historical archeology of the real Jesus', it displaced historical events with fictional ones.

Opus Dei Beyond the Fiction

The Dan Brown novel published in 2003 by Doubleday, included prefatory material that claimed its portrayal of *Opus Dei* was accurate and alleged that Christianity, and the Catholic Church in particular, is a 'hoax', invented by the fourth-century Roman emperor Constantine, according to Marc Carroggio, who managed *Opus Dei*'s Rome office of media relations at the time (Carroggio et al. 2006: 1).

Contrary to the fiction, the actual *Opus Dei* organization, though it has little visibility, never set out to be a secret organization or a cult. Founded in 1928 in Latin America, and in the USA in 1949 in Chicago, currently it registers more than 87,000 members worldwide, both men and women ('Members' n.d.), with about 3,000 members in the USA, none of whom are monks ('*Opus Dei* in the U.S.' n.d.). According to *Opus Dei*, 'Freedom and personal responsibility' are key aspects of membership ('Message' n.d.) and the organization 'commits itself to provide its members the spiritual support and guidance they need to respond faithfully to God's call' (Coverdale n.d.).

When the founder was canonized in 2002, 'an audience of 350,000 over-flowed St. Peter's Square, stretching to the Tiber river' according to the press office of the organization (B. Finnerty, personal interview 15 January 2006). The organization manages what it calls 'numerous' educational and charitable initiatives; that is, seven hospitals, 15 universities, 36 K–12 schools and 97 vocational-technical schools worldwide. Pope Benedict is a member, and he blessed both a statue of the founder, when it was installed in the Vatican, and Bishop Javier Echevarria Rodriguez, the current head of the organization. In September 2006, Bishop Rodriguez visited New York, Montreal, Toronto, Vancouver, San Francisco and Houston in what the *National Catholic Reporter* called a 'victory tour' for the organization, which had seen a growth in membership after the film. The same article claimed that the leaders of *Opus Dei* refer to the increase in members as the '*Da Vinci Code* bump' ('*Opus Dei* head on pastoral visit' 2006).

Further, as Marc Carroggio, Brian Finnerty and Juan Manuel Mora observed, the case raised issues in media ethics, though they did not use those exact words. Leaders of *Opus Dei* asked, 'What responsibilities do the entertainment industry have to be sensitive and fair in the portrayal of different religious, ethnic and social groups? And how can offended parties respond, defending their own rights, while respecting freedom of expression and the freedom of the market-place?' (Carroggio et al. 2006).

When the novel was published in 2003, the organization tried to 'ignore the book as much as possible', according to spokesmen for *Opus Dei*. They took a strategically responsive, rather than defiantly reactive or defensive stance. Members of the organization thought the book so poorly written and crafted, from a literary standpoint, and so ludicrous from an historical standpoint that they thought no one would read it. Then it became a global bestseller. Within nine months, they had received such a flood of inquiries, they posted a statement on the organization's website that *The Code* was a fictional work, unreliable, not credible; they also created a resource list to answer questions.

Opus Dei's Crisis Management Plan

When *Opus Dei* learned that Sony bought the film rights to the novel, they were less sanguine. Ron Howard's film version of *The DaVinci Code* opened on 19 May 2006, with a marketing budget of $40 million in the USA alone. *Opus Dei*'s strict disciples collaborated with the American Catholic Bishops to disseminate information about what had been identified as a 'secret' organization countering the image by raising its public profile. Similar responses to the book were launched by Bishops in Mexico, Poland and Brazil (Carroggio et al. 2006).

The communication offices of the organization divided their responses into two phases. In Phase A, 2004–2005, they avoided confrontation or any style of 'polemic', because they knew 'controversy' would generate more publicity for the film and spread farther the negative image they sought to undermine. In 2004, the chief priest leading *Opus Dei* requested that the name the organization not be used – not a realistic request as Hollywood saw it. Then Father Tom Bohlin requested a meeting with Amy Pascal, head of Sony film at the time. Though the meeting was declined, Sony sent a letter. During this time, Sony did not communicate any information of substance about the film to *Opus Dei*, which learned about the release of the film through the press, along with millions of other readers, viewers and potential filmgoers (Carroggio et al. 2006).

Did Sony have an ethical obligation to communicate with the group they were depicting in a false light? Media ethics would suggest that any group, however much they were on the margin, should be granted some basic rights by the mainstream media. There is a further consideration under the burden of corporate social responsibility. Should a global multimedia empire such as Sony offer a public apology for giving offence to religious groups? Should Sony retract the insult by refusing to produce the film, allowing another corporation to pick it up and garner the profits? What about the Buddhist values that describe qualities of inner being, theories of dependent origination, that all members of society bear similar obligations of universal responsibility to work for social harmony and to uphold a mutual respect and tolerance for all religions?

Apparently, the global media power did not do as it said. Two days prior to the movie's release, *Opus Dei* issued a press release accusing Sony of violating its own internal code of ethics. The press release pointed out that the Sony Code of Conduct, approved by the senior management of the corporation on

28 May 2003 contained the following assertions and declarations of universal social responsibility:

> Personnel (of Sony) are required to give careful consideration to cultural and regional differences in performing their duties (section 1.3);
>
> No Personnel may make racial or religious slurs, jokes or any other comments or conduct in the workplace that create a hostile work environment (section 2.4);
>
> With respect to publicity, Sony commits itself not to engage in false publicity that misleads or slanders others (section 3.4). (Hurtado 2006)

When religious groups are belittled in media fiction or caricature, what the Dalai Lama terms a 'secular' or 'universal' code of ethics should prevail, one that precludes giving offence to religious groups in a world where many people are not religious (Dalai Lama 2001: 180–186).

Phase B was in 2006, after the producer Ron Howard said that the organization not only would be mentioned, but that its fictional depiction 'would be faithful' neither to history nor to any fact *but to the novel* (emphasis mine). This statement propelled the organization into a more aggressive posture regarding the anticipated film. They created their own media ground and tried to draw the audience onto that ground, rather than be forced into a reactive mode. They started to present their own identity to the public using all forms of media, beginning with a strategic session calling together people from the media relations offices of New York, London, Paris, Madrid, Cologne, Lagos and Montreal.

The meeting of the global offices of *Opus Dei* media relations people determined that there was an organizational identity crisis precipitated by this film that had to do first with the fundamental beliefs that define Christianity, secondarily with the image of Catholics and third with their organization. Many Christians link their identity with the belief that Jesus Christ was the son of God the Father. Catholics' most contested belief is that the body and blood of Christ continues on materially in this world in the sacramental wine and bread. *Opus Dei*'s sacred beliefs have to do with the papal succession direct from St. Peter, whom Christ commissioned to be the rock upon which the Church would be built. So as the *Opus Dei* media relations people created a strategy of resistance, they focused on the most universalizable or primary belief, not the tertiary one, which many Christians would dispute.

The novel and film were a marketing phenomenon that could not be stopped, and those parodied were wise to recognize that fact and respond accordingly. The only action they could take would be to neutralize the negative image by implementing 'a communications plan that would be worldwide in its scope, Christian in its content and positive in its tone' (Carroggio et al. 2006).

The principle objectives of the crisis communication plan designed to neutralize the negatives were to differentiate the organization's identity from the fiction, to renew its request to Sony to 'avoid giving offense to Christians by a free decision, not through pressure or threats [. . .] nobody would utter words of censure' (Carroggio et al. 2006).

The timeline over 2006 included an interview with one international news agency, the 'first official answer' to Ron Howard's interview published in *Newsweek* that featured the movie on the cover. The interview reiterated the organization's message: that the fiction offended Christians, that religious beliefs ought to be respected and that Sony had been asked to respect their religious beliefs. On 14 February 2006, Sony Pictures launched its own website, www.davincichallenge.com, where the film producers invited *Opus Dei* and all world Christians to comment.

Opus Dei responded by observing that they had asked Sony to avoid the offence, not to provide web space for people to respond to the offence and observed, 'we refused to join this "mediated" dialogue on their sponsored website, and instead continued the dialogue on our own terms' (Carroggio et al. 2006).

A coalition of the US Catholics formed an initiative they called 'DaVinci Outreach' (davincioutreach.com), and produced a Q&A book, *The DaVinci Deception*, the best-selling book and film precipitated a flurry of other publications and a film (Carroggio et al. 2006).

Rather than call for a film boycott of *The Code* by Catholics, the offended believers used mass media not only to resist, but to recruit. They adapted web designs originally formatted by Dan Brown's film organization for evangelization of nonbelievers. Reaching ordinary Catholics with information about the *Opus Dei* organization, they provided key copy points for priests and ideas about how to integrate the conflict into sermons, so that they could counter the anti-Christian messages in the film from the pulpit (Carroggio et al. 2006).[3] While opposition among Catholics to the film as prejudicial and degrading has been 'building', according to *Opus Dei*'s website, the proactive media counter-offensive waged by the Catholic Church was organized, media-savvy and globally accessible to both pro- and anti-Christian factions.

The Media Coverage

In the three months prior to the release of *The Code* film, mainstream media focused their collective lens on *Opus Dei*: on 18 April 2006 Diane Sawyer broadcast live for *Good Morning America* from the *Opus Dei* offices in Manhattan. In June of 2006, Chris Mathews devoted a full hour to *Opus Dei*. Other stories appeared on all three networks, including NBC's *Meet the Press*, Fox's *Greta Van Sustern* and programmes on CNN. Print media were equally zealous: stories appeared in *The New York Times*, on the Associated Press, *The Los Angeles Times*, *The Washington Post*, *The Wall Street Journal* and other news print forms. A cover story in *Time* magazine of 24 April 2006 put the 3,000 member *Opus Dei* organization located on Lexington Avenue into the midst of the media frenzy. MSNBC featured a web exclusive. 'It's like trying to feed an army', according to Brian Finnerty, in charge of media relations for *Opus Dei* (B. Finnerty, personal interview 1 May 2006).

On 19 April 2006, one month to the day prior to *The DaVinci Code* film release, *Opus Dei* released a half-hour video of its own, profiling members of the organization: and made the DVD easily obtainable, free on its website (www.opusdei.org). One priest member, based in Rome, a graduate of the 'real Harvard', as he put in on his website, maintained a blog (Pentin 2005). Father John Wauck, a priest and member of *Opus Dei*, poked fun at the movie by pointing out that 'the real Silas' was Silas Agbim, a stockbroker from Nigeria living in Brooklyn with his wife Ngozi. They hosted a reception on 15 May 2006 in New York for Harambee, an *Opus Dei* educational charity raising funds for Africa. The reception was staged at the Dahesh Museum in NY, which is located across the street from Sony Corporation, which produced the film (B. Finnerty, personal interview 1 May 2006).

The Catholic Exchange of *Opus Dei* published a book-length response to Frequently Asked Questions, *The DaVinci Deception*, to address the errors in *The DaVinci Code*. And a coalition of Catholic groups including the high profile Catholic League, led by spokesman William Donahue, made a series of media appearances. To make amends, Doubleday published *The Way* on 9 May 2006, a collection of points for prayer written by *Opus Dei* founder, Saint Josemaria Escriva (B. Finnerty, personal interview 1 May 2006).

In a reputation management campaign that the Italian Newspaper *La Stampa* called 'Operation Transparency', the organization opened up to the press about what went on at its headquarters, *Opus Dei* arranged for journalists to tour 'the real Murray Hill Place', in New York on the corner of Lexington Avenue and 34th Street, which the novel depicted as the worldwide headquarters. According to Brian Finnerty, head of media relations for the New York facility, when 'dozens of journalists' visited, they missed the 'torture chambers' mentioned in the book (B. Finnerty, personal interview 1 May 2006). Rather, they found the offices of the Regional Vicar of the USA, a 30-room conference centre, another centre for university students and young professionals and accommodations for the team that manages the facility. The centre estimated that about 10,000 people annually attend retreats, conferences, cultural lectures and the like at the facility (B. Finnerty, personal interview 1 May 2006).

Opus Dei's strategy targeted not merely its belittlement by Sony in the film. In their response, the organization attempted to normalize its fundamentalist image, portray its strict observance as mainstream. They did so by emphasizing a public image acceptable to the universal mediated secular culture through a variety of tactics and media products, relaying what they deemed were the 'facts' about its identity. Their primary goal was to counteract the charges that they were extreme or a sect of Catholicism. The St. Josemaria Institute of Chicago produced a documentary, *Passionately Loving the World: Ordinary Americans Living the Spirituality of St. Josemaria*. The documentary consists of interviews with members of the lay organization throughout the USA 'whose lives have been touched by *Opus Dei*'s founder' (B. Finnerty, personal interview 1 May 2006). Clips of the film were picked up as news and run on CNN and ABC. The website on which the DVD could be ordered was activated on 15 April 2006, and 'within hours', according to the organization's media relations spokesman, 'we began receiving orders for the DVD from around the world: Trinidad and Tobago, Kuwait, India, Australia, Canada, South America, Europe,' and 'even one order from Wichita, Kansas' (B. Finnerty, personal interview 1 May 2006).

Through the Catholic Exchange, *Opus Dei* prepared a media kit, including 'homily helps', a diocesan plan for Adult Faith Formation Coordinators, Directors of Religious Education, key copy points about the errors in the Code for priests and deacons, and a month's worth of lessons for discussion groups in parishes, along with the posters and advertising materials to publicize the sessions, in addition to materials for Youth Ministers, all available without charge on website www.davinciantidote.com.

The organization made unprecedented use of its website to communicate both proactively and reactively. The website offered information in 22 languages, and recorded more than three million visits.

On 6 April 2006, the Communications office of *Opus Dei* in Tokyo, sent a letter addressed to Sony Corporation and its shareholders, asking that a final version of the movie not contain references that might offend. The religious group offered to give them information about the 'real *Opus Dei*', and petitioned the directors of Sony about the possibility of including a disclaimer in the soon to be released film that 'any similarity is purely coincidental', to stress the difference between the fiction in entertainment and the reality. This action, 'would be a gesture of respect towards the figure of Jesus, to the history of the Church and to the religious beliefs of viewers' (B. Finnerty, personal interview 1 May 2006). Once the letter was put on the *Opus Dei* website, it was picked up by media worldwide. By putting the letter on the website, according to media relations officials, *Opus Dei* hoped that when the movie was released, everyone would recognize it in the language of the organization's news release as a 'comedy of errors' about Christianity. Because Sony stonewalled the inquiry, saying it would not release information about the film, *Opus Dei* appealed again to Sony, to its 'great tradition' and sense of 'social responsibility', to attach a preface to the film, a disclaimer that the work is fiction ('Open letter to Sony' 2006). They were joined in their appeal by the conservative Catholic League for Religious and Civil Rights. Sony refused the idea of a disclaimer. *Opus Dei* released several statements expressing 'sadness', according to the letter, because the novel and film imply that 'the Christian Faith is founded on a lie, and the Catholic Church has over the centuries employed criminal and violent means to keep people in ignorance' (B. Finnerty, personal interview 1 May 2006).

Seizo Inahata, Information Officer for *Opus Dei*, Japan, argued in his appeal to Sony, that by acknowledging that in the media today the 'name of God' is 'used to justify hatred and violence', the producers could make a firm purpose of amendment ('Open letter to Sony' 2006). The *Opus Dei* media relations office in Japan saw in 'The public declaration . . . of unresolved problem' (B. Finnerty, personal interview 1 May 2006) another opportunity to pull the attention away from the film itself, towards their own identity and get into the news with the differences between the two. When they failed to elicit a response from Sony, they issued a release quoting Sony's words back to them, writing that 'its businesses have direct or indirect impact on the societies in which it operates' and that 'there can be no prosperity for a company that does not consider the environment and society' (Hurtado 2006).

The letter was part of *Opus Dei*'s overall reputation management strategy, to 'treat the media as an ally', respond to the flood of media inquiries, and thereby 'generate a worldwide public dialogue' (B. Finnerty, personal interview 1 May 2006). To counter the producers' marketing push consisting of mass media advertisements, in both traditional print and digital media, *Opus Dei* concluded that it did not have the means to compete. So the Information Office strategy was to respond to marketing with information, open conversation with journalists, giving priority to all requests for interviews (B. Finnerty, personal interview 1 May 2006).

Third, the *Opus Dei* organization generated news and fed it to the media. The United States Conference of Catholic Bishops' Communication Campaign produced a one hour documentary, which NBC ran in the third week of May 2006, in prime time, designed to coincide with the release of the film. Titled *Jesus Decoded*, the website is instructive, providing information about how to obtain the DVD of the documentary, with a sample trailer for viewing on the website. The film *Jesus Decoded* aims to 'bring authentic Catholic teaching about Jesus Christ back into focus' (Vlazny 2006). The theoretical construct of the lens and the gaze in mediated communication, elevates the principle of what a woman should look at, and how she should be viewed. The relationship between subject and object in media analysis is further played out in the advertisement for the film, presenting a strong visual contrast to the visual cliché, the eyes of The Mona Lisa, used to advertise Howard's film of Brown's novel, cropped in publicity blurbs, so they resemble the eyes of a woman veiled by a *burkha* – everything else is hidden but the eyes.

In stark contrast, the full face of Christ, eyes wide and open as a Byzantine Icon, look straight into the reader's in the advertisement for the UCCB film, promising to restore the word 'Mystery' to the religious connotation, as opposed to the mediated context, where the word connotes the conspiracy.

Carroggio, Finnerty and Mora concluded that through ecclesial cooperation, building an alliance with journalists by creating news and being transparent to all inquiries for news and interview with authoritative spokespersons, they succeeded in creating a global awareness about the 'unfair' portrayal of Christianity, the Catholic Church, and the *Opus Dei* organization. 'Public opinion is putting the DaVinci Code in its place', according to a media relations staffer for the organization (B. Finnerty, personal interview 1 May 2006). Though their strategies worked in many respects, they never did succeed in getting a direct line of communication to Sony: everything was filtered first through news, then advertisement, then the book, the film, the web. They said, 'The *DaVinci Code* has given us many headaches [. . .] we have to recognize that the decision to communicate our point of view openly and positively, in a proactive way, has generated' an opportunity to lead a discussion that they would not otherwise have had (Carroggio et al. 2006).

The lessons learned, according to the three global media relations people is that by being Christian in tone and style, they eliminated the 'sterile dynamic of confrontation' (B. Finnerty, personal interview 1 May 2006). Finally, the leaders of the organization wished that media ethics would prevail:

That the powerful may be more respectful. That they may freely decide to improve their strategies and become less arrogant and more open [. . .] upholding respect does not reduce business or lower the quality of art. The powerful in our society are often big communications corporations. With more power comes more responsibility. In the field of communications, the profit motive cannot be made absolute, to the detriment of the work of journalists, creative writers, or the audience [. . .] An African writer, Margaret Ogola, describes maturity as the realization that we are capable of offending, of wounding others, and acting in consequences (Carroggio et al. 2006).

Conclusion

In the *Opus Dei* case, the negative portrayal was resisted by the organization's own strategic communication, and the organization of fundamentalist Christians negotiated the meaning of the insult, not so much for believers or insiders, nor for the secularists or outsides, but for the fence-sitters, those who might be likely to join, and 'discover' something new about their own religious self by living their faith in a 'lay worker' organization.

The quest for belief that matters to the self, found not in public texts interpreted over the ages, but in the rubble of public culture, the shard, the artifact, in the search through historical evidence, archival and archeological, is repositioned as news by a continuous stream of multimedia enterprises that reflect, reiterate, copy and reinforce one another. From searching for objective truth by authentic seekers, to projecting bias that cultivates ideas among outsiders that there is a global conspiracy of opposition forces, expressed in fundamentalist Christian-mediated productions, there have been instances where other fundamentalist groups such as the one described here flocked to the production precisely because it contained some allegation against The stranger or the Enemy.

Consider the popularity of Mel Gibson's *The Passion* among those in the Middle East audiences who are anti-Semitic. In the case of the cartoons of the Prophet Muhammad, people died in street riots in several Muslim states. What *Opus Dei* did to mute its resistance and use media relations to capitalize on the notoriety created by the film, while successful, did nothing to dent the profits of the producers or the profitability of the genre of religious conspiracy, from a Hollywood standpoint. They can be said to have succeeded because they positioned the locus of control within their own media, and made that accessible worldwide.

Though they communicated to the site of production, they realized the limits of their power or ability to influence producers of anti-Christian messages. Instead, they offered audiences an alternative reality: by producing their own narrative, they reframed the question. Those who were opposed to them would remain opposed, and profit handsomely from their opposition. Those who were with them stayed with them, perhaps enjoying their 15 minutes of fame. The target publics were those potential believers who would, because of the contested image of the strict disciples, find the *Opus Dei* way of life neither arcane nor anachronistic, but an appealing counter-cultural statement about fundamentalism as a way of life.

Notes

1   See www.odan.org and 'awareness network' to deprogram followers. The average time for sainthood is 17–27 years after the death of the individual, allowing ample time for biographical scrutiny and several major miracles.

2   Using lawsuits as a publicity tactic is as old as Ivy Ledbetter Lee, the so-called father of the public relations industry in the USA circa 1920.

3   Response productions included 'DeCoding DaVinci' by Amy Wellborn, 'The DaVinci Hoax' by Carl Olson, and 'Solving the 2000 Year Old Mystery' by Grizzly Adams (a documentary) among others.

References

Anderson, B. (1983), *Imagined Communities*. London: Verso.
Badaracco, C. (1998), 'Cultural resistance and literary identity: Merton's reading notebooks', *The Merton Annual*, 10, 193–204.
Badaracco, C. (2006), *Quoting God: How Media Shape Ideas about Religion*. Waco, TX: Baylor University Press.

Carroggio, M., Finnerty, B. and Mora, J. M. (2006), 'Three Years with *The DaVinci Code*', paper presented to the 5th Professional Seminar for Church Communications Offices, 27 April 2006, Rome, Italy. Retrieved 27 August 2008 from <http://www.opusdei.us/art.php?p=15986>.

Coverdale, J. F. (n.d.), 'The vocation to *Opus Dei*', retrieved 27 August 2008 from <http://www.opusdei.us/art.php?p=11401>.

Dalai Lama (2001), *Ethics for the New Millennium*. New York Penguin Group, pp. 180–186.

Hoover, S. M. (2006), *Religion in the Media Age*. London: Routledge.

Hurtado, M. S. (2006), 'Sony's other code', press release, 17 May. Retrieved 3 August 2008 from <http://www.opusdei.us/art.php?p=16332>.

Jeffrey, D. L. (2003), *Houses of the Interpreter: Reading Scripture, Reading Culture*. Waco, TX: Baylor University Press.

Lannstrom, A. (ed.) (2004), *The Stranger's Religion*. South Bend, IN: University of Notre Dame Press.

'Members' (n.d.), *Opus Dei* website, retrieved 27 August 2008 from <http://www.opusdei.us/art.php?p=43>.

'Message' (n.d.), *Opus Dei* website, retrieved 27 August 2008 from <http://www.opusdei.us/art.php?p=12224>.

Norby Bonde, B. (2007), 'How 12 cartoons of the Prophet Mohammed were brought to trigger and international conflict', *Nordicom Review*, 28(1), 33–48.

Nord, D. P. (2004), *Faith in Reading*. New York: Oxford University Press.

'Open Letter to Sony' (2006), April 6. Retrieved 3 August 2008 from <opusdei.us/art.php?p=15075>.

'*Opus Dei* head on pastoral visit' (2006), *National Catholic Reporter*, 29 September. Retrieved 31 August 2008 from <http://findarticles.com/p/articles/mi_m1141/is_42_42/ai_n26707508>.

'*Opus Dei* in the U.S.' (n.d.), *Opus Dei* website, retrieved 27 August 2008 from <http://www.opusdei.us/sec.php?s=379>.

Pentin, E. (2005), 'Decoding *Opus Dei*', *Newsweek*, 24 March, cover.

'*The Da Vinci Code*, the Catholic Church and *Opus Dei*' (2006), November 16. Retrieved 28 August 2006 from <http://www.opusdei.org/art.php?w=32&p=7017>.

Vlazny, J. (2006), 'We respond to *Da Vinci Code* by speaking the truth in love', *Catholic Sentinel*, 28 April. Retrieved 27 August 2008 from <http://www.sentinel.org/node/7646>.

Wolfsfeld, G. (2001), 'The news media and peace processes: The Middle East and Northern Ireland', US Institute of Peace, *Peaceworks*, 1(1), 5–13.

Part III

Locations

Chapter 10

African Traditional Religion, Pentecostalism and the Clash of Spiritualities in Ghana

J. Kwabena Asamoah-Gyadu

Introduction

Religious fundamentalism is usually discussed in the context of Western Christian evangelicalism and Middle Eastern militant and political Islam. The word 'fundamentalism', Jürgen Moltmann and Hans Küng have pointed out, was originally used in reference to particular developments within North American Protestantism 'which in the face of all modern and liberal adaptations of the church, sought to go back to the biblical "fundamentals" of the Christian faith: to fundamentals of faith which were interpreted in a very arbitrary way' (Moltmann and Küng 1992). In a Preface to a special issue of *Concilium* on fundamentalism, the two authors serve us well in their recognition that 'fundamentalist symptoms and developments analogous to this movement within Protestantism can also be found in the sphere of Roman Catholicism and Eastern Orthodoxy' (Moltmann and Küng 1992). Although there is no explicit reference to primal or indigenous religious traditions, an observation by the authors that 'fundamentalism is a challenge to all religions and confessions' is a very significant one (Moltmann and Küng 1992). I will assume that the reference to 'all religions and confessions' cannot preclude such non-missionary religions as those of the indigenous peoples of Africa. This chapter is dedicated to drawing attention to this fact using the encounter between African Traditional Religions (ATRs) and Christianity in Ghana as its point of entry into the discussion.

Within sub-Saharan Africa, Judaism, Islam and Christianity and such world religions as Hinduism and Buddhism are all 'missionary' religions. That means they have had to encounter different forms of indigenous religions in one way or another. Indeed in Africa, as elsewhere including places like Australia where indigenous peoples have been displaced, it is these traditional religions that played 'religious hosts' to all the other missionary religions, particularly

Christianity and Islam, which were encountered prior to the colonial era. Religion has grown in very many directions in postcolonial Africa leading to religious pluralism with its attendant competition for space and attention from the practitioners of the different faiths. Religious fundamentalism usually thrives in competitive environments and in Ghana, the geographical location of this study, the growth of Christianity especially the Pentecostal/charismatic varieties, has clearly put traditional religion under siege. Pentecostal/charismatic churches demonize traditional religion as devilish and practitioners of traditional religion now reject Christianity as an inherently foreign faith that has been used 'to dominate and exploit Africans' (de Witte 2007: 16). The acrimonious encounters that have taken place between Christianity and traditional religions since the middle of the twentieth century are not merely sociopolitical. It is usually cast as 'the battle of the gods' for spiritual supremacy and so it has very deep spiritual connotations for adherents on both sides of the religious divide. This chapter scrutinizes some of the spiritual connotations of these perennial hostilities between African Christianity and ATRs based specifically on clashes over sacred periods of silence in Ghana. We will find in this study a shift in the Western understanding of religious fundamentalism. The siege under which Christianity in particular puts traditional religions has angered African religio-cultural activists who are increasingly adopting what may broadly be described as 'fundamentalists' tactics in their bid to redeem a religious heritage that does not have a single centre in terms of representations. African religions are very local in nature with each tribe and ethnic group having its own deities and supernatural entities. Thus in this paper, we have a broader view of fundamentalism than is generally available in Western thought. We will note for example that Accra, the capital of Ghana, is now a cosmopolitan city. It is therefore, as I will note below, becoming increasingly difficult to enforce traditional taboos that are not accommodated in the Constitution of a postcolonial state. The same could be said of various urban and sub-urban communities where religious clashes have occurred. Further, in the Christian imagination, traditional religion is associated with Africa's dark and uncivilized past and so its values are treated with disdain and considered irrelevant in contemporary society.

Sacred and Secular Realities and Fundamentalism in African Cultures

The encounter between missionary religions and indigenous religions must be understood as occurring between religions and cultures due to the inseparability between religion and culture within non-literate cultures. The issues involved are deeply religious and theological. African traditions, for example, do not generally distinguish between sacred and secular realities. There are therefore no known vernacular words that translate 'religion' directly. Thus among the Akan of Ghana, for example, a proverb seeking to explain the origin of religions simply says, *obi nnkyere abofora Nyame*, 'a child knows God by instinct'. In these traditional cultural contexts, religion and life form an integral whole with no dichotomy between what is sacred/holy and what is secular/profane. This is very succinctly articulated by Yale Divinity School Gambian scholar of African religion, Lamin O. Sanneh:

> A basic and persistent trait of African societies is the importance of religion. It falls like a shaft of light across the entire spectrum of life, fused and undifferentiated at one end, and refracted and highly refined at the other. From casual, daily, and spontaneous contexts to somber, highly structured public occasions, it is the focus of elaborate and detailed interest. In art and ritual, in speech, work and leisure, in field, home and travel, on land or on water, in health and in sickness, in need and in contentment, religion occurs with authoritative force. African communities have consequently lived, moved, and had their being in religion (Sanneh 1990: 64).

Agitations, reactions and fights for the preservation of pristine and valued religious ideas – the stock-in-trade of religious fundamentals – are thus simultaneously, fights for the preservation of ancestral cultural values, at least in the African context. It is usually lost on scholars, that as the host of missionary religions and in the desire to preserve cultural heritages and sanctities, ATRs have generated their own brands of fundamentalists too. The forces of formal education, Western-style development and modernization and growing religious pluralism together with the importance of modern media for the dissemination of religious ideas have contributed to the feeling that traditional culture and therefore religions are under siege. The traditionalists are fighting back on all fronts and the mass media have become the new frontiers within which representatives of the various religions now pursue their fundamentalist ideas. The growing public presence of Pentecostal/charismatic Christianity in particular through the mass media has extrapolated the antagonism between Christians and traditionalists in Africa to another level.

Religious Fundamentalism and Media in Context

The expression 'fundamentalist' is used here very broadly to refer to conscious personal and institutional commitments to defend particular religions against others. Usually the 'other' is seen as threat to one's fundamental beliefs, religious practices and survival. In Ghana, several clashes have occurred between Christianity and ATRs because since the nineteenth-century missionary era, to be a Christian has always meant abandoning ATRs with all its resources of supernatural succor in order to embrace the former. Historically, one of the best known clashes between the two religions was the invasion of a sacred grove by a first-generation Methodist Christian gentleman, Akweesi, in defiance of the traditional priests and deities at Mankessim in the Central Region of Ghana around 1850. Akweesi's actions led to the collapse of 'Nananom Pow', 'shrine/grove of the gods' when Methodism was only about 15-years old in the then Gold Coast (Crayner 1979). In modern Ghana, clashes of that nature have continued to occur between the two religions. Some recent high profile ones have taken place over questions relating to whether Christians have the right 'to drum or not to drum' during impositions of sacred silence in honor of the gods prior to the celebrations of traditional religious festivals (Asamoah-Gyadu 2005a).

Believing that they owe no ontological commitment or allegiance to the gods or spiritual entities of the various traditional deities of the land, and that the traditionalists have no religious authority over them, some churches in Ghana have continued loud drumming and singing during these sacred periods of silence to the chagrin and consternation of their ATR compatriots. Discussions of these matters are now regularly featured in the newspapers, on radio and television programmes dedicated to the exchange of ideas on religion and culture. Sometimes representatives of some religions have used media opportunities to get at others. In the early 1980s, a neo-traditional movement led by a defrocked Roman Catholic priest, Vincent Kwabena Damuah, spent large amounts of its Tuesday night radio programmes challenging the claims of Christianity and castigating it as a neo-colonialist religion. In one more recent case involving Christianity, Rev. Augustine Annoh Yeboah, then General Secretary of the Christ Apostolic Church told traditional religious authorities to 'go to hell' with their religious injunctions during a television broadcast. This was during the 2004 imposition of ritual bans on drumming and noise-making prior to the celebration of the traditional festival *Homowo* in Accra, the capital of Ghana. Hell did indeed break loose following the open provocation. The premises of the Christ Apostolic Church were violently attacked and this left in its trail broken glass windows and injuries to not a few people.

Thus in contemporary Africa, it is difficult to discuss the encounters among religions without reference to the media. Media institutions and representations constitute an important site of conflict between religious groups and these tendencies have been heightened in the contemporary hi-tech world in which we live (Hackett 2006: 166–187). Based on the premise that the mass media now constitute one of the principal locations 'for the propagation and self-representation of religious groups', Rosalind I. J. Hackett has explored the role modern media have played in the inter-religious tensions and conflicts that have characterized Nigerian society since the late 1970s (Hackett 2003: 47–63). The mass media, she points out, 'have the capacity to construct new geographies both real and imaginative, and to (re)shape perceptions of social reality and para-social contact' (Hackett 2003: 49). Hackett's work ably demonstrates that public discourse on religious conflicts has been elevated to a national level in Nigeria by the expanding mass media regime. The media, as she points out, 'now constitute an important interface/discursive site for the negotiation of difference and representations of the Other' (Hackett 2003: 51). Hackett's observations made in the context of the difficult relationship between Christianity and Islam in Nigeria are equally reflective of the relationships between Christianity and ATRs in Ghana, especially since the resurgence of Pentecostal/charismatic Christianity from the late 1970s.

The Pentecostal/charismatic churches and movements dominate the use of the mass media. Where programmes serve evangelistic purposes such as the issue of home videos by such churches representations of traditional religions are always negative (Asamoah-Gyadu 2007: 224–243; Ukah 2003: 203–231). Marleen de Witte's observation on the need to study the repercussions of such media representations is useful for our purposes:

> The point is that charismatic Christian and traditionalist leaders operate and manifest themselves in a single religious arena, in which they seek to convince widely overlapping audiences of their claims to authority and authenticity. In other words, they compete for the same 'metaphysical space.' This arena is increasingly constituted by the mass media and so are the modes of being present in it (de Witte 2007: 13).

Thus it has become common for conflicts between religious groups to be linked with media representations. The negative representation of ATRs in Christian-dominated media in Africa has played some role in the rise of traditional religious fundamentalism discussed in this chapter. The core issues, however, relate to the rights of existence and recognition of ATRs in the light of the challenge from religious pluralism. The media has served to portray the fact that traditional religion has gradually become a minor faith in African countries like Ghana where official statistics puts its following at 8.5 per cent of a population of twenty million people as against Christianity's 62 per cent.

Christ and Culture

H. Richard Niebuhr articulated the relationship between the church and society in terms of three main attitudes: first, 'Christ against culture', in which there is an uncompromising affirmation of the sole authority of Christ over the Christian and the resolute rejection of culture's claims to loyalty. Second is the 'Christ of culture' position that accommodates the demands of culture in a religiously inclusive manner and third, 'Christ above culture', which encourages an almost full disengagement between Christ and the 'world' of materialism and its attraction as the locus of the devil's activity. The approach of Pentecostal/charismatic Christianity to traditional religions discussed in this chapter is a kind of synthesis between the 'Christ against culture' and 'Christ above culture' attitudes. In the Christ against culture attitude which is most pronounced in Pentecostal/charismatic relations with non-Christian religions, 'the counterpart of loyalty to Christ' is the 'rejection of cultural society' leading to disengagement between Christians and non-Christians (Niebuhr 1951: 47). The 'world' as Niebuhr explains is seen by proponents of the 'Christ above culture' position 'as a realm under the power of evil; it is the region under the power of darkness, in which the citizens of the kingdom of light must not enter . . .' (Niebuhr 1951: 48).

In an African context where religion and life remain inseparable entities, a rejection of the world as the realm of the devil inevitably means a rejection of traditional religion as demonic. The perception of the world as the realm of the devil, as far as African Christianity is concerned, fits the African religion and culture and all it stands for. This is a position that has very clearly been articulated by Birgit Meyer in her work, *Translating the Devil: Religion and Modernity among the Ewe in Ghana*. This attitude to non-Christians in Africa, Meyer establishes, has its roots in Pietist Protestantism. Through diabolization, Awakened Pietists drew boundaries between themselves and others, but at the same time integrated others into their world as representatives of evil. The missionaries as Meyer explains therefore exported to Africa 'a model of how to conceptualize and treat the "pagans" in the framework of their Pietist world-view, according to which the Ewe [traditional Africans] were servants of Satan' (Meyer 1999: 52). The result was that a strict boundary was drawn between the two religions of Christianity and traditional faiths through 'diabolization.' Thus, once African Christians had accepted the missionary position they were expected to acknowledge 'the superiority of Christianity and reject their old ways as Devil worship' (Meyer 1999: 56). This 'Christ above culture' approach to traditional religion has been sustained in contemporary African Christian practice and the response from the traditionalists has been to resist attempts to demonize them by using any available means, including the media to reassert themselves as custodians of culture.

Picketing for the Gods

The immediate context of this discussion is the following example of clashes between Christianity and ATR in Ghana: On Tuesday, 26 April 2005, a group of Ga-Dangme peoples of Accra the capital of Ghana and its environs organized a massive demonstration in the city. The Ga-Dangme's constitute one of the major traditional ethnic groups in Ghana and they trace their ancestral roots to present day Eastern Nigeria. They demonstrated against a perceived disrespect for their religious traditions by Christians, particularly, those of the Pentecostal/charismatic variety for whom 'joyful noises' constitute an inseparable part of regular worship. Following the demonstration, partici- pants presented two copies of their petition to the relevant authorities, one to

Parliament and the other to the President of the Republic, John A. Kufuor at the seat of government, the Castle, Osu. According to the substance of their petitions, first, the demonstrators wanted only the indigenous language of the Ga-Dangmes, to be taught in Accra basic schools. There are reasons for this. Language is the primary vehicle for the preservation of culture, religion and tradition so the neglect of language could lead to the death of culture. The relocation of the capital from Cape Coast in the Central Region to Accra in the postcolonial era meant that the city had become cosmopolitan, a veritable melting pot of peoples and languages from across the country.

These developments including the teaching of other Ghanaian languages in Accra's basic schools, the Ga-Dangme's consider, are detrimental to their cultural interest. Second, they wanted Ga-Dangme traditional religious beliefs and customs to be respected by the 'outsiders' who have come to live in Accra. In effect the demonstrators were asking for governmental enforcement of religion-related traditional taboos and injunctions emanating from the *Naa Wulomo*, the chief priest of the Ga-Dangme traditional area. The immediate underlying reason for this particular petition was the persistent refusal of some Christian churches to observe and comply with the ritual injunctions relating to annual bans on drumming and noisemaking imposed as part of the celebration of *Homowo*. *Homowo*, literally 'hooting at hunger', is the traditional festival of the Ga-Dangme. The ban is imposed in May, four clear weeks prior to the celebration of *Homowo* by the Ga-Dangme Traditional Council (GTC) under the leadership of the *Naa Wulomo*. It is a sacred period for the observance of religious reverential silence required by the gods and the *Naa Wulomo* as the two communicate so that the ensuing year would be one of abundance in food, health and prosperity. These are the ends to which African religious rituals are generally directed and they are the focus of festivals.

Thus, we have in these encounters a complex clash not simply of spiritualities but also of the tensions between tradition and modernity. The traditional authorities consider the refusal of the churches to observe the ban on drumming and noisemaking very provocative. On occasion they have taken the law into their own hands to enforce it. Sometimes, the politicians have issued statements in support of the position of the traditional religionists but this has been done out of political convenience and not because traditional taboos can be upheld by modern constitutional law. For example a former Minister of Interior, Nii Okaijah Adamafio, issued a statement in the *Daily Graphic* of 9 June 1998 that read in part: 'It is wrong for certain people to assume that practices such as the ban on drumming and noisemaking is fetish and therefore of no significance to society'.

Nii Okaijah Adamafio belongs to the Ga-Dangme stock, and at the time, was also a member of parliament for one the most populous constituencies in Accra. His only option in the matter was to side with his people against the churches. We will therefore be reading too much into his statement if it is seen as a 'government position'. The Accra Metropolitan Assembly, as with all local governing councils in Ghana, has bylaws on noise decibels. These laws affect churches, entertainment houses, funeral and birthday parties, picnics and other social activities that involve noisemaking. But silence imposed in the name of religion is not ordinary or mundane silence. Thus, what we are confronted with is also not a contestation over mere silence. It is a deeply spiritual issue for both sides – traditional religionists as well as Christians – and that is what these reflections focus on. In what follows, I draw on two main examples, the Ga-Dangme one and another that occurred in the Nzema traditional area of the western region of Ghana in the early 1990s. I argue that these clashes are not new and that they date back to the nineteenth-century missionary era when Christianity was seen as a religion hostile to traditional religion because, as we have noted, to become a Christian in Africa, has always meant abandoning the indigenous faith with its belief in gods and deities. As one gospel-life music from the Pentecostal/charismatic stable has recently captured the Christian position:

> All other gods, they are works men;
> You are the most High God
> There is none like you
> Jehovah, you are the Most High
> Jehovah, you are the Most High God.

The hostility between Christians and traditionalists has been taken to another level by Pentecostal/charismatic Christianity in which testimonies relate how people have been 'exorcised' from the demonic influences of traditional religious beliefs and practices. Thus in Pentecostal/charismatic preaching, gospel-life music and in the African film industry also inspired by the demonization of traditional gods and spirits, African traditional religion has survived in the imagination as the domain of the Christian devil or Satan. The non-observance of the requisite silence for the traditional community puts lives in danger as the anger of the gods could be expressed in ways that affect cosmic and communal harmony. The result, when that happens, is hunger, disease and suffering as punishment from the gods. The Christian community, as I will point out, sees the observance of these traditional bans differently. In their submissions on the matter, the Ga-Dangme peoples refer especially to the fact that Pentecostal/charismatic churches notoriously flout traditional injunctions prohibiting drumming and noisemaking during those 'sacred hours' of the year. For the Christian community, observing them means submitting to the authority of traditional gods they do not believe in. In other words, the Christian community considers the imposition of the bans to be an infringement of their religious rights and in breach of one of the most critical articles of faith as outlined in the Mosaic Decalogue: 'I am the LORD your God . . . thou shall have no other gods before me' (Exodus 20: 2).

Sacred Periods

In *Christianity in Africa*, Ghanaian theologian Kwame Bediako points out that ATRs have a strong affinity with nature (Bediako 1995: 95). The natural environment is virtually enchanted as the abode of various gods and divinities. Thus selected mountains, rivers, the sea, rocks and trees, may all have taboos related to them depending on which deities inhabit such natural phenomena. As sacred places and objects these items of nature are also locations of religious ritual. African traditional festivals are usually founded upon the roles that these natural phenomena have played in the religious lives of the people. Usually, they are places where what Mircea Eliade calls *hierophanies*, manifestations of the sacred, have occurred. Such sacred places also have a direct relationship with how traditional communities eke out a living. If the traditional economic activity is fishing for example, then the festival and its associated taboos are likely to be related to prohibitions on fishing during particular periods. The *Homowo* festival, for example, has to do with the planting, growing and harvesting of millet a basic ingredient for the traditional staple food of the Ga-Dangmes. Tradition has it that through the providence of their deities during a particularly acute period of hunger, millet became the crop through which the situation was arrested. Similarly, many farming communities in Ghana have sacred days on which people are not allowed to farm. They are the 'sabbaths' of those communities. Thus the ritual bans associated with traditional festivals are common in Ghana. They are set apart as sacred periods of quiet and silence for the performance of rituals associated with the traditional economies through which communities eke out a living. The gods and ancestors of the various traditional areas are the custodians of the land and festivals are held to acknowledge their benevolence and seek their interventions against evil, hunger and want in ensuing years.

Clash of Spiritualities in History

Violent clashes between Christians and traditionalists over festival customs and taboos date back to early missionary times. Reference has already been made to Meyer's work among the Ewe of Ghana. In the book, *The Presbyterian Church of Ghana 1835–1966*, Noel Smith also reports how one nineteenth-century missionary teacher of the Presbyterian Church at Akropong-Akwapim in Ghana, J. A. Mader, will provocatively send his students to fetch manure from the community's sacred grove. When a traditional priest confronted him on one occasion he publicly flogged the priest. Madder did not die at the instance of the gods as the indigenous community thought he would. The act led to some significant conversions because in the minds of the Christian community, their God had triumphed over traditional deities (Smith 1967: 90–91).

This was an extreme case of denigrating traditional beliefs. With time the historic mission churches have learnt to accommodate traditional injunctions and so clashes between the two religions are now very minimal. The situation has been greatly helped by the interventions of the Christian Council of Ghana and its constant dialogical engagements with representatives of traditional religions. With the rise of the Pentecostal/charismatic movements however, there has been a resurgence of such conflicts over the last two decades. Most Pentecostals belong to the Ghana Pentecostal Council but the relationship between the latter and the traditionalists has not been consistent and cordial. Pentecostalism, with its ardent desire to prove the reality of the God of the Bible through emphasis on miraculous and powerful acts, has been most uncompromising in its dealings with traditional religion (Asamoah-Gyadu 2005b). In the early 1990s, the Global Revival Ministries, one of the new Pentecostal churches, was banned from operating in the Akropong-Akwapim traditional area because one of the church's pastors had led a group to burn down an ancient traditional shrine. The traditional authorities are now usually the aggressors when it comes to enforcement of traditional taboos. This indicates some desperation on the part of traditional religious practitioners to preserve what is left of their weakening influence in the modern religiously pluralistic nation state. In traditional African societies, religion, governance, life and existence have always been inseparably linked. Multi-culturalism, constitutional democracy, and more importantly for our purposes, religious pluralism has gradually rendered traditional religious authority irrelevant in many African countries.

Pentecostal Christianity in particular, with its fundamentalist approach to the gospel, has taken the resistance to traditional religions to another level by openly challenging the authority of the gods. After all, Christ is supposed to be against culture. On Sunday 31 May 1998, for example, a group of traditionalists from the Korle Gonno area in Accra invaded the premises of the Lighthouse Chapel International located within the same geographical area. Lighthouse is one of the new Pentecostal churches that have sprung up in African cities since the late 1970s. The invasion led to the vandalization of property and many worshippers were seriously injured. Rijk van Dijk explains the reasons behind the aggression of the traditionalists:

> [Lighthouse Chapel] was accused of not respecting the imposed ban on drumming in an utter and provocative denial of traditional values. Supported by the [Ghana] Pentecostal council, the church claimed that modern religious liberties needed to be upheld, and these permitted them to make music during church services whenever they wanted, and that true Christianity could not be involved in obeying 'animistic' rituals. The traditionalists in turn voiced their opposition to the noisemaking, which accompanied so many Pentecostal meetings. They pointed to the fact that the making of loud music by Pentecostals during their night vigils usually went on throughout the

entire night and that in many parts of the city numerous complaints against the practice had been filed with local assemblies (van Dijk 2001: 2).

Contrary to the impression given by van Dijk in the paper on this subject, the clashes between Christianity and traditional religionists are not contests over mere silence. The problem of the Christian community is with observing 'silence in worship' imposed in the name of gods they do not believe in and by religious authorities who are considered 'representatives' of the devil. Thus, the impression that it is only Pentecostal/charismatic churches that refuse to observe annual bans on drumming and noisemaking is not entirely correct. There is a whole gamut of traditional practices that Christians have problems with and the issue of 'sacred silence' is only one of them. In *The Position of the Chief in the Modern Political System of Ashanti*, Kofi A. Busia cites a number of instances of such conflicts. In 1941, the Ashanti Confederacy Council issued a decree to reinforce an old traditional custom that forbade Ashantis from farming on Thursdays because it is the sacred day of *Asaase Yaa*, Mother Earth. The Christian response was that the law was offensive to 'Christian conscience'. On 16 October 1942, Christian churches in Ashanti sent a memorandum on the relation between Christians and the Ashanti state to the *Ashantihene*, paramount chief of the Ashantis. The memorandum read in part:

> We recognize that this is an observance closely linked with ancient beliefs of the Ashanti people; beliefs which, however, are not to our mind wholly compatible with the Christian belief in God. Our members, if they observe the day, cannot do so for the ancient Ashanti reason. The question arises, should they be asked to observe the day out of respect for beliefs of others in the community? We feel that we cannot ask this of our members, in that to refrain from work on Thursday would be to them a confession of faith in *Asaase Yaa* and her relation to harvest and family and therefore a denial of the Fatherhood and providential care of God (Busia 1968: 24).

Historically, therefore, the clash between Christianity and indigenous religions is over spiritualities. 'Spirituality' here refers to 'lived religion', that is, those rituals, beliefs, practices, observances, ways of life and worship that give a particular faith its distinctive identity as evident in the way practitioners conduct their daily affairs. The observance of periods of rest from the exploitation of natural resources and noisemaking as part of indigenous spirituality have been part of traditional religions since ancient times. In the run up to the celebration of the *Bakatue* festival of the people of Elmina for example, the community is enjoined by religious tradition to cease fishing from the Benya lagoon. Ecologically, this allows the lagoon to replenish its stocks of fish, but for the traditional community, it is observed in deference to the lagoon deity, Nana Benya. In the rest of this paper, I use a particular clash between the Church of Pentecost and the traditional authorities of the Half Assini area over injunctions related to the *Kundum* festival. I proceed on the premise that religious beliefs or spiritualities are at the centre of these and they are fallouts from the radical opposition that traditional religions and Christianity have formed since the missionary era.

Church of Pentecost and the *Kundum* Festival

The *Kundum* festival is celebrated by the Nzemas of Half Assini in the western region of Ghana. *Kundum* is a sacred dance that according to Nzema mythology is done in honour of the gods of the land. In the early 1990s there was a violent clash between traditional religious authorities of Half-Assini and the Local Council of Churches (LCC) led by the Church of Pentecost (CoP). The LCC was made up of all the churches at Half Assini – Methodist, Presbyterian, Christ Apostolic, Roman Catholic and the CoP. This clash was over an injunction imposed on drumming and noisemaking by traditional authorities for the stipulated period prior to the celebration of the *Kundum* traditional festival. The LCC 'decided to continue their normal worship practices including drumming despite [the] ban by the traditional authorities'. The battle lines were drawn as reported by the leader of the CoP, Pastor Sintim Koree who led the Christian resistance:

> The ministers decided that the God they are serving could not be limited by man-made rules and demonic practices and influences, which form the basis of the *Kundum* festival. They therefore took a firm decision and met all the congregations of the churches in a joint Local Council of Churches' meeting hosted by the Methodist Church and informed them of their intent. While the traditional authorities began to beat their gong-gong to restrict the churches and all other religious groups from drumming, the ministers also thought it wise to continue their normal way of worship (Koree n.d.: 2).

Following this decision, the churches defied the traditional order not to drum. The authorities led by the chief of Half Assini then moved in to seize the drums of the churches. The interpretation of the pastor of the CoP on the implications of this action is very instructive:

> After the seizure of our drum, the congregation entered into an intensive prayer session for the Lord to strengthen us in order to stand to face the problem, which had started. We foresaw that the battle, which had just begun, would not be a nine-day wonder. We anticipated a life-long battle before us – the battle between light and darkness. War has escalated between two powers, the power of God and the power of Satan. The power of darkness had rule over the place for a long time and we believed it was now the appointed time for us through the Holy Spirit and the power of God, to

wage war against these domineering and territorial evil spirits of Nzemaland (Koree n.d.: 4).

The matter eventually ended up in court and the churches were charged with doing acts 'with intent to provoke the breach of the peace, and having behaved in a manner whereby the breach of the peace was likely to be occasioned'. The CoP decided to use its remaining drums to worship in defiance of the court action. The pastor of the CoP worked with the interpretive framework that the situation confronting him was similar to the one in which Shadrach, Meshach and Abednego found themselves in the book of Daniel. In Pastor Koree's inter-pretation, 'one of the worst diseases that afflict the Church today is the ten-dency to take sides with the [people] of the world in the face of persecution, atrocities, threats, intimidation or promise of reward at the expense of known biblical truths and convictions. Regrettably, many men and women that would have been mightily used by God have been drowned in the calm sea of com-promise' (Koree n.d.: 14). In a press statement issued in the *Daily Graphic* of Saturday, 8 January 1994, the CoP described the *Kundum* festival as dedicated to 'dwarfs' and Christians should not be placed in a situation in which they have to bow down to such gods. Thus Pastor Okoree and his church invoked the 'Christ against culture' position that ruled out any form of engagement with representatives of traditional religion.

Re-invoking the Spirit of Elijah

These were very bold decisions, and from the point of view of the local Christian community, God vindicated the stance of the pastor of the CoP. The church and its members went through long periods of harassment and molest-ation at the hands of the traditional authorities. Two main incidents following these confrontations are worth recalling. In the first incident thunder struck the chief's palace when Pastor Koree and his elders were taken there and physically manhandled. In the second incident a sub-chief who had seized the church drummer's seat took it to his house. He had taunted the congregation that 'if your God is powerful, let him come for the seat himself'. After about a year, according to the report, he accidentally sat on that particular chair. His whole genital area began to rot from that moment. He did eventually make a connec-tion between his own blasphemous statement and his predicament, asked for forgiveness on his hospital bed and died a couple of minutes after the confes-sion. The churches at Half Assini led by the CoP obviously claimed victory over the traditional religious powers and according to the report, this increased Christian conversions in the town.

In the end, the CoP was banned from operating in the town but according to the pastor at the centre of the drama, it was important for him to 'operate in the spirit of Elijah' in order to prove that God was still alive and had not changed.

In that story involving Prophet Elijah, he wanted to prove the powerlessness of Baal and its prophets who had come to wield considerable influence over Israel. In the ensuing context the prophets of Baal failed to conjure fire to burn a prepared sacrifice, a feat which Elijah did by calling on the more powerful God who consumes by fire. The success of Elijah led to the worship of God by the people and as an ultimate sign of his triumph, Elijah had the prophets of Baal killed (I Kings 18). Thus in taking the approach of religious confrontation, Pastor Koree was identifying with a biblical icon as far as the relationship between the God of Israel and Baal was concerned.

Silence and Spirituality

We observed earlier that Christian conversion in Africa has meant, to use the words of St. Paul, first and foremost a turning away from the gods to serve the living and true God, the father of the Lord Jesus Christ (I Thessalonians 1:9). Since the ban on drumming and noisemaking relates directly to the worship of traditional deities, the Christian thinking has been that obeying these injunctions implied a tacit approval of the worship of lesser deities that was tantamount to compromising the Christian faith through a breach of the First Commandment. So although the misunderstanding itself is not new, it is only with the rise of the Pentecostal churches that it is becoming very prominent. In contrast to formal worship in historic mission denominations, Pentecostal/charismatic worship tends to cherish noisemaking as an important part of religious experience. Worship here is thus unordered and sometimes even 'chaotic'. Pentecostal services are noisy by nature and to insist on their not drumming or making noise for a whole month virtually denies the Pentecostals something that lies at the core of meaningful worship, that is, to 'make a joyful noise unto the Lord' (Psalm 66:1). 'The Lord inhabits the praise of his people' (Psalm 22:3) is a passage often quoted to encourage worshippers not to feel inhibited in their shouts of praise and screams unto the Lord. To that end, noisemaking has become part of Pentecostal worship.

Historic mission denomination church liturgies tend to be ordered and prayers are usually read. Until some of these churches started introducing reforms under pressure from the Pentecostals, even *ododow mpaebo*, spontaneous mass praying, would be conducted in very hushed tones. The argument in favour of such subdued praying is also located in the Bible: 'God is in his holy temple let the earth keep silent before him' (Habakkuk 2:20).

During the 2003 ban on drumming and noisemaking in Accra, a Methodist minister, Rev. Georgina Mensah, was in the news for taking an innovative approach to the problem. She set aside a parallel period of 'silence' in her church during which time she gave teachings to the members on the 'theology of silence in Christian spirituality'. To justify the need for silence as a mark of mature spirituality, historic mission churches also make references to Prophet

Elijah's experience in which contrary to his own thinking, God never revealed himself in noise or violent winds. He did so in the proverbial 'still small voice' (I Kings 19:12). In response, noisemaking in historic mission church worship is usually restricted to a segment called 'praise and worship', which was borrowed from the Pentecostal/charismatic traditions. In fact many mainline churches place notices in front of the altar telling early worshippers 'this is God's house, sit silently, and pray quietly'.

Thus prayers in Pentecostal/charismatic churches are according to the spirituality of the tradition, expected to be spontaneous and loud. There is no 'order' in drunkenness and it is the commotion caused by the 'drunken' disciples on the day of Pentecost that attracted the crowd. Moreover, on leaving the presence of the Sanhedrin in Acts, the Apostles prayed loudly, and as we are told, the place in which they were meeting was *shaken*, and they were all filled with the Holy Spirit (Acts 5:31). The use of tongues does not allow silent praying and so loud prayers accompanied by screams, shouts, loud cries, stamping of feet and ejaculations is considered an essential part of Pentecostal/charismatic worship and prayer culture. Even when congregational prayers are summed up by prayer leaders, worshippers are expected to approve what is being prayed on their behalf with shouts of approval: 'Amen', 'Hallelujah' and 'Praise the Lord'. Nevertheless, Pentecostal/charismatic traditions believe in silence too, but often for different reasons. When services in this tradition go silent, then it is expected that the Lord will 'speak'. Such divine intervention occurs either through a prophetic utterance, words of knowledge or spontaneous individual adulations towards God for being present among his people.

Whether we are looking at Christianity or traditional religions therefore, the bottom line is that, silence seems to play an important part in spirituality. The issue, as I see it from the problem in Ghana, is whether traditional religionists have the right to impose periods of silence on the Christian community or not. Pastor Sintim Koree stated the matter clearly:

> What is the *Kundum* festival and why can Christians not abide by its associated rituals and taboos and to forgo drumming during the periods of the ban? ... Drumming, although part and parcel of the mode of worship of many Christians, especially among the Pentecostal and charismatic churches, its absence in the churches for a period does not hinder the presence and the power of God among the saints. After all, God is present wherever two or three have gathered. Christians in the Jomoro traditional area, specifically Half Assini, know that drumming can be exempted from their mode of worship without changing their relationship with the Almighty God. However this silence must be observed if only if they do it out of their WILL and by the inspiration of the Holy Spirit, who leads us to DO and to WILL, according to his divine purpose (Koree n.d.: 5).

What the Christian community takes issue with, as outlined in the position of

Pastor Koree, is similar to the one taken by the Ashanti Christians in the 1940s. They felt that obeying traditional injunctions imposed in the name of deities is a sign of submission to the authority of those gods. The issue, as we have noted earlier therefore, is not one of the place of silence in religious worship, practice or spirituality. In the experiences of most religions, landmark experiences have usually taken place when the founders have 'withdrawn' from the mundane world into seclusion for meditation. The major celebrations of various religions are then built around such experiences such as the temptations of Jesus in the wilderness, the revelatory experiences of the Buddha and Muhammad in the caves where the Qur'an was revealed to him. Silence in religion, it seems to be a general belief of religions, creates the auspicious environment for the renewal of faith and revelation.

The position taken by most historic mission denominations seems to be something like this: rather than being a weakness, the abstinence from drumming and noisemaking must be seen as a major strength. Those who abstain make the same argument that Peter made during his long exposition following Pentecost: 'God does not dwell in houses made with human hands'. In other words, the people of God may need temples and synagogues to worship, but true religion, as far as Christianity is concerned, depends on things more profound than the availability of buildings or in the context of this paper, drumming, shouting and noisemaking. God is above the logic of noisemaking and inability to literally make noise does not detract from faith, it enriches it, because silence is an important aspect of Christian worship. For many years, churches in the former Soviet Union had to worship as underground congregations because of the hostility of the communities in which they had to exist. That presupposed that they did not have to make noise yet it did not make their services poorer than those who had the liberties and luxuries of noisy worship services. With respect to the position of the church, it is worthy to note that Jesus did not always insist on his rights. He stood silent before Pilate. The approach of the Christian church may be to recognize that God could be active, even in silence. In the end, the silence of Jesus proved a more powerful weapon in the midst of humiliation than calling upon angels to fight on his behalf.

However, from the Christian viewpoint, the action of the LCC in Half Assini led by the CoP also proved a valuable point: that the Kingdom of God comes with power. It is not being suggested that the action of provocative resistance ought to be a paradigmatic Christian response to the imposition of traditional taboos on whole communities. The same Jesus Christ who violently drove out those desecrating the Temple in Jerusalem is the same Christ who, as the Lamb of God, stood before his accusers dumb (Isaiah 53). The CoP action reveals something about African Christianity and its ability to resist the compromises that have bedeviled their counterparts in the West as they relate to society. In many cases, the moral and theological relativism of the churches in the West have weakened Christian witness and subdued the moral voice of the church in modern Western society. Irresponsible confrontations with African traditional society with respect to ancient beliefs could undermine the inevitability of religious pluralism and peaceful co-existence. Nevertheless, the CoP position of showing the power of God proved the viability of the gospel of Jesus Christ and the reality of the supernatural as an important aspect of Christianity. Sometimes life in Africa can be so precarious that calling on the power of God to deal with situations becomes the only option open to people. Constitutionally though, Ghanaians are permitted freedom of religious association. This means the current constitution of Ghana recognizes the religiously pluralistic state of the nation. If noisemaking were a part of religious practice this would be allowed within the limits of the law. This means the right to worship is constrained by the rights of other people to live in peace.

Conclusion

In this chapter we have looked at a different paradigm of religious fundamentalism. In Africa, religious aggression has not involved only missionary or world religions, but also indigenous religions that served as hosts of missionary activity. The tolerant attitude to missionary religions associated with traditional religions has come under strain due to religious pluralism and particularly in Africa, Christian evangelization efforts. Religious tolerance and coexistence have come under great strain in Africa due in part to the rise of Pentecostal/ charismatic Christianity. In the developing economies of African countries like Ghana with its constitutionally prescribed ways in which religions must co-exist, faiths must necessarily work together. The difficulties that African Christians face as they deal with African religions are very theological. As Niebuhr notes, when Christians meet Christ they do so as 'heirs of culture' which they cannot reject because 'it is part of them'. They can withdraw from its more obvious institutions and expressions', he notes, 'but for the most part they can only select – and modify under Christ's authority – something they have received through the mediation of society' (Niebuhr 1951: 70). In that vein the challenge remains how to carry out religious activity within an atmosphere of religious and democratic liberties and yet respect each other's right to serve their ultimate sources of reality in a world that will continue to be pluralistic and diverse as far is religion and culture are concerned.

References

Asamoah-Gyadu, J. K. (2005a), 'To drum or not to drum: Traditional festivals, Christianity and clashes over religious silence in Ghana', *Trinity Journal of Church and Theology*, 15(2), 106–116.
Asamoah-Gyadu, J. K. (2005b), *African Charismatics: Current Developments*

within Independent Indigenous Pentecostalism in Ghana. Leiden, Netherlands: Brill.

Asamoah-Gyadu, J. K. (2007), 'Blowing the cover: Imaging religious function-aries in Ghanaian/Nigerian Films,' in L. S. Clark (ed.), *Religion, Media and the Market Place*. New Brunswick, NJ: Rutgers University Press, pp. 224–243.

Bediako, K. (1995), *Christianity in Africa. The Renewal of a Non-Western Religion*. Edinburgh: Edinburgh University Press.

Busia, K. A. (1968), *The Position of the Chief in the Modern Political System of Ashanti*. London: Frank Cass.

Crayner, B. J. (1979), *Akweesi and the Fall of Nananom Pow*. Accra: Methodist Book Depot.

De Witte, M. (2007), *Spirit Media: Charismatics, Traditionalists and Mediation Practices in Ghana*. Unpublished Ph.D. Thesis: Free University of Amsterdam.

Hackett, R. I. J. (2003), 'Managing or manipulating religious conflict in the Nigerian media', in J. Mitchell and S. Marriage (eds), *Mediating Religion: Conversations in Media, Religion and Culture*. London: T&T Clark, pp. 47–63.

Hackett, R. I. J. (2006), 'Mediated religion in South Africa: Balancing airtime and rights claims', in B. Meyer and A. Moors (eds), *Religion, Media and the Public Sphere*. Bloomington, Indiana: Indiana University Press, pp. 166–187.

Koree, S. S. (n.d.), 'God who answers by thunder' [unpublished manuscript].

Meyer, B. (1999), *Translating the Devil: Religion and Modernity among the Ewe of Ghana*. Edinburgh: Edinburgh University Press.

Moltmann, J. and Küng, H. (1992), 'Fundamentalism as an ecumenical challenge', *Concilium*, 3, retrieved 25 June 2008 from <http://www.concilium.org/english/intro923.htm>.

Niebuhr, H. R. (1951), *Christ and Culture*. New York: Harper and Row.

Sanneh, L. (1990), 'New and Old in Africa's Religious Heritage', in A. F. Walls (ed.), *Exploring New Religious Movements: Essays in Honor of Harold W. Turner*. Elkhart, Indiana: Mission Focus, pp. 63–82.

Smith, N. (1967), *The Presbyterian Church of Ghana: 1835–1960*. Accra, Ghana: Waterville Publishing House.

Ukah, A. F.-K. (2003), 'Advertising God: Nigerian Christian video-films and the power of consumer culture', *Journal of Religion in Africa*, 33(3), 203–231.

Van Dijk, R. (2001), 'Contesting silence: The ban on drumming and the musical politics of pentecostalism in Ghana', *Ghana Studies Review*, 4, 31–64.

Chapter 11

Discursive Construction of Shamanism and Christian Fundamentalism in Korean Popular Culture

Jin Kyu Park

Introduction

Like some other chapters in this volume, this one documents a trend where students of religious fundamentalism are becoming concerned with non-Western cases of fundamentalist phenomena. Today we know that our interests lie beyond 'a single worldwide fundamentalist movement' but in 'global (multiple) fundamentalisms' (Lawrence 1998). Given that religious funda-mentalism is in nature an 'organized religious reaction to secular modernity' (Marty and Appleby 2004[1994]: 1), the diverse paths to modernity in many parts of the world make it difficult to identify consistencies between those movements. Indeed, it should be noted that there are variable ways to be 'modern', because modernity itself is a historical product of what we call 'the West' and non-Western routes to it must necessarily be multiple and dis-similar (Featherstone et al. 1995). But at the same time, it becomes possible and necessary to uncover similar patterns among them, driven by the growing interconnectedness of a late capitalist world. At this point, therefore, our task is to explore the diverse local specifics, while at the same time giving attention to globalizing trends.

With this in mind, this chapter looks at a recent television series *Wang-kkot Seon-nyeo-nim*[1], which became very controversial in Korean society. Part of the significance of the series came from the fact that it brought into relief contemporary struggles in the religious landscape of South Korea. Two forms of religious tradition are evolving along distinct paths in South Korea today: Protestant Christianity and a resurgent traditional shamanism. Protestant fun-damentalism in Korea, a well-known example of successful localization of the 'new' Christian fundamentalism stamped 'made in the USA' (Brouwer et al.

1996: 11), sees itself as being significantly challenged in the public sphere, despite its prominent accomplishments during the country's rapid modernization process over the latter half of the twentieth century. At the same time, an indigenous religious shamanism, ignored and discriminated against by mainstream society during the period of modernization, is gaining new social and cultural significance.

Wang-kkot Seon-nyeo-nim and the popular discourses provoked by it provide an interesting case for the examination of how these two different, yet related, religious movements are discursively constructed as well as how they now confront each other in the mediated realm. The qualitative data used in this analysis were collected through several methods, including in-depth interviews with 11 members of the series' production crew and 27 audience members. The show's content was textually analysed and, in addition, comments posted on the discussion board of the show's official website were also reviewed. In short, by analysing the text's representations and accompanying discourses on it, this chapter pursues three goals. First, it argues that this programme is a case in which a local reaction to a global fundamentalism is emerging in the context of reflexive deliberation on modernity. Second, it shows how religious traditionalism can be a useful resource for such reactions. Finally, it demonstrates how the realm of popular culture becomes engaged in the whole process.

Wang-kkot and the Representation of Religion in Korea

The daily half-hour episodes of *Wang-kkot* ran on MBC, one of Korea's three major television networks, weekdays at 8:25 p.m. From its first episode, the show created much controversy and public discussion online and offline. Audiences and journalists used words like 'unconventional', 'novel', 'extraordinary' and 'bizarre' in their comments about the series, and the discussion about it concentrated on its assumed sensational impacts on society. The controversy was mainly focused on the fact that *Wang-kkot* was the first prime-time television drama which dealt with shamanism as a main subject. It was not the first time that shamanism had appeared in television drama, but its role was usually limited to a minor dramatic device involving a shaman's divination of the future. Since it told a shaman's story directly and treated shamanism as a main theme, *Wang-kkot* was thought to break the conventional codes of South Korean television drama.

Chowon, the main character, is a graduate student in Korean literature. She suffers from an unknown illness, later revealed as *mubyung*[2]. She also has supernatural powers such as foreseeing the future and diagnosing other people's diseases. It is soon revealed that she was adopted when she was a newborn baby – a fact that has been kept a secret from her – and her natural mother is a famous *mudang*[3]. Her mother has chosen to abandon Chowon in the hopes that in this way her daughter might escape her shaman lineage. As Chowon's secrets are disclosed, her life gets tougher. Her family has to give her up to her biological father because her adoptive grandfather, a committed Christian, does not want a *mudang* in his family. Her engagement to a young Ph.D. of a socially established family also suffers because her fiancé's parents no longer approve of the marriage. In spite of her tremendous efforts to free herself from her condition, she continues to suffer from it and, in the end admitting her destiny, she decides to receive *narim-kut*[4] and become a *mudang*.

The most unusual aspect of the series was the positive portrayal of shamanism not typical in Korean television drama. The first episode began with a scene in which Yong-Hwa (Chowon's mother) in her white shaman costume knelt before her altar on which shamanistic gods were enshrined. The scene portrayed the details of the ritual with mysterious music. In another scene where she made divination for a wealthy businessman, he paid respect to her in awe. The series also challenged the notion that shamanism is mere superstition outmoded in our high-tech era, by pointing out the contradictory attitude towards it among Koreans. While Yong-Hwa was portrayed as looked down upon by many people, her clients were depicted as significant figures in business and politics. For example, in one episode a middle-aged gentleman, whom people called 'chairman', asked Yong-Hwa for a divination on his plan to run for an important political position. He did not hesitate to take her advice not to run.

Challenging negative ideas about shamans and shamanism, the text attempted to deconstruct existing stereotypes and construct an image of 'modern' shamanism. Yong-Hwa teaches *feng-shui* at a community cultural centre, in her modern-looking outfits in place of the shaman's traditional clothes. After receiving *naerim-kut*, Chowon returns to her graduate study to become a 'scholar-shaman'. This challenges the generally accepted link between *mudang* and their traditional functions such as divination or *kut*, which are seen as non-intellectual. The repetitive theme music used when Yong-Hwa's grief was expressed was not derived from Korean folk music, but a French *chanson* which would sound more 'Western' to Korean ears than US popular songs.

Several moments in the series resulted in fierce public controversies, and they were related to representations of shamanistic mysticism. The second episode began with a nightclub scene in which Chowon suddenly fainted at the sight of a group of ghosts sensually dancing on loudspeakers. Afterwards she suffered physical symptoms, including high fever and lethargy. She also made bird sounds and she became obsessed with flowers, which are indicative of a shaman-related illness. Chowon even mysteriously survived a suicide attempt. As she got to know that the illness was *mubyung*, she tried to kill herself by crashing her car. Hit by a huge trailer truck, she lost consciousness as her car rolled off a high cliff into a deep abyss. At that moment, a mystical voice came to Yong-Hwa's ears, while she was preparing her routine worship, saying, 'Your daughter is trying to kill herself'. Terrified, Yong-Hwa desperately prayed to her gods to save her daughter. As the car fell down, a mysterious bubble carried Chowon up into the air and safely laid her down onto the ground.

The most controversial moment during the series was Yong-Hwa's coming back to life from death. In her deep grief that she could not tell Chowon that she was her birth mother, Yong-Hwa stayed away from the shrine and became mentally deranged as a spiritual punishment. She starved herself, hoping that she would be able to watch over her daughter as a guardian spirit after death. In the next episode, mysteriously coming to know that Yong-Hwa was dying, one of her apprentices found and took her to a hospital only to hear the doctor pronounce her dead. However, while being moved into the mortuary, she miraculously came back to life.

Another controversial moment was an episode that portrayed a shamanistic *kut* ritual. The description of the ritual was highly detailed and the entire episode was devoted to the ritual's full process. It was a comprehensive illustration of shamanistic costumes, instruments, equipments and procedures, realistically dramatized with the help of advisory shamans. The scenes were rich in sight and sound, showing colourful flags, archery, shamanistic dancing and flaming torches. This provoked a critical reaction from viewers who objected to shamanism being shown in such detail in a family-time television drama. Even among the production crew, some expressed the cynical opinion that the episode was like a 'documentary' on shamanism.

Another unusual aspect of the drama was that the positive portrayal of indigenous shamanism was juxtaposed with a rather unfavourable description of Protestant Christianity. Many Protestant viewers were uneasy that the show depicted Chowon's adoptive grandfather – a devout Christian believer – as greedy and pitiless and a key reason for Chowon's harsh life. When the grandfather saw Chowon climbing up a mountain and praying in a shamanistic way before a big rock he realized that her illness was related to shamanism. He immediately raged at Chowon's adoptive parents:

> I already told you. Didn't I? This is because you didn't listen to me. If you had listened and been going to church sincerely, this would not have happened. I always told you to commit yourselves to the Lord, but you two didn't listen. That's why you had the recent troubles. Kick her out of this family! I mean it. If you don't, I'll stop paying for Taewon's [Chowon's brother] tuition. You have my word! (*Wang-kkot Seon-nyeo-nim*, episode 48, first aired 18 August 2004).[5]

Many Christian viewers vigorously objected to these lines, and complained that the series created a negative image of Protestantism. Some claimed that the programme was a conspiracy by the secular culture to damage Christianity's status in Korea. Other religions also appeared in the drama but, unlike Protestantism, were presented in a neutral way. Chowon visited a Protestant church to pray for her illness, but she also stopped by a Buddhist temple and a Catholic church. The latter two locations seemed to only provide a symbolically religious atmosphere, without further meanings attached.

Public and Cultural Elites' Discourse on *Wang-kkot*

The representation of shamanism and Protestantism in the series was said to be very unusual and, furthermore, not consistent with the production conventions of the genre. Generally, daily evening series in Korea fall within the genre of 'home drama' – a format that must be appropriate for every member of family. Home drama is expected not to be 'experimental' or 'innovative' so as to be 'comfortable' for everyone to watch. In other words, a daily series in Korea is supposed to be 'safe' in a number of ways, including its choice of subject matter, narrative development, visual representation, and so on. In that regard, *Wang-kkot* was never 'safe' in its treatment of shamanism and Protestantism, its storyline, and its representations.

Such codes of the genre are an outcome of the history of television production in the Korean context and, more importantly, of the general public's television experiences and expectations. TV producers then are not willing to risk breaking them. Presumably, they would do so only when they are convinced that a favourable reaction will profitably balance the risk. According to Kellner (1997), challenges to the codes of media culture should be in accordance with social changes that 'lead media producers to conclude that audiences will be receptive to new forms more relevant to their social experience' (106). In this sense, it is of interest to explore how *Wang-kkot*'s producers, as cultural elites, discursively legitimated the programme's code-breaking and how those legitimations are related to the changing religious landscape of contemporary Korea.

In the planning stages, the programme's attempts at code-breaking were initiated mostly by a single individual, the screenwriter, who had long been preparing a shaman's story and researching shamanism with the help of experts. She was one of the biggest names in the drama scriptwriting field, known for her sensationalistic choices of subject matter. Indeed, there was uneasiness among the production crew about the plan that the new series would be a story about a shaman and that *mubyung* would be a crucial motif of its plotline. However, despite the worry, the proposal was approved by the network based on their confidence in the writer's commercial appeal, an acknowledgment that the sensationalistic approach to religion in general and shamanism in particular would be controversial, but also commercially appealing.

Although sensationalism may explain the code-breaking, the production crew did not willingly admit that it was a key motivation. Instead, they legitimatized the choice of shamanism by focusing on certain meanings of the religion. Because they professionally must be sensitive to what would be acceptable to the general public, the meanings of shamanism they identify provide a useful way to map out the religion's symbolic location in the society.

The most frequently mentioned meaning of shamanism by crew members was its value as a tradition. As an indigenous religion, shamanism symbolizes traditionalism, which may diminish its status as a religion. Instead, it is perceived as a set of traditional cultural practices. This way of characterizing shamanism allowed the crew to sidestep the problem of portraying a religion in television drama, which might violate the notion of objective balance in a situation of religious pluralism. An administrative crew member articulated this view:

> Shamanism is not necessarily equal to religion. That's why we could come this far in spite of the earlier worries. It is our folk culture, our traditional faith. It is a sort of religious faith, but at the same time it is a folk custom deeply embedded in our lives. [. . .] It is not a matter of believing or not. It is something that is being dismissed, something that is disappearing. That's why we thought it's worth trying (Personal interview 28 December 2004).

The production team also noted that the indigenous culture of shamanism also signifies 'alternativeness' in Korean society. They emphasized that shamanism was an alternative to other established religions like Christianity and Buddhism. They recognized that if the series had chosen other religions, they could not have done what they could do with shamanism. This was articulated in the director's rationalization of the choice of shamanism over other religions:

> The fact that shamanism is under a veil makes people more imaginative. If it had been Christianity, we could not have done what we've done here. Because it was shamanism, which people are not familiar with, and because people just loosely think of it as something like talking with the dead or talking with ghosts, they can have more imagination, and we also, as producers, can use our imagination in making it. [. . .] Therefore, it was possible to make something new. If it had been Christianity or Buddhism, this drama couldn't have given a feeling of something new (Personal interview 28 December 2004).

Because shamanism is 'alternative' to other established religions in the landscape, its symbolic representation within popular culture is also 'alternative' to representations of other religions. For producers, this notion of 'alternativeness' seemed to reduce the difficulty in breaking with genre convention.

In addition, 'alternativeness' indicates shamanism's minority status in Korean society. The marginal status shamanism has long held offers some advantage because an accepted responsibility of the media in Korea is to represent social minorities. This rationale was used by some administrative staff members of the show when they defended themselves against criticism that shamanism was not an appropriate subject for a television drama.

Along with shamanism, the producers from the beginning took Protestant Christianity into consideration in production decisions. In their legitimation of their representation of shamanism, Protestantism was frequently invoked, juxtaposed against shamanism. Shamanism's marginal position in the society was compared and contrasted with the hegemonic position Protestantism has long enjoyed, and shamanism's rare presence in popular culture was compared to the symbolic prominence of the 'foreign' religion.

Yet, from the beginning, the production team was concerned about the possible reactions from Christian audiences. Because Protestantism has been central to the marginalization of shamanism and Protestants form a substantive group of television viewers, it could be predicted that shamanism in this drama could be offensive. Moreover, Christians are known to be very active when the media bring up a controversial issue involving their religion[6]. The production team attributed the low rating of the first few episodes to the 'unconditional rejection' of the series by Protestant viewers. Although they were not able to provide any clear evidence of this, they supposed that the disappointing ratings were due to the group's strong, although unorganized, rejection of the programme.

For members of the production team who were afraid of Christian response, representation of shamanistic mysticism was a big concern. While they say mysticism as an attractive feature of shamanism for the purposes of representing it in popular culture, they were concerned about the social responses and realized that their television drama was pushing against a boundary. The team played with this boundary of what would be acceptable to the society in their representation of mysticism. In this, Christian viewers' potential reaction was one of the most important grounds they thought about.

The biggest scandal of the series clearly illustrated this. The incident which became 'the highlight' of *Wang-kkot*'s unconventionality was about how to represent Yong-Hwa's death and resurrection, and its result was the unprecedented departure of the show's scriptwriter. According to the original script, Yong-Hwa was to be found dead by her family. Her body would be put into a coffin after being washed and shrouded, as her family prepared for her funeral. On the next day, hoping for a miracle, they would conduct *sosaeng-kut*, a shamanistic rite of resuscitation. On the third day, when the coffin was in transit, her brother was to stop people and shout that he heard a sound coming from the inside. They would urgently open the coffin and would be surprised to find that she was alive. They then were to quickly take her to the emergency room.

This caused a big controversy within the production team. The administrative staff requested that the writer rewrite the script, but to no avail. They finally decided to replace her with a new writer. The executive producer, who was the final decision-maker in this matter, explained his decision:

It is not possible. She [Yong-Hwa] is not Jesus. Television drama must be a story that is plausible. It is not plausible that a dead person rises up from the coffin in which she has been locked for three days, right before being put into a crematory fire. Well, it might be possible. There may be one case or two like this among six billion people in the world, but it's not something general (Personal interview 6 January 2005).

The reference to Jesus was frequently repeated by many other production crew members in talking about this incident, revealing the prevalence of Christian symbolism of resurrection after three days among not only Christians but also the general public. In this situation, the series' administrators believed that the original script would have seriously crossed a boundary. Although they had broken with conventional codes of the genre to some degree, the media professionals were not able to completely ignore Christian viewers.

While Christian viewers' responses to *Wang-kkot* in general were not as aggressive or organized as the producers had feared, their criticism towards the show was significant, both online and offline. Most negative comments on the official homepage's discussion board were posed by viewers claiming to be Christian. The Korean Association of Church Communication, a Protestant group, released a public statement arguing that recent trends in popular culture were 'pathological', and pointed to this series as an example of 'the wicked perspective that leads to lowbrow culture' (Korean Association of Church Communication 2004).

What does *Wang-kkot*'s representation of religion mean to late modern Korea? What does the adversarial relationship between shamanism and Protestant Christianity manifested in and around the drama reveal about the country's changing religious landscape? How are the fundamentalist characteristics of the two religions related to the change? What made the drama's producers, as cultural elites of the society, certain that the unconventional representation of religion in the serial would work for their audiences? To answer these questions, it is necessary to understand the social, cultural and religious context of contemporary Korea. The next two sections will contextualize the relationship between the two religions, and relate it to these religions' fundamentalist characteristics.

Shamanism and Christianity in Modern Korea

Considering its similarities with the original form of shamanism in Siberia, which is characterized by spirit possession and spirit mediumship, Korean shamanism is generally regarded as an authentic expression of the larger category (Kim 2003, Choi 1998, Hogarth 1999). The role of the shaman, or *mudang*, is central. Shamans are religious specialists, predominantly female, claiming to have mystic abilities with which they mediate between spirits and humans. Another term for shaman, *mansin*, literally meaning 10,000 spirits, points to a role as mediating agents capable of controlling all the numerous spirits. As this term implies, the Korean shamanistic pantheon is characterized by its multitude of spirits, which has a strict hierarchy from gods to ancestors, to sundry ghosts (Hogarth 1998).

The religion does not have any organizational structure, except for some cooperative associations of shamans. Instead, it relies on individual practice; there is no regular meeting or gathering place, and the personal relationship between a shaman and clients is the only functional mechanism in the religion. Thus, clients usually do not have a sense of membership related to a particular shaman or to shamanism in general; they just want to consult a shaman with a good reputation. It is generally believed that shamanism has existed since the beginning of the Korean nation and therefore has provided the foundational ethos of the nation, on top of which every foreign religion and culture is over-laid (Kim 2000).

Despite its long and engaging history, a negative discourse on shamanism has long existed. Although shamanism had not been part of the religious mainstream even before modernity was introduced, the introduction of Western modernity was the critical point for the negative discourse about it. The modern, or Western, rationalistic dichotomy first introduced the notions of 'true' and 'fraud' religion into Korean culture, according to which shamanism was classified as superstitious practice rather than a religion.

During the modernization process, this dichotomous classification strategy was consistently employed by a number of agents. In the nineteenth century, the introduction of Christianity was a serious setback for shamanism, because American missionaries refused to accord it legitimate status. They defined it as a pre-modern, primitive superstition that should be overcome for the sake of the nation's enlightenment and progress. The same discursive strategy was used during Japanese colonialism (1910–1945). Colonial scholarship defined it as a practice of lower culture instead of a religion. After liberation, especially during the Third (1961–1972) and Fourth (1972–1979) Republics of the authoritarian Park Chung-Hee regime, the government's drive for industrial-ization made the social and cultural environment even tougher for shamanism. As part of the regime's 'Superstition Eradication Project', many shrines were destroyed, and the public ritual was banned or confined only to some designated areas.

Shamanism, in the process of modernization, was stripped off of its status as a religion and was not able to benefit from the guaranteed privileges enjoyed by religions in Korea's religiously pluralistic context. As a consequence, 'while many religious leaders, mostly Buddhists and Christians, enjoyed powerful political connections, shamans continued to survive on the periphery of Korean society' (Hogarth 1999: 327).

Understanding Christianity is a key to mapping the religious landscape in modern Korea. Comprising both Protestantism and Catholicism, Christianity not only constitutes the largest religious group, but is also more visible than others due to its urban location, well-established organizational structures, and more visible and active practices. Korea is a well-known case in which Christianity achieved a prevalent status after a relatively short period of time. Since the late eighteenth century, when Roman Catholicism first came to the Korean peninsula, and the late nineteenth century, when Protestant missionaries arrived from the USA, Korea has developed into 'the world's second largest source of Christian missionaries, only a couple of decades after it started deploying them' (Onishi 2004: A-1). The growth of Christianity in Korea is recognized as a 'remarkable case' (McGrath 2002: 30), often contrasted with its decline in the West.

The growth of Christianity in Korea is aligned with the rapid process of modernization. The religion is closely associated with the adoption of modernity and it has effectively responded to the country's modernization process. In the era of Western missions, modernization was an intentional effort of the early Protestant missionaries. Their active introduction of modern civilization was central to their project of 'cultural imperialism' (Kim 1999), which intended to lower the barrier erected by the Joseon Dynasty against foreign religious ideas. Missionaries built hospitals and schools, as well as churches, which functioned as crucial apparata for the spread of an episteme of modernity. Because of these efforts, Protestantism was 'presented only as a part of the modern world' (Kim 1999: 210) instead of as a foreign religion. With this strategy, Christian missionaries were able to expand their own influence and also to weaken the power of traditional religions like Confucianism and Buddhism, as well as shamanism and folk beliefs (Jang 1999). In doing so, Christianity was at the centre of breaking pre-modernity and of spreading the modern ethos during the earlier stage of modernization. During the Japanese colonialist period, Christianity became associated with nationalism. It produced many leaders who took the lead in the anti-colonial movement, and to become a Christian was a way to express hostility towards Japan, which enforced worship at Shinto shrines.

Christianity's role in modernization was also significant after Liberation from Japan. Rhee Syngman, the first President of the Republic of Korea, was himself a Christian, and the majority of higher rank officials were from the Christian community. Since then, an amicable relationship between Christianity, in particular Protestantism, and the secular authorities continued through the 1970's and 1980's when authoritarian regimes ruled the state (Park 2003). Even though there was a Christian political activism led by liberal Christian groups, symbolized by *Minjung sinhak*, the Theology of the People[7], which was one of the core anti-government movements during that time, Christians have generally been a social group that did not criticize, but instead supported established political power, even the authoritarian regimes of Rhee Syngman, Park Chung-Hee, Chun Doo-Hwan and Roh Tae-Woo. This is accounted for by common interests shared by the conservative Christian community and the regimes, such as anti-communism, national security and the goal of modernization in terms of economic growth (Clark 1997).

Through the end of the twentieth century, Korean Protestantism saw rapid growth in both membership and social power. Ideas of rationalism, objectivism and individualism promoted by modernity were more compatible with Christianity than other religions. The insecurity that many people felt in the process of class mobilization, possibly because of rapid social change and the establishment of capitalist structures, resulted in the growth of the religious population. In the process of urbanization, Protestant churches with more active proselytizing efforts better served the need for identity and community among those who migrated into urban areas looking for a job and a better life (Yoon 1997). These efforts produced a number of mega-churches founded on the basis of charismatic ministerial leadership, like The Full Gospel Central Church in Seoul, known as the world's largest church, with a congregation of over half a million. More importantly, with its growing membership, Christianity could accomplish 'a strong organization and a religio-cultural hegemony' (Yoon 1997: 273).

Religious Changes and Late Modernity

Since the late 1980s, as Korea has entered a late modern condition in which the 'hyper-' rapid modernization and its unexpected social expenses have been critically reassessed, the social statuses of Protestant Christianity and shamanism have begun to switch. One of the central points of an emerging counter-modernity discourse is that Korean modernization was mainly initiated and influenced by foreign powers. The economic crisis in 1997 and the IMF trusteeship which followed was the moment in which Koreans had to begin to understand and manage the pressure to incorporate the nation into the global economic system. It was during this time that Koreans fully realized that the modernization process might not be structurally wholesome and that their exalted economic growth was in fact quite fragile. They also had to recognize that the hegemony of capital was replacing the hegemonic power of the authoritarian state, especially in the form of a greater degree of foreign capital (Shin 2000), which accelerated the establishment of late capitalist economic and social structures.

As this global influence makes further inroads in economic, academic and cultural spheres, nationalism that characterized Korean history in the twentieth century is being further strengthened. Cultural nationalism has emerged as a result of the effort to re-establish Korean identity and pride in the midst of rapid Westernization. While they still have not given up the aspiration for a Westernized life, to many Koreans globalization is perceived as 'evil' (Alford 1999) and nationalist discourses call into question the relationship with the USA, particularly its support of the former dictatorial regimes, as well as more recent involvement in forms of transnational capitalism (Palais 1998, Larson et al. 2004).

In this situation, Christianity's hegemonic position begins to be challenged. The link between Protestantism and pro-Amercanism, as well as its theological and political conservatism, is becoming more visible in public discourse. Christianity has become a primary target of public attention, more so than any other religion in Korea (Korean Association of Church Communication 2004). The secular media, which have been cautious not to violate their canons of 'balance' and objectivity in the multi-religious context, increasingly has joined and encouraged the symbolic creation of anti-Christian sentiments. The Christian community claims that it is now facing a 'crisis' in which public hostility is increasing and its membership, particularly among the young, is declining. Within the Christian community, a reflexive movement has begun to 'reflect on, and regret their earlier role as promoters of pro-American and anti-Communist ideology as well as the part Christians had played in glorifying Western civilization' (Ro 2002: 55).

The crisis of Korean Christianity is connected to its fundamentalist characteristics. While most churches claim to abide by evangelicalism, Korean Christianity is known to be closer to fundamentalism in nature (Shin 2004, Lee 2002). It is by origin fundamentalist because the original US missionaries' conservative theology was rooted in the fundamentalist side of the church (Brouwer et al. 1996). Also, Christianity in Korea, especially its Protestant branch, is characterized by 'emotional, conservative, Pentecostal, individual-istic, and other-worldly' characteristics (Suh 1985: 11), all related to the new 'global' Christian fundamentalism (Brouwer et al. 1996)[8].

The public's criticism against the movement has revealed two aspects, both of which demonstrate Christian fundamentalism's position in the Korean con-text. The most widely used label for Christianity is as an 'extremely exclusivist' group. This exclusivity is at the centre of the general hostility towards the religion. It is thought of as a religion that has no tolerance towards other religious traditions and religious ideas, which leads to it being labelled as 'dogmatic' and 'religiously fanatical'. This is the characteristic that was most directly addressed by the character of the grandfather in *Wang-kkot Seon-nyeo-nim*. Christianity in Korea is criticized by the public as an obvious example of Woodhead and Heelas' (2000) 'religion of differentiation' that at the sociological level 'take[s] the form of tightly-bounded communities which differentiate themselves both from other religious communities and from "the world"' (28).

The other frequent accusation against Christianity focuses on its being a Westernizing agent in the modern history of Korea, that it has taken part in destroying traditional cultures and values. Because of its link with Westerniza-tion and 'Americanness', it has become a frequent target of the anti-modernity and anti-globalization discourses, which have often been presented in forms of anti-American sentiments. People come to realize that Korea has a dependent relationship with the US and Protestant churches have taken a great role in the process. In the late modern context where modernity and modernization are questioned, the link of Christianity to Westernization turns out to be a symbolic stigma attached to the religion.

While Christianity faces this identity crisis, shamanism not only survives, but is experiencing a 'revival' (Hogarth 1999: 352). This revival of interest began in the late 1980s (Hogarth 1999, Tangherlini 1998), when the symbolic representation of the shamanistic was used by both the authoritarian government and the anti-government democratization movement. Although their political goals were quite contrary, both camps attempted to legitimatize their town efforts by equally employing 'Koreanness', an important value associated with the indigenous religion.

Moreover, since the 1990s, the revival of interest has extended from the purely political realm to the realm of everyday life. Shamanism or shamanistic practices have now become pervasive in people's ordinary culture. The practice of shamanism, traditionally confined to the private realm, has become open and public. The red and white flags indicating a shaman's residence and *yeok-sulwon*[9] hang in many neighbourhoods, even in urban settings. Advertisements with shamans' photos and striking copies are displayed nearly everywhere in public spaces, on public buses and in tabloid newspapers. Shamans and *yeoksul-in*[10] no longer wait at home for customers; they build divination booths and offer services in public places such as crowded subway stations and shopping malls. Shamans also make the most of diverse communication devices in their efforts to recruit customers. Today they offer divination services to customers over the phone as well as the internet with a minimal charge.

With these new methods, shamanism has enhanced its accessibility in society, which works well particularly for younger generations. Indigenous religion used to be thought of as a practice for older generations, but more and more young people are engaging in it and forming a new culture around it. For younger generations who do not have much experience with the traditional way of practising shamanism, the enhanced mediated accessibility to shamanism and its public presence provide an opportunity to practice it in their own way. In the streets frequented by young people, a number of *saju* cafes[11] catch the attention of young customers, whose numbers have increased in recent years. On the internet, almost every major portal site has a section for 'today's horoscope' and there exist numerous websites exploring shamanism and the shaman cosmology.

Although it is not formally a fundamentalism, the resurgence of shamanism in Korea is worth considering in our discussion of religious fundamentalism. Korean shamanism is a form of religious traditionalism, a primary dimension of fundamentalist movements in their attempt to preserve their distinct identity by retaining traditional values and recovering the sacred past. Korean shamanism has long been associated with cultural nationalism (Hogarth 1999), which has been reinforced when its symbolic meaning was utilized by many political groups for their own purposes. Its pantheon demonstrates its nationalistic meanings: from Dangun, the believed progenitor of the Korean nation, to all the founders of the various royal dynasties, to spirits of military heroes famous for their patriotic achievements. Prominent shamans regularly perform rituals just wishing for the security and welfare of the state dressed with traditional costumes. Shamans' shrines are usually decorated with a variety of nationalistic objects such as *Taegukgi* (Korean national flag), portraits of Dangun and other traditional symbols.

The resurgence of shamanism as a religious traditionalism can be explained first by its link to the revival of national identity in the context of globality. It can be argued that Korean shamanism's nationalistic features fit well with implicit and explicit resistance to Westernization and globalization among Koreans. In the globalized world, asserting national identity by giving new meanings to traditionalism is a common phenomenon in rapidly modernizing, or westernizing, societies (Smith 1981). Religion is an important arena in which the revival of ethnic and national identity takes place (Hopkins et al. 2001), and shamanism clearly functions as an expression of cultural nationalism and ethnic identity and the resistance against globalizing power (Hoppai 1996, Pentikäinen 1997). Thus, the resurgence of shamanism is understood in terms of the emergence of a 'post-traditional shamanism' or a 'postmodern shamanism', as it has emerged as a reaction to the failure of modernity and modernity's enforced rejection of cultural tradition (Hoppal 1996, Lindquist 2005).

Second, shamanism means alternativeness in Korean society, which rejects the fundamentalist characteristics of the established religions. Particularly, as *Wang-kkot* has clearly demonstrated, shamanism's alternativeness directly targets Christianity's fundamentalist core. While a religious fundamentalism prescribes certain norms and rules to members based on its theological dogmas, shamanism does not and can thus be regarded as a rather individualistic, personalized practice. Shamans function in their clients' lives not as religious leaders but as counsellors on a very practical basis compared to leaders in organized religions, who function on a more dogmatic and moral basis.

Shamanism is thus positioned as an alternative in the late modern religious landscape of Korea, in which both the public detestation of organized religion, particularly fundamentalist Christianity, and the interest in alternative spirituality are continuing to grow. It works especially well with younger generations who have their own style of cultural practice, of which the religious/spiritual domain is an important part. It also has a potential to be connected with the 'alternative spiritual movements' or putative 'new age movements,' which attempt to satisfy the spiritual desire of those who are seeking a form of religion and spirituality alternative to conventional organized religion.

Conclusion

This chapter has explored how an unconventional mediation of shamanism and Christianity by a popular television programme could be possible and how the mediated religion reflects late modern change in contemporary Korea. It has suggested that this change involves reflexive reactions against modernity and against religious fundamentalism (in the form of Protestant Christianity) as a product of the modernization process in the non-Western context.

This case study gives some insights into the discussion of the dynamic relations among religious fundamentalism, popular culture, and modernity. First, this study shows a case in a non-Western context where a Western, global, religious fundamentalism faces a fierce local reaction in the time of reflexive deliberation on modernity. Korea is a well known example of the new Christian fundamentalism's successful localization, as the religion has taken an active role in the country's exceptionally speedy industrialization by dispensing capitalist messages, comforting the middle class, and inspiring the working class. It may be particularly persuasive evidence of the thesis that 'the new Christian fundamentalism is a core element of Western civilization' (Brouwer et al. 1996).

Yet the case suggests that our attention should go further than to the mere internationalization of Christian fundamentalism, and the finding that globalizing effects in the religious domain do not always go on without any local resistance. The imported religion now comes to face an ever-increasing opposition in the public sphere. This situation seems to be a product of the late modern condition of contemporary Korea that is characterized by the coexistence of pre-modern, modern, and post-modern elements, produced by the recent and ongoing experience of rapid modernization and globalization (Koo 2002). The emerging ambivalence towards modernity and globalization creates a new circumstance for the social status of global (and globalizing) religion.

This case also illustrates that a religious traditionalism, which has been considered to be a primary element in fundamentalist movements, can be utilized as a useful resource in the local reaction *against* a global fundamentalism. The television series and the discursive rationalization by its producers and viewers are based on a symbolic mapping of religion in contemporary Korea, which has a clear demarcation between Christianity and shamanism. The dualistic juxtaposition of Christianity and shamanism reveals a confrontational relationship between the two religions in late modern Korea, respectively representing global fundamentalism and religious traditionalism. The oppositional relationship, or cultural war between them, in turn means that there are two major camps competing in the late modern religious landscape in Korea, and that shamanism as a traditionalism works well to challenge the hegemonic status of global fundamentalism. It appears that in this circumstance shamanism and its symbolic meanings may stand for the postmodern religious/spiritual sensibilities that are used to oppose its counterpart.

Finally, it should be noted that the cultural war between the two camps becomes visible in the media and popular culture. The mediated realm seems to play a vital role in the whole process of confrontation. The role of the media in the symbolic recreation of religion in the public sphere is important in that people's perception of a religion is largely influenced by the symbolic resources provided by the media. The television drama *Wang-kkot* is one of many cases where this changing religious mapping and the social locus of fundamentalism in late modern Korea are both reflected and reconstructed in the mediated realm.

However, this does not mean that we can argue that the media solely initiate or create this change, or that media representations of religion purely reflect the change. The relationship between the media and religious fundamentalism needs a more complex theoretical and empirical configuration. But it seems apparent that the realm of popular culture and the media becomes more engaged in the process and its significance continues to grow. In particular, since religious change in a non-Western context necessarily involves external influences and internal responses in this globalizing/globalized world, the mediated realm is a key site where the dynamics between the global and the local become evident thus increasing its significance for our understanding of religious fundamentalism.

Notes

1   Literally translated, the show's title means 'Big Flower Angel'. This strange title was one of the things that drew people's attention. In the rest of the chapter, it is shortened to *Wang-kkot*, as it was frequently referred to by the audience. The 174-episode daily series was telecast five days a week from June 2004 to February 2005.

2   Spirit sickness or possession sickness, indicative of supernatural notification to assume the role of shaman (Harvey 1979: 293).

3   A Korean word referring to shaman. This word carries a derogatory nuance in regard to shamans.

4   A shamanistic ritual of initiation where the shaman candidate invites possessing spirits to descend into him/her. After this ritual, the candidate takes on the role of a shaman.

5   All interview quotes and quotes from episodes of the show were translated from Korean by this chapter's author.

6   Protestant communities frequently had protests and boycotts against the media when they raised ethical problems within Protestant com- munities. They have often shown a confrontational view on popular culture by claiming that the negative allegations against them were satanic efforts to harm their social reputation.

7   A liberal theology developed in the 1970's in Korea, which is often
     compared with Liberation Theology but, unlike it, the *Minjung* theo-
     logians deny any association with Marxism.
8   According to Brouwer et al. (1996), there are four attributes that define
     the new fundamentalist Christianity: 1) Personal 'born again' relation-
     ship between the believer and Jesus; 2) The text of Bible as literally
     inerrant; 3) Mandated strict standards for personal behaviour and 4) The
     tendency to look for God-centred interpretations of history.
9   A place for divination based on *Juyeok*, a book of eastern philosophy on
     cosmology. Although *yeoksul* (divination based on *Juyeok*) is different
     from shamanism, for ordinary people, the difference between the two
     is not that important compared to the similar function that both provide
     for them.
10   Practitioners of *yeoksul* (see note 9 above).
11   Coffee shops that have several *yeoksul-in* whom people can consult if
     they want.

References

Alford, C. F. (1999), *Think No Evil: Korean Values in the Age of Globalization*.
    New York: Cornell University Press.
Brouwer, S., Gifford, P. and Rose, S. D. (eds) (1996), *Exporting the American
    Gospel: Global Christian Fundamentalism*. New York: Routledge.
Choi, J-S. (1998), *Hanguk-ui Jonggyo, Munhwaro Ingneunda (Reading
    Korean Religion as Culture)*. Seoul, Korea: Sagyejeol.
Clark, D. N. (1997), 'History and religion in modern Korea: the case of
    Protestant Christianity', in L. R. Lancaster and R. K. Payne (eds), *Religion
    and Society in Contemporary Korea*. Berkeley, CA: University of California,
    pp. 169–195.
Featherstone, M., Lash, S. and Robertson, R. (eds) (1995), *Global Modernities*.
    Thousand Oaks, CA: Sage.
Harvey, Y. K. (1979), *Six Korean Women: The Socialization of Shamans*. New
    York: West Publishing.
Hogarth, H. K. (1998), *Kut: Happiness through reciprocity*. Budapest,
    Hungary: Académiai Kiadó.
Hogarth, H. K. (1999), *Korean Shamanism and Cultural Nationalism*. Seoul,
    Korea: Jimoondang.
Hoppal, M. (1996), 'Shamanism in a postmodern age', *Electronic Journal of
    Folklore 2*, retrieved 4 August 2005 from <http://haldjas.folklore.ee/
    folklore>.
Hopkins, D. N., Lorentzen, L. A., Mendieta, E. and Batstone, D. (eds) (2001),
    Religions/Globalizations: Theories and Cases. Durham, NC: Duke
    University Press.

Jang, S. (1999), 'Protestantism in the name of modern civilization', *Korea Journal*, 38(3), 187–204.

Kellner, D. (1997), 'Overcoming the divide: Cultural studies and political economy', in M. Ferguson and P. Golding (eds), *Cultural Studies in Question*. London, UK: Sage, pp. 102–120.

Kim, C. (2003), *Korean Shamanism: The Cultural Paradox*. Burlington, VT: Ashgate.

Kim, S-K. (2000), 'Hanguk-ui bosujeok gaesingyo-wa musokshinang grigo jabonju-ui (Conservative Christianity, shamanism and capitalism in the contemporary Korean society)', *Damron 201*, 3(3), 39–74.

Kim, S-R. (1999), *Hanguk Mugyo Yeongu-ui Yeoksajeok Gochal (Historical Exploration of Korean Mugyo Studies)*. Seoul, Korea: Cheongnyoensa.

Koo, B-M. (2002), 'Preface', in J. Lewis and A. Sesay (eds) *Korea and Globalization: Politics, Economics and Culture*. New York: Routledge, pp. vii–x.

Korean Association of Church Communication (2004), 'Gui-shin-i pan-chi-neun se-sang, eonron-ui chaik im' ['World full of ghosts, media's responsibility'] (press release), retrieved 5 January 2005 from <http://www.chpr.org/subpage4.htm>.

Larson, E. V., Levin, N. D., Baik, S. and Savych, B. (2004), *Ambivalent Allies?: A Study of South Korean Attitudes Toward the U.S.* Santa Monica, CA: RAND.

Lawrence, B. B. (1998), 'From fundamentalism to fundamentalisms: A religious identity in multiple forms', in P. Heelas (ed.), *Religion, Modernity and Postmodernity*. Oxford: Blackwell, pp. 88–101.

Lee, W-K. (2002), 'Jong-gyo sa-hoe-hak-jeok gwan-jeom-e-seo bon han-guk gyo-hwoi-wa geun-bon-ju-eui' ['Korean church and fundamentalism in the perspective of sociology of religion'], *Jong-gyo-yeon-gu* [*Religious studies*], 28, 29–67.

Lindquist, G. (2005), 'Healers, leaders and entrepreneurs: Shamanic revival in Southern Siberia', *Culture and Religion*, 6(2), 263–285.

Marty, M. and Appleby, R. S. (2004[1994]), 'Introduction', in M. Marty and R. S. Appleby (eds), *Accounting for Fundamentalisms: The Dynamic Character of Movements*. Chicago, IL: University of Chicago Press.

McGrath, A. (2002), *The future of Christianity*. Oxford, UK: Blackwell

Onishi, N. (2004), 'Korean missionaries carrying word to hard-to-sway places', *The New York Times*, A–1.

Palais, J. (1998), 'Nationalism: Good or bad?', in I. H. Pai and T. R. Tangherlini (eds), *Nationalism and the Construction of Korean Identity*. Berkeley, CA: Institute of East Asian Studies, University of California, pp. 214–28.

Park, C. (2003), *Protestantism and Politics in Korea*. Seattle: University of Washington Press.

Pentikäinen, J. (1999), 'The revival of shamanism in the contemporary north', in T. Kim and M. Hoppal (eds), *Shamanism in Performing Arts*. Budapest, Hungary: Akademiai Kiado.

Ro, K-M. (2002), 'New religions and social change in modern Korean history', *The Review of Korean Studies*, 5(1), 31–62.

Shin, Y. D. W. (2004), 'Bok-eumju-eui? algobomyeon gideukgwonju-eui' ['Evangelicalism? Indeed vested-interest-ism'], *Hankyeore*, 21, 536.

Shin, K-Y. (2000), 'Globalization and class politics in South Korea', in J. D. Schmidt and J. Hersh (eds), *Globalization and Social Change*. London: Routledge, pp. 143–57.

Smith, A. (1981), *The Ethnic Revival in the Modern World*. Cambridge: Cambridge University Press.

Suh, D. K. (1985), 'American missionaries and a hundred years of Korean Protestantism', *International Review of Missions*, 74.

Tangherlini, T. R. (1998), 'Shamans, students, and the state: Politics and the enactment of culture in South Korea, 1987–1988', in I. H. Pai and T. R. Tangherlini (eds), *Nationalism and the Construction of Korean Identity*. Berkeley, CA: Institute of East Asian Studies, University of California, pp. 126–47.

Woodhead, L. and Heelas, P. (eds) (2000), *Religion in Modern Times: An Interpretive Anthology*. Malden, MA: Blackwell.

Yoon, S-Y. (1997), *Hyundae Hanguk Jongyo Munhwa-ui I-hae* [*Understanding Contemporary Korean Religion*]. Seoul, Korea: Hanwool.

Chapter 12

Christian Fundamentalism and the Media in India

Pradip N. Thomas

Introduction

While it is tempting to portray Christian fundamentalism in India in terms of the military struggles in numerous 'tribal' states located in North-Eastern India, where assorted bands of Christian Baptists and other Christian groups committed to autonomy and independence based on a separatist Christian identity are involved in struggles against a perceived de facto Indian/Hindu state, that is only one aspect of a larger, more complex phenomenon. I have argued elsewhere that the terrain of Christian fundamentalism and its strategies are, in fact much wider and need to be defined in the main as a communicative strategy directed towards the strengthening of Christianity in India via soft strategies involving broadcasting, education, Christian mission, Christian mobilization, aid and development work and international advocacy and mobilization. These diverse opportunities for spreading the Word involve the spaces and places of globalizing India as much as its hinterlands where modernity has scarcely touched the daily rhythms of life. In this chapter, I explore Christian fundamentalism in India as a phenomenon that includes: 1) Christian separatism based on armed struggle against the state; 2) Christian involvement in domestic politics; 3) Spiritual warfare; 4) Spatial strategies including the embrace of the city of Chennai and 5) Christian broadcasting. This is by no means a composite strategy. Different groups adopt one or more of these strategies. What is clear is that each of these options is based on a literal understanding of the 'Great Commission' and on a clear understanding of the nature of the adversary. In the case of military strategies, the adversary is the state that, in the recent past, has aided and abetted the project of Hindu nationalism and attempted to subvert 'indigenous' identities. With respect to politics, it is the perceived need to counter mainstream exercises of power through Christian representation and involvement in local and national politics.

Spiritual warfare is directed towards defeating the principalities and powers that exist in the Hindu spirit world. The embrace of city-space through the acquisition of real estate, worship in malls, advertising, icons, mega-events such as crusades and rallies are the means to counter secular, non-Christian presence and Christian broadcasting is directed towards claiming Christ as Lord of the airwaves, a significant aspect of their cultural and communicational strategy. It is this multi-faceted approach that makes the study of Christian fundamentalism in India a fascinating phenomenon on its own right (see Thomas 2008).

This chapter is based on a larger study on Christian Fundamentalism and the media in India that I have been involved with. That study is based on a political-economy approach that is undergirded by a Bourdieuean framework. Bourdieu's project of constructivist structuralism attempted to bridge the differences between the objective and the subjective, between agency and structure, between cultural idealism and historical materialism and was an attempt to theorize the mutually constitutive connectivities between social structures and actors. I was involved in field work in Chennai, India in December 2005 and January 2006 where I carried out a series of interviews with evangelists, Christian media producers, theologians and a variety of Indian Christians.

Christian fundamentalism in India is partly an indigenous project manifested through the politics of Christian separatism in North-East India, a variety of cultural and spatial strategies and, also, a project that is significantly supported by exogenous interests, mainly Pentecostal and neo-Pentecostal ministries located in the USA in particular. The reasons for the rise in Christian fundamentalism in India are manifold. Its growth coincides with the global growth and spread of Pentecostal and neo-Pentecostal ministries, the search for 'certainty' in the light of the vagaries and insecurities of economic globalization, aggressive global mission strategies adopted by para-church organizations such as AD 2000 and a response to the rise of Hindu nationalism in India. It is also an outgrowth of dissatisfaction with the ministries offered by traditional churches – in particular the Roman Catholic, Protestant and Orthodox churches.

While there has been the odd attempt by the mainstream church in India to assess the growth of these new churches, in general no serious efforts have been made to understand or counter their growth. In fact, it would seem that the strategy adopted by the mainstream churches is to accommodate a variety of conservative positions thereby lessening opportunities for members to leave the church. In personal conversations with members belonging to the Protestant church hierarchy in India, I was given to understand that in the context of Hindu nationalism and attempts by nationalist Hindus to call into question the validity of the Indian-Christian hyphen, the cause of Christian unity took precedence over the admonition of recalcitrant Christian groups committed to Christianizing the nation. In 2006, the Pew Forum on Religion and Public Life released a survey entitled, *Spirit and Power: A 10-Country Survey of*

Pentecostals based on a random sampling of publics in countries located mainly in the South including India. This study is by all accounts, the first comparative global survey of Pentecostalism – a religion 'made to travel' (Dempster et al. 1999), and that is the most significant expression of global Christianity today. The survey attempts to assess the global salience of 'distinctions' that mark 'renewalist' traditions – speaking in tongues, belief in divine healings, divine revelations and stance on moral issues such as homosexuality and divorce. The section on 'renewalists and politics' is particularly intriguing and offers a glimpse of the emergence of a robust Christian politics, the growing belief in the need for greater correspondences between Christianity and politics:

> Majorities of renewalists in every country surveyed say that it is important to them that their political leaders have strong Christian beliefs. In six of the 10 countries, at least three-quarters of Pentecostals share this view; in the other four countries, at least two-thirds of Pentecostals agree with this position. Charismatics, as well, share the conviction that political leaders should have strong Christian beliefs (Pew Forum on Religion and Public Life 2006: 7).

The 2006 Pew Study on global Pentecostalism includes statistics on the growth of Pentecostalism and neo-Pentecostalism in India – information that confirms some of the findings in Paul Parathazham's (1997) survey of 4,558 neo-Pentecostals from 328 neo-Pentecostal churches in nine cities in India. What is interesting about Parathazham's study is that it explicitly tries to explore the motives behind Catholic charismatics leaving the Catholic Church and joining neo-Pentecostal churches. The study shows that the Catholics who leave their church joined neo-Pentecostal churches because of their need for a more relevant and fulfilling God-experience, experience of fellowship, support during crisis and the need for certainty in troubled times. While Prior (2007: 121), quoting information from this survey, has observed that, 'the Indian Catholics who are joining Pentecostal churches are mostly urban, educated and middle class', the fact remains that given the profusion of these churches in urban, semi-urban and rural contexts, members belong to a variety of socio-economic strata. The ability to reach out to both the victors of globalization and to their victims remains a strength of these new churches. Economic globalization has led to the growth of a significant section of Christian businessmen and women, whose wealth has alienated them from the mainstream churches that often confess publicly to a complex, anti-market ideology while functioning, for all practical purposes, within the boundaries of the global market economy.

To most observers of religion and politics in South Asia, it is the many varieties of Islamic and Hindu fundamentalism and, to a lesser extent, Buddhist fundamentalism that defines the terrain of religious fundamentalism on the sub-continent. Christians have often featured as victims – as martyrs in blasphemy cases in Pakistan or as targets for Hindu fundamentalists in India. While the covert violence of Christian mission, in particular, the attempt to Christianize through the provision of education, access to health facilities and other material and monetary inducements has led to Christian converts being described as 'rice Christians', there is in general widespread respect among all religious communities for certain aspects of Christian mission, in particular the provision of a variety of services inclusive of health and education throughout the length and breadth of the country. The critique of Christian mission varies from the benign critiques of Christian mission famously articulated by Mahatma Gandhi to the more strident critiques that have emerged in the more recent past. Arun Shourie, a journalist and former minister in the 2000–2004 Hindu nationalist Bharatiya Janata Party (BJP)-led coalitional National Democratic Alliance (NDA) government, has written among the most trenchant, post-colonial critiques of Christian mission focused on the theology, activities and pronouncements of the mainstream Catholic Church. Shourie (1994, 2000) offers a historical reading and critique of mainstream Christianity's mission by stealth. In hindsight, it is a major oversight on Shourie's part to have entirely missed out on the role of the many 'new' churches in India to whom the mantle of fundamentalism sits easy. However Shourie's critique does point to a core issue in Christianity in India today – the fact that mainstream churches do accommodate and have made their peace with their members who believe in the inerrancy of scriptures, the superiority of Christians, a Christians-only eschatology, Christian validation of conversion and a triumphalistic understanding of the Christian faith. A recent book by the journalist Edna Fernandes (2006), *Holy Warriors: A Journey into the Heart of Indian Fundamentalism*, offers at best a partial and tenuous glimpse of Christian fundamentalisms in India including a history of the Inquisition in Goa and Christian mission and separatism in Nagaland, a state located in North-East India that has, for over half a century, been involved in a struggle for independence.

Christian Separatism

It is important that we recognize the struggles in North-East India as one aspect of a larger struggle to claim India for Christ. Christianity remains the religion of the majority in a number of the 'hill-states' in North-East India including Mizoram, Meghalaya, Nagaland and there are significant groups of Christians in other states in that region. The Christianizing of North-East India that began in the 1850s led to Welsh Presbyterians, English and American Baptists and Catholics having a significant presence and influence in this area. These states, inclusive of Nagaland, Mizoram, Meghalaya, Tripura, Manipur buffering and bordering China, Myanmar and Bangladesh, have been strategically significant to the Indian government and a variety of 'insurgencies' have led to bloody counter-operations by the Indian army and frequent accusations of military abuse of the civilian population. At the very same time, organizations like the predominantly Baptist National Liberation Front of Tripura and the National

Socialist Council of Nagaland have been accused of organizing mass conversions to Christianity and of encouraging conflict with other Christian groups in the region. While Mizo insurgency has ceased, the conflict in Nagaland, Manipur and Tripura remains. As Edna Fernandes (2006: 169) observes in her account of Christian fundamentalism in Nagaland, 'The Baptists clearly backed the Nagas in their claim for sovereignty. [. . .] An independent Nagaland for Christ seemed to fit in very neatly with the Baptists' own plans for the region – a spiritual nerve-centre which would export the Word into neighbouring countries'. Subir Bhaumik (2004: 234) in an article on separatist movements in North-East India has observed that:

> Christianity reinforced and complemented, rather than supplanted, the sense of distinct ethnicity and otherness among Nagas and the Mizos. Separatist groups such as the Naga National Council (NNC) and the Mizo National Front (MNF) laced their separatist rhetoric with free use of Biblical imageries – and the MNF even christened its (first) military operation *Operation Jericho*.

Christian missionaries from North-East India continue to play a significant role in Christian mission in North, East and Central India. The Zoram Baptist Mission (ZBM) from Mizoram has, for instance, been involved in converting indigenous groups in Madhya Pradesh. As one of their mission handbooks states:

> ZBM, with the help of God, is planning to plant fifty local churches in the Madhya Pradesh field by the year 2000. Thousands of villages in Betul, Hoshangabad and East Nimar districts north of the Tapti River are the home of four lakhs (400,000) aboriginal Korku and Gond tribals. Along with them are more than a million Hindus and Muslims (Rammawia 1992: 98).

Christian Involvement in State Politics

When compared with the close relationships forged between politicians and conservative Christianity in other parts of the world – Paul Mbiya (Cameroon), Frederick Chiluba (Zambia), Efrain Rioss Montt (Guatemala), Laisenia Qurase (Fiji), Bill Skate (PNG) and George Bush (USA) – the situation in India, at least at the federal level, is not of real concern. However at a state-level, in the majority Christian, so-called 'tribal' states in North-East India, and some of the states in Southern India, this relationship is much stronger. The leaders of the two major Pentecostal denominations in Tamil Nadu, South India, Ezra Sargunam and M. Prakash are aligned with the two major political parties in the state – and depending on the party in power, one or other leader often occupies a position on the State's Minority Commission, as a representative of all Christians in the state. Christians are a minority vote bank in most of the country, although in states where they are a significant minority, bloc voting can make a difference. While there is to date scant evidence to suggest that these leaders are actively involved in the advocacy of socially conservative policies, their commitment to mission, evangelism and conversion has taken them on a collision course with Hindu nationalists and secularists. Christian conservatives have become the de facto spokespersons for Indian Christians, featured on Capitol Hill at the US Commission on International Religious Freedom and the US State Department's annual report on International Religious Freedom. These leaders have played a major role in the consolidation of independent and Pentecostal churches and have used their political power to leverage the government of Tamil Nadu to repeal the bill against 'forced conversions' and to lobby for the legitimization of Christian conventions and rallies that are a platform for conversion. The *Every Tribe, Every Tongue* conference that was held in Chennai in January 2005 and organized by Ezra Sargunam, was a celebration of indigenous converts belonging to 'tribal' groups located all over India. The fact that leading members of the ruling Congress party and the state party, the Dravida Munnetra Kazhagam (DMK) politicians were involved in the opening ceremony indicates that those in favour of secular India, in their haste to undo the excesses of Hindu nationalism, ignore the part played by minority religious politics in undermining the fabric of secularism in India and fail to understand the 'multiplicity' that is at the very core of Indian Christianity. A number of these Christian leaders feature regularly on Christian cable and satellite channels where they reinforce their brand of conservative Christianity. The ex-President of the Minorities Commission in the state of Tamil Nadu, M. Prakash, and founder of the South India Soul Winner's Association, is also the President of the Synod of the Independent Churches of India (1,700 churches) and is the national coordinator of the Trinity Broadcasting Network. A former chairperson of the State's Minorities Commission, Ezra Sargunam leads the Evangelical Church of India and is a vocal supporter of conversion. The present chief minister of Andhra Pradesh (AP), the largest state in South India, Samuel Rajasekhar Reddy is a Seventh-Day Adventist who has allegedly provided tacit support for Christian missions, including Christian broadcasting. His controversial support for Christian mission in his state, in particular church growth on the Hindu pilgrimage route to one of the better known temples in South India, Tirupati, has made him a target for Hindu nationalists. The Christian Broadcasting Network's Indian operations are based out of Hyderabad, the capital of Andhra Pradesh.

Spiritual Warfare

'Operation Jericho', the code that was used by the Mizos in their first major military operation against the Indian army, was first used in connection with an

Allied bombing sortie on the German-occupied Amien's Prison in February 1944 but has since then become firmly associated with the strategies of 'spiritual warfare'. For instance, 'Prayer in Evangelism' is described as a global battle against Satan:

> Spiritual warfare prayer is God-directed intercession using the resources of Jesus Christ given to the whole Church in order to overcome obstacles by the power of the Holy Spirit to facilitate the evangelization of the whole world (2 Corinthians 10; Ephesians 6:12) (Lausanne Committee for World Evangelisation 2004).

Spiritual warfare is a strategy that addresses the need for conversion and repentance but is also a means by which the superiority of the Christian spirit over other extant spirits is maintained, fortified and reinforced.

The obstacles to Christian mission include other religious traditions and the symbolic mediations of these traditions via priests, shamans, rituals and practices, images and the territorial spirits that resist the Christian message. The defeat of Hindu supernaturalism and its diverse spirit world is seen as an essential aspect of the Christianizing of India. As Susan Bayly (1994: 749) has observed:

> These believers want to reassert their primacy over the rich supernatural terrain of south India with its living pantheon of divinities, warrior heroes and cult saints. For them, Jesus, the Virgin, and the Christian Saints must be made known to a wider world as fierce figures of power with the capacity to contend as warriors in the crowded and menacing supernatural landscape of contemporary South India.

For the Hindu converts to Pentecostalism, the need to overcome the malign influence of the Hindu spirit world remains an entirely rational imperative given that this world is part of their 'plausibility structures' and its presence is real in their negotiations of day to day life. The vanquishing of evil spirits is part of the repertoire of Pentecostalist preachers. Evil spirits in other words may have been banished by the rationalists and the intellectualized pastoral elite belonging to the Church of South India but for ordinary people their destructive presence is real enough. As Thomas (2003: 379) has observed in a study of Dalits and Pentecostalism in Kerala:

> The Dalits saw in Pentecostalism powerful continuities with those folk elements which are part of their past culture, although they would not explicitly say this. These included the spirit-filled worship, which have strong emotional elements, the transmuted elements of spirit possession in worship centered on the third person of the Trinity, the whole aspect of faith healing and exorcism which Pentecostalism offered.

Lionel Caplan (1991: 372), in a study of Christian fundamentalism in urban
Madras (now known as Chennai), contrasts the ready willingness of Pentecostal preachers to combat the spirit world against the rationalized Christianity
practised by the mainstream churches that does not recognize the supernatural
in popular Indian Christianity:

[The Pentecostals] do not deny the reality of such (evil) forces which by
intention, or otherwise, bring adversity. In this respect, they provide a strong
contrast with the orthodox churches and their missionary predecessors. In
South India, as in virtually every part of the missionized world, Protestant
evangelists turned their backs on such concerns. The essential Christian
doctrine of belief in the authenticity of miracles was suspended. Whereas
Hindus had resort to a variety of deities and ritual specialists to protect
them, the missionaries refuted and eliminated the agencies by means of
which converts to Protestantism and their descendents sought protection
from these dangerous powers.

Within evangelical and neo-Pentecostal traditions, spiritual warfare prayers are
often complemented by 'strategic level spiritual warfare' and 'spiritual mapping'. Not only is training for spiritual warfare a reality in India – as for
example training camps organized by the Youth With a Mission's 'School of
Intercession Worship and Spiritual Warfare' (YWAM Extreme!! n.d.). Christian
groups have taken spiritual mapping seriously, as for instance in Chennai, where
the para-church organization Last Days Harvest Ministries (n.d.) describes the
obstacles to Christianizing mission in the following words:

1) The Theosophical Society in Adyar who are Freemasons which include
women, are open to all gods including Baal and Astoreth, 2) The
Kapaleswara temple in Mylapore to the Hindu God Siva and, 3) The
Parthasarthy Temple in Triplicane to the Hindu God Vishnu.

In the same vein, Chennai's largest Pentecostal church, the New Life Assemblies
of God (NLAG), and their Yo Team that specifically caters to youth describe
their mission strategy as follows:

The youth are in the forefront of the battle and this is the generation of
God's Generals. The sounds of war, the wail of people in pain, the cry of
lands in distress and the atmosphere of vigilance we see are the trumpet call
to the end times. At NLAG, God is in the process of raising up a **New
Generation** sold out for Him to see His glory rest upon their lives and in this
land. Rise up and join this **Warrior Tribe**. As a church these days we have
been praying for the land and blew the trumpet over St. Thomas mount
and at the peripheral of the city, declaring victory over the land . . . ('City
Shakers' n.d.).

Prayer walks organized by the Friends Missionary Prayer Band are means by which spiritual warfare is carried out. Their monthly publication *Friends Focus* describes one of their activities in a suburban area in Chennai – New Washerampet:

> We prayed to God and bound the filthy, suicidal and murderous spirits. We asked God to take this place in his hands, bring his presence and set the people free; and to revive the church. We blessed this place in Jesus' name. Like this we prayed for New Washerampet, Ennore, Alamathy, Keeldon-daiyur, Neemam and Naduveerpattu. And we are expecting great blessings in these areas. . . . We should arrange prayer walks in the frontiers of mission where the strongholds of Satan keep people in bondage for hundreds of years (Friends Missionary Prayer Band 2005: 13).

In other words, at the heart of this contestation between new Christian groups and the rest are their attempts to prove that the power of the Christian God is stronger than that of the Hindus. Faith healing, exorcism, miracles are a part of this competition (Bergunder 2001). There are also deliberate attempts to take over the heart of Hindu Chennai through spiritual warfare. As one website claims:

> Mylapore and Triplicane are two of the oldest towns of Chennai and the Apostle Thomas ministered in these towns. According to tradition, the apostle was martyred by the king of Mylapore. The apostle must have established strong churches grounded on God's Word in these areas, but over a period of time they have backslidden and profaned God's Word. The glory and presence of God departed because of the sins of the forefathers, and the door was wide open to the enemy to come in and establish strong-holds which are controlling the city (Last Date Harvest Ministries n.d.).

Pentecostal healers in Chennai routinely 'anoint' products – from oils to books and other products which are then sold to the faithful and used as forms of protection – as talismans against evil. In globalizing India where the religious market has become a dominant reality, anointed religious products have become the means by which certain Christian groups maintain their share of the religious market. Just as products featuring the Hindu God Ganesh are available in every imaginable texture, so organizations like the Chennai-based Jesus Calls sell anointed books, DVDs and CDs including books such as *The Gifts of the Holy Spirit* and *Secrets for Success* that are endorsed on their 24-hour television channel Rainbow TV (Photo 12.1). A pioneering conservative evangelical para-chruch organization set up by D. G. Dhinakaran in the early 1970s, it is today a family concern with a multi-million dollar budget. The power of prayer is however the key spiritual warfare strategy used by Jesus Calls. Prayer itself is a commodified process and there are six partnership plans

இயேசு அழைக்கிறார் ஜெப கோபுரம்
Jesus Calls
PRAYER TOWER

Photo 12.1 Jesus Calls is the oldest, largest, wealthiest evangelical mission in India with extensive trans-national operations. It is based in Chennai and was founded by Brother Dhinakaran. The mission has a formidable communications ministry that includes broadcasting, print and new media. (**photo by Pradip Thomas**)

through which their prayer ministry can be financially supported. As their website states:

> The Prayer Warriors, when they pray for the sick, apply the oil which is specially prayed upon by The Dhinakarans for the Lord's anointing. According to the promise 'let them pray over him, anointing him with oil in the name of the Lord; and the prayer of faith will save the sick, and the Lord will raise him up, and if he has committed sins, he will be forgiven' (James 5:14, 15), the Lord honours their faith and delivers the sick and those in bondage ('Prayer & Counselling' n.d.).

Testimonials reinforce the power of prayer and deliverance that are symbiotically related, the one reinforcing the other.

However, and in spite of the best efforts of Pentecostal and neo-Pentecostal missionaries, the sacred topography and diversity of Tamil sacred sites that are grounded in locality, intricately related to the life-worlds of local people, steeped in neighbourhood history is difficult to breach. In fact, temples that are widely known and specialize in curing specific types of possession by evil spirits and that offer an expansive and sophisticated affinity to gods and goddesses than with any singular, all-powerful God, are resistant to subversion (Shulman 1980). Chennai is steeped in Hinduism in a sense that Christianity is not. Pentecostalism's engagement with the spirit world is global. In Latin America and Africa, studies have shown that Pentecostalism's validation of the spirit world meshes with traditional, pre-Christian understandings of this world based on struggles between different gradations of good and evil.

Christian spiritual warfare is but one aspect of a larger, extensive and intensive, well-funded Christian fundamentalism project in India, although its specifics are, for the most, relatively unknown within and for that matter outside India. One can of course argue that in a country that has more temples than schools, significant religious diversity and a population of Indian Christians that accounts for a mere 2.4 per cent of the total population, the strategies of Christian fundamentalists will not amount to much. Furthermore, in the context of the contemporary religious market, traditions of spiritual warfare are associated with all the major religious traditions in India – Hinduism in the context of the rise of Hindu nationalism and Islam in the context of its own battles on the sub-continent.

The Pentecostal/neo-Pentecostal Embrace of the City

One of the key strategies adopted by these groups is the embrace of the city by Pentecostal and neo-Pentecostal groups. One of the interesting features of the new churches is their spatial presence in Chennai, their embrace of the official city and the unintended cities, the rural and the urban, their being part of and catering to a globalizing Chennai and Chennaites (Manokaran 2005, Prakash 2002). There is a real sense in which Pentecostalism intrinsically is a religion that was made to travel for it is part of the flows of the global, at home in a crowded market area as in a gleaming mall (Dempster et al. 1999, Cox 1996). Mendieta (2001: 20) observes that, '. . . religion appears as a resource of images, concepts, traditions and practices that can allow individuals and communities to deal with a world that is changing around them', in the midst of places and shopping, leisure and recreation, production and consumption, an observation that captures the new church in changing Chennai. Malls, as for instance the Abirami Mall in the suburb of Kelly's Corner in Chennai, host the Power Church with its accent on Gospel Rock and a congregation that consists of young professionals from the IT and other sectors in the new economy. This culture is an emerging one and there are other malls in Chennai that are being used by the new churches. There are intentional efforts to reach young professionals – from call-centre workers to software professionals. The cell church movement in India is an organic expression of church growth in the era of globalization. Since church planting and the harvesting of souls are fundamental objectives of the new churches, members belonging to tightly knit cell churches are involved in enabling the viral replication of these cells. A number of these new churches may be termed indigenous churches that espouse indigenous theologies although as many are influenced by the Health and Wealth

Gospel linked to the Faith movement. Stephen Hunt (2000: 344), in a perceptive essay on the Health and Wealth Gospel, observes that the success of this model relates to its value-addedness:

> Pentecostalism serves to develop attributes, motivations and personalities adapted to the exigencies of the de-regulated global market. [. . .] It has integrated the urban masses into a developing economy through the protestant work ethic and active citizenship. [. . .] At the same time, the mobile new professionals and the educated in mega-cities carry a work ethic that *results* from a strict Pentecostal upbringing. [. . .] The explanation for the success of the Faith movement is that it can adapt itself to such complexities. This makes it a global 'winner'.

The re-taking of the Hindu heartlands of Chennai features in the literature of neo-Pentecostal groups in Chennai and Christian forums exist in the heart of these emblematically Hindu suburbs.

Transformation for Chennai City involving concerned Christians is not a new movement. As early as 1996, leaders in Chennai City have been meeting together to see how the Whole Church can take the Whole Gospel to the Whole City. In the late 90s, Chennai City was divided into 12 zones and pastors fellowships began to be formed in geographical areas of the city that had a focus on bringing transformation. Various networks have been formed of which some continue to operate to this day.

This includes banners and posters of conventions, faith-healing gatherings, rallies and crusades that are posted on public and private spaces – trees, as adverts on three-wheeler taxis (auto-rickshaws), stickers on cars, banners that are strung across roads. These new churches, in other words, have begun to have a public presence in Chennai and feature in its symbolic economy. Sharon Zukin (1995: 23–24) has observed that:

> [T]he symbolic economy features two parallel production systems that are crucial to a city's material life: the *production of space*, with its synergy of capital investment and cultural meanings, and the *production of symbols*, which constructs both a currency of commercial exchange and a language of social identity.

Not only are churches like the New Life Assembly of God church located on the key highway leading to the city of Chennai; the re-location of Jesus Calls, the oldest and perhaps best known of the evangelical organizations from its present location on Greenways Road to a landmark property on Rajaji Salai (the heart of the city) previously owned by the TIAM group, one of Chennai's largest business houses, stands as an example of the claiming of public space by these new churches. It must be pointed out that the presence of traditional churches in the urban cityscape of Chennai remains strong. However it is clear that in the 'new' Chennai, these new churches have begun to claim public space. The heart of the city along with its suburbs and hinterlands now host any number of Christian churches and Christian para-church organizations. One can argue that this religion has travelled well to the centres as well as to the peripheries of Chennai. Not only are these new churches networked in an informational sense, they are structured along corporate lines:

> [T]he decentralisation of management; the sub-contracting of operations to constellation of ancillary small and medium-sized businesses; and the networking of corporations linking their elements to each other and to their auxiliaries. The result is the formation of complex, hierarchical, diversified organizational structure . . . (Castells 1989: 168).

This structure is evident in Jesus Calls, the New Life Church and the Youth With a Mission Chennai among other church and para-church organizations that are intentionally grounded in the new globalizing Chennai, and its flows – material, resources, images, information, personnel – between the local and the global. These churches have adapted to the culture of work and social mobility in globalizing Chennai. They have valourized, bought into, and reinforced globalization as an inevitable reality that needs to be exploited by the church in the context of the fulfilment of the 'Great Commission'.

New migrants to the cities formed the bulk of the congregations of the early Pentecostal churches in Chennai. This trend has continued, although it is now complemented by settled congregations catering to the needs of the urban upper and middle classes. Chennai and its suburbs alone has upwards of 2,500 churches – consisting of indigenous churches, house churches and a variety of Pentecostal and neo-Pentecostal churches that, according to some observers, make it the fastest growing hub of Christianity in South Asia. Numbers can of course be disputed but the sheer numbers of churches listed in church directories available in Christian bookshops point to their growing presence. Raj and Selvasingh (2004: 10) have observed that, 'Chennai is privileged to have the highest number of churches of all the cities in South Asia. In 1994, there were about 1,400 churches in Chennai . . . in 1999 . . . 1,864 churches . . . small churches (formed) "by the influence of the Pentecostals"'. Mega churches include the New Life AOG church in Saidapet, Chennai with its 35,000 members and 10,000 at sitting services. The clearest evidence however of church growth in Chennai is the *Chennai Christian Directory* (2000) which lists 3,000 churches and para-church organizations in this city inclusive of the Beulah Church (8 churches), End Time Zion (14 churches), Marantha Full Gospel Church (27 churches), Moving Jesus Mission (3 churches), Pillar of Fire Mission (6 churches), the Village Evangelism of Indian Mission (5 churches), Indigenous Churches (645), Assemblies of God (120) among very many other churches in Chennai. This directory also lists 46 Bible colleges, 23 Christian media centres, 122 Christian magazines in English and Tamil and 114 church planting missions. There is every reason to believe that there has been a further growth in these sectors of late (Thomas 2007a).

Christian Television

Today, there are, broadly speaking, five avenues for Christian television in India: 1) The occasional space on the national broadcaster *Doordarshan* for Christian programmes; 2) transnational satellite channels including GOD TV, CBN, TBN, MiracleNet and Daystar TV that are available via cable; 3) Christian programming on a variety of secular cable channels available throughout the country (e.g., Raj TV, Zee TV, Vijay TV and other channels); 4) stand-alone indigenous Christian cable channels such as Blessing TV, Angel TV, Shalom TV, Jeevan TV and the free, 24-hour DTH channel Rainbow Television that features programmes from the Chennai-based Jesus Calls organization and 5) web-based telecasting – for instance 'Jesus Calls' 'Num.TV'. Webcasting remains an evolving reality in India with limited audiences. Pentecostal and charismatic organizations have a dominant presence in all forms of Christian broadcasting in India.

What are some aspects of Christian television in India that can be termed 'fundamentalist'?

Muscular Christianity and the Gospel of Prosperity

These channels, often backed by indigenous and exogenous Christian organizations and agencies, frequently feature content that is supportive of a triumphalistic, muscular Christianity based on a promise of health and wealth for all those who are Christian. At the very same time, it offers an uncertain future for those who either do not belong to the Christian faith or are opposed to it. This agenda is for instance foregrounded in Pat Robertson's *700 Club* as well as through Alec and Wendy's current affairs round up on GOD TV. Frameworks for understanding global politics, the war in Iraq, global terrorism and democracy are frequently drawn and boundaries clearly delineated. For a Christian audience in Chennai not previously exposed to Biblical justifications for right-wing politics, such programmes, sandwiched between Joyce Meyer's homily on 'familial strife' and Sam Chelladurai's 'prosperity theology', offer justifications for a range of issues from Christian Zionism to easy understandings of the causes and nature of evil in contemporary societies. The Christian conception of evil and good is different from its understanding in Hinduism, where the accent is on the continuities between evil and good rather than their separateness. The truth of these stories has been revealed to God's anointed. In a situation characterized by the mainstream church's distance from interrogations of global and national politics, the primary Christian version of politics on public display is that advocated by televangelists. The average Christian in India has a very conservative understanding of politics in the Middle East – and these channels, CBN and GOD TV in particular, routinely privilege and sanction the divisive policies and politics of the Israeli government and reinforce stereotypes of Muslims and people of other faiths. Pat Robertson's open critique of Hindus and Hinduism on his syndicated programmes has led to a number of condemnations from Hindu nationalists. These channels, and television in particular, tap into, and are sustained by, the core message of economic globalization: that the pursuit of individual wealth and profit-making are premier virtues, over and above the pursuit of communitarian futures. Sam Chelladurai's ministry, the Assemblies of God Churches, Brother Dhinakaran's ministry, that of PowerHouse and numerous other ministries celebrate the health and wealth gospel. The MTV style Gospel rock music on GOD TV with its bland and repetitive lyrics is also on offer at the PowerHouse and the Vineyard, where young IT professionals and stock brokers rock to an anodyne version of Christianity. The lyrics may be modern, but in essence they are a throwback to the triumphalist hymns of yore that celebrated the primacy of the Christian God (see Thomas 2007b).

Representations

While most Christian channels avoid any direct criticism of Hinduism, unlike on Christian websites where the most disrespectful descriptions of other religions are on display, there is an implicit message that Hinduism is a lesser religion, mired in superstition and destined to be marginalized by the Christian message. There is an endless circulation of persecution stories of Christian missionaries in India, noticeably on K. P. Yohanan's *Gospel for Asia* radio broadcasts but also on Pat Robertson's CBN. Benny Hinn's video of the crusade held in Bangalore in November 2005 begins with God's miraculous delivery of the crusade from anti-Christians who tried to get the government of India to ban the evangelists from entering the country. While there has been persecution of Christians in India, one rarely comes across information on what these missionaries were doing in the heartlands of Hindu India in the first place. Missionaries who deem it a virtue to topple deities in a Hindu temple can be expected to be persecuted. Persecution, and the battle of these evangelists against Satan, adds to the allure and the mythos of these modern day Crusaders riding into battle against heathen hordes. Praying for a secular government in India is also rather widespread on these channels. At the *Every Tongue, Every Tribe* conference that was held in Chennai in January 2006, God was exhorted to change governments in numerous BJP-governed states. There is a strong belief in the power of prayer to change lives and situations. The fact that India had in 2004 changed governments from one that was led by Hindu nationalists to a Congress-led coalition was directly attributed to the 'hand of God' and the power of prayer.

Appropriating India for Christ

Given the demand for Christian television and the need for professional programming, established musicians and production staff from the Tamil film industry including playback singers, sound technicians and camera persons are involved in the creation of Christian programmes. An example of a Bollywood singer turned 'Born Again' Christian is the playback singer Vijay Benedict (Photo 12.2) who is a regular on Christian TV and is a major attraction at evangelical conventions such as those organized by the itinerant global Christian rallyist Benny Hinn, and the *Every Tongue, Every Tribe* conference (Photo 12.3). Benedict and other singers have played an important role in adapting Bollywood and MTV music styles and the creation of crossover styles of Indian Christian popular music. Given the extraordinary influence of film music in India, such personalities have contributed to strengthening the market for contemporary Indian Christian popular music. In Benedict's case the songs are often couched in an 'India for Christ' thematic – and the sessions include flag-waving patriotism. The spectacle often includes the appropriation of the tri-coloured Indian

Photo 12.2 Born-again Bollywood singer Vijay Benedict at the *Every Tongue, Every Tribe* conference held in Chennai in January 2006. The names in the foreground are of tribes in India present at the conference. The conference was the largest ever Christian mission conference devoted to 'tribal mission' organized by the Pentecostal Church in India. (**photo by Pradip Thomas**)

Photo 12.3 Pirated Christian CDs and VCDs for sale in Chennai outside the *Every Tongue, Every Tribe* Conference. (photo by Pradip Thomas)

flag by Christians, a symbolic wresting of the flag from the Hindu nationalists and its anointing for a Christian nation. 'Saving the Nation for Christ' is a broad thematic and the stage at live events is often festooned with Indian flags.

Christian Media and Proselytization

I had, while on fieldwork in India during December 2005 and January 2006, attended an evening worship at the Assemblies of God mega-church in Saidapet, Chennai where there was a special segment devoted to a project – the 'My Hope Campaign' supported by the Billy and Franklin Graham Ministries. Representatives from this organization presented the project. The project was a series of 30-minute-long television programmes *Mathew and Son* that was to be shown on channels in Chennai during the Christmas season. The objective of this exercise was to recruit as many people as possible to organize an event around these programmes. The congregation was asked to invite non-Christians in particular to watch these programmes: 'If you have a television, invite unbelievers to your home. You could call them for tea or dinner and while they are at your home, you could ask them to watch the *My Hope* television broadcast on various channels on primetime, in different Indian languages' (*My Hope India* 2005). They were asked to each invite 10 people, watch the programme, present a testimony and follow up with those who expressed an interest in 'Christ'. The representatives were on a whirlwind tour of Chennai churches that day. A 'how to' video was shown that took the congregation step at a time through this process. Similarly, Pastor Thangiah of the AOG church in Bangalore provided the logistics and support for Benny Hinn's campaigns and frequently endorses such campaigns and is featured on GOD TV. It is in this sense that one can conclude, that despite the complexity that characterizes the new church environment in Chennai, it remains a receiving city of global imports of conservative Christianity. As Rory Alec of GOD TV concluded after a recent visit to the Chennai regional headquarters of GOD TV, 'it is an extraordinary hour for India and more now than ever, we have a power and authority and responsibility, indeed I could add the word "urgent", that Christians and particularly our viewer's work with the God channel to get it to every household as quick as we can' (Alec n.d.).

Christian broadcasting in India, transnational as well as local channels, offers the space for identification with a Christian '*umma*' far beyond the boundaries of the territorialized nation state.

Conclusion

Christian broadcasting is in itself, one aspect of a larger, well-funded, multi-faceted, global Christian mission strategy aimed at reaching the unreached living in the '10/40 window', the area of the world that extends 10 to 40 degrees North of the equator and that includes all of the nations of North Africa, the Middle East, South Asia, South East Asia and China. As the tenor and shape of public Christianity in India changes from 'humble', reticent traditions of Christian mission to the more aggressive, there is bound to be a rise in tensions between Christians and members of other faiths. As this chapter reveals, it is clear that Christian fundamentalists are on a collision course with Hindu nationalists and secularists. Given the unwillingness of the mainstream churches to rein in and/or counter some of the more belligerent Christian groups in India, inter-faith confrontations are bound to become even more pronounced in the years ahead.

References

Alec, R. (n.d.) 'Partner Connect India', *GOD TV South Asia Magazine*, retrieved 24 March 2008 from <http://uk.god.tv/Publisher/Article.aspx?ID=1000026177>.

Bayly, S. (1994), 'Christians and competing fundamentalisms in South Indian society', in M. E. Marty and R. C. Appleby (eds), *Accounting for Fundamentalisms: The Dynamic Character of Movements*. Chicago/London: The University of Chicago Press, pp. 726–769.

Bergunder, M. (2001), 'Miracle healing and exorcism: The South Indian Pentecostal movement in the context of popular Hinduism', *International Review of Mission*, Jan–April, 90, 103–112.

Bhaumik, S. (2004), 'Ethnicity, ideology and religion: Separatist movements in India's Northeast', in S. Limaye, R. Wirsing and M. Malik (eds), *Religious Radicalism and Security in South Asia*. Honolulu, HI: Asia-Pacific Center for Security Studies, pp. 219–244. Retrieved 16 December 2007 from <http://www.apcss.org/Publications/Edited%20Volumes/ReligiousRadicalism/PagesfromReligiousRadicalismandSecurityinSouthAsiach10.pdf>.

Caplan, L. (1991), 'Christian fundamentalism as counter culture', in T. N. Madan (ed.), *Religion in India*. New Delhi: Oxford University Press, pp. 366–381.

Castells, M. (1989), *The Informational City: The Space of Flows*. Oxford, MA: Basil Blackwell.

'Church in India responds to Pentecostals' (1997), Catholic World New Website, retrieved 18 December 2007 from <http://www.cwnews.com/news/viewstory.cfm?recnum=4866>.

'City Shakers' (n.d.), NLAG Website, retrieved 19 June 2008 from <http://www.nlag.in/youth/youth.htm>.

Dempster, M. W., Klaus, B. D. and Petersen, D. (eds) (1999), *The Globalization of Pentecostalism: A Religion Made to Travel*. Irvine, CA: Regnum.

Fernandes, E. (2006), *Holy Warriors: A Journey into the Heart of Indian Fundamentalism*. New Delhi: Penguin/Viking.

Friends Missionary Prayer Band (2005), *Friends Focus*, 1, 9, pp. 9–13.

Hunt, S. (2000), ' "Winning Ways": Globalisation and the impact of the Health and Wealth Gospel', *Journal of Contemporary Religion*, 15(3), 331–347.

Lausanne Committee for World Evangelisation (2004), 'Prayer in evangelism: Lausanne occasional paper no. 42', *Proceedings of the 2004 forum for world evangelization*, Lausanne Movement, Pattaya, Thailand, pp. 1–52. Retrieved 12 January 2007 from <http://www.lausanne.org/documents/2004forum/LOP42_IG13.pdf>.

Manokaran, J. N. (2005), *Christ & Cities: Transformation of Urban Centres*. Chennai, India: Mission Educational Books.

Mendieta, E. (2001), 'Invisible Cities: A Phenomenology of Globalisation from below', *City*, 5(1), 7–26.

My Hope India (2005), 'Mathew and Friends Manual', Secunderabad, India.

Parathazham, P. (1997), 'The challenge of neo-Pentecostalism: An empirical study', *Vidyajyoti*, 61, 307–320.

Pew Forum on Religion & Public Life (2006), *Spirit and Power: A 10-Country Survey of Pentecostals*. Washington, D.C.: The Pew Forum on Religion

Prakash, G. (2002), 'The urban turn', *Sarai Reader*, 2–6.

& Public Life, pp. 1–233. Retrieved 11 March 2007 from <http://pew forum.org/publications/surveys/pentecostals-06.pdf>.

'Prayer & Counselling' (n.d.), Jesus Calls Website, retrieved January 22 2007 from <http://www.jesuscalls.org/prayer/prayer.asp>.

Prior, J. M. (2007), 'The challenge of the Pentecostals in Asia part two: The responses of the Roman Catholic Church', *Exchange*, 36, 115–143.

Raj, V. S. and Selvasingh, J. W. (2004), 'Churches in Chennai: Characteristics of churches in Chennai', *Ethne*, 3(8), Jan–March, 10.

Rammawia, F. (1992), 'Tribal evangelisation: A Madhya Pradesh story', in S. Lazarus (ed.), *Proclaiming Christ: A Handbook of Indigenous Mission in India*. Madras: Church Growth Association of India – CGAI, pp. 63–68.

Shourie, A. (1994), *Missionaries in India: Continuities, Change, Dilemmas*. New Delhi: Rupa & Co.

Shourie, A. (2000), *Harvesting our Souls: Missionaries, their Designs, their Claims*. New Delhi: ASA Publications.

Shulman, D. D. (1980), *Tamil Temple Myths: Sacrifice and Divine Marriage in the South Indian Saiva Tradition*. Princeton, NJ: Princeton University Press.

Last Days Harvest Ministries (n.d.), 'Strategic level spiritual warfare prayer', Appius Forum Website, retrieved 16 December 2007 from <http://www.appiusforum.com/mapping.html>.

Thomas, P. N. (2007a), 'Pentecostals and Christian broadcasting in globalizing Chennai: Past & present', paper presented at the global seminar *The Mediation of Religion: Historical Perspectives from the Ancient World to the Present*, Ayala Museum, Makati, Philippines, 25–27 June.

Thomas, P. N. (2007b), 'Christian fundamentalism and the media in South India', *Media Development*, January, 23–31.

Thomas, P. N. (2008), *Strong Religion/Zealous Media: Christian Fundamentalism and the Media in India*. New Delhi: Sage.

Thomas, V. V. (2003), 'Pentecostalism among the Dalits in Kerala from 1909 to the Present: A Subaltern Reading', D.Th. thesis, Pune, India: Union Biblical Seminary.

YWAM Extreme!! (n.d.), 'School of Intercession Worship and Spiritual Warfare', retrieved 21 March 2007 from <http://www.ywamextremesoip.com/pages/School%20of%20Intercession%20Worship%20and%20Spiritual%20Warfare>.

Zukin, S. (1995), *The Cultures of Cities*. Cambridge, MA: Blackwell Publishers.

Index